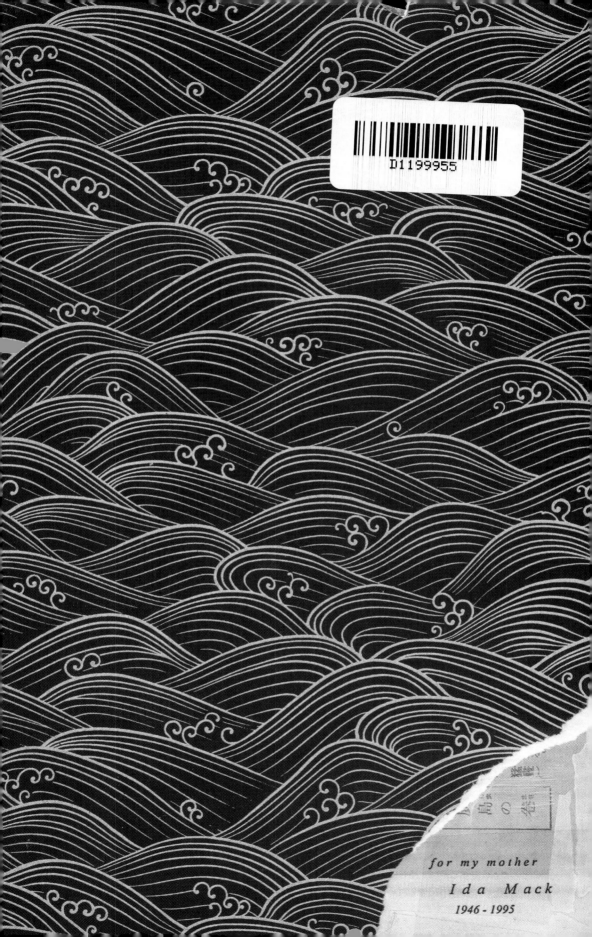

for my mother

Ida Mack

1946 - 1995

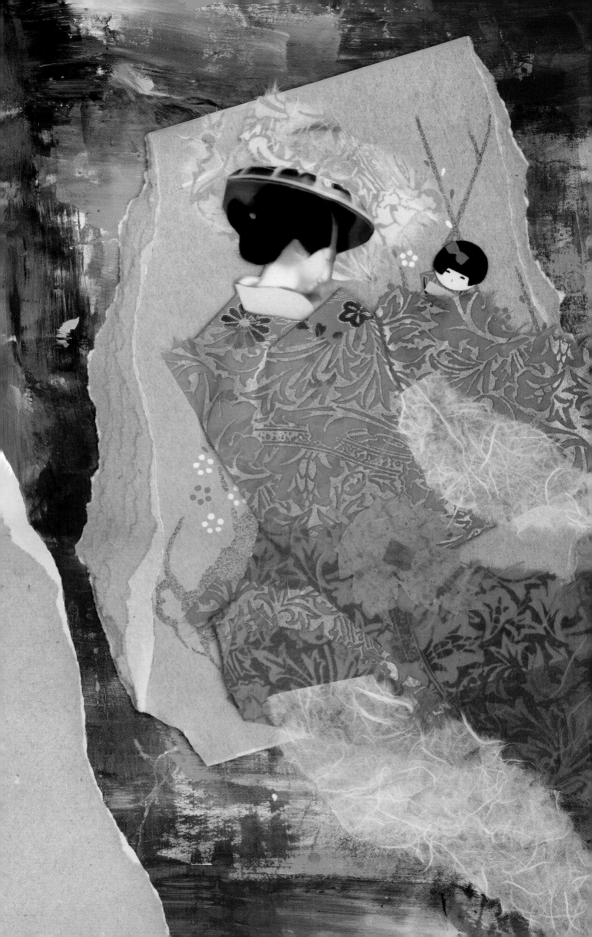

kabuki

Dreams

Film output by Kell-O-Graphics

KABUKI Dreams is published (Nov. 2001) by Image Comics,
1071 N. Batavia St. Ste A, Orange, CA 92867.
It presents KABUKI stories originaly published as The Kabuki Color
Special(1995), Dreams of the Dead(1996), Kabuki 1/2(1999), and new work.
Kabuki and all related characters, their distinctive likenesses, and entire contents
are Copyright and TM 2000 David Mack.

book design by

David Mack

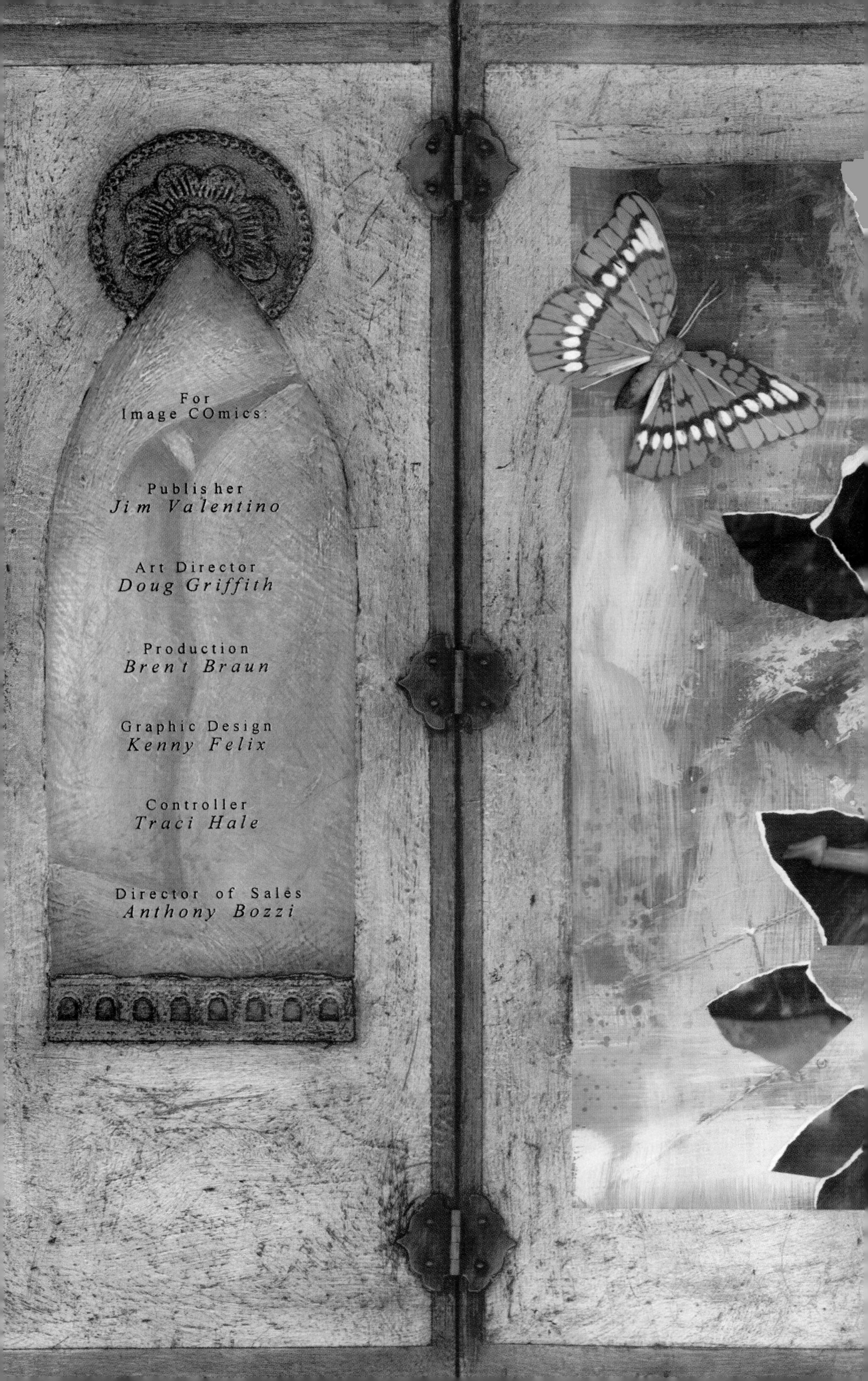

For
Image COmics:

Publisher
Jim Valentino

Art Director
Doug Griffith

Production
Brent Braun

Graphic Design
Kenny Felix

Controller
Traci Hale

Director of Sales
Anthony Bozzi

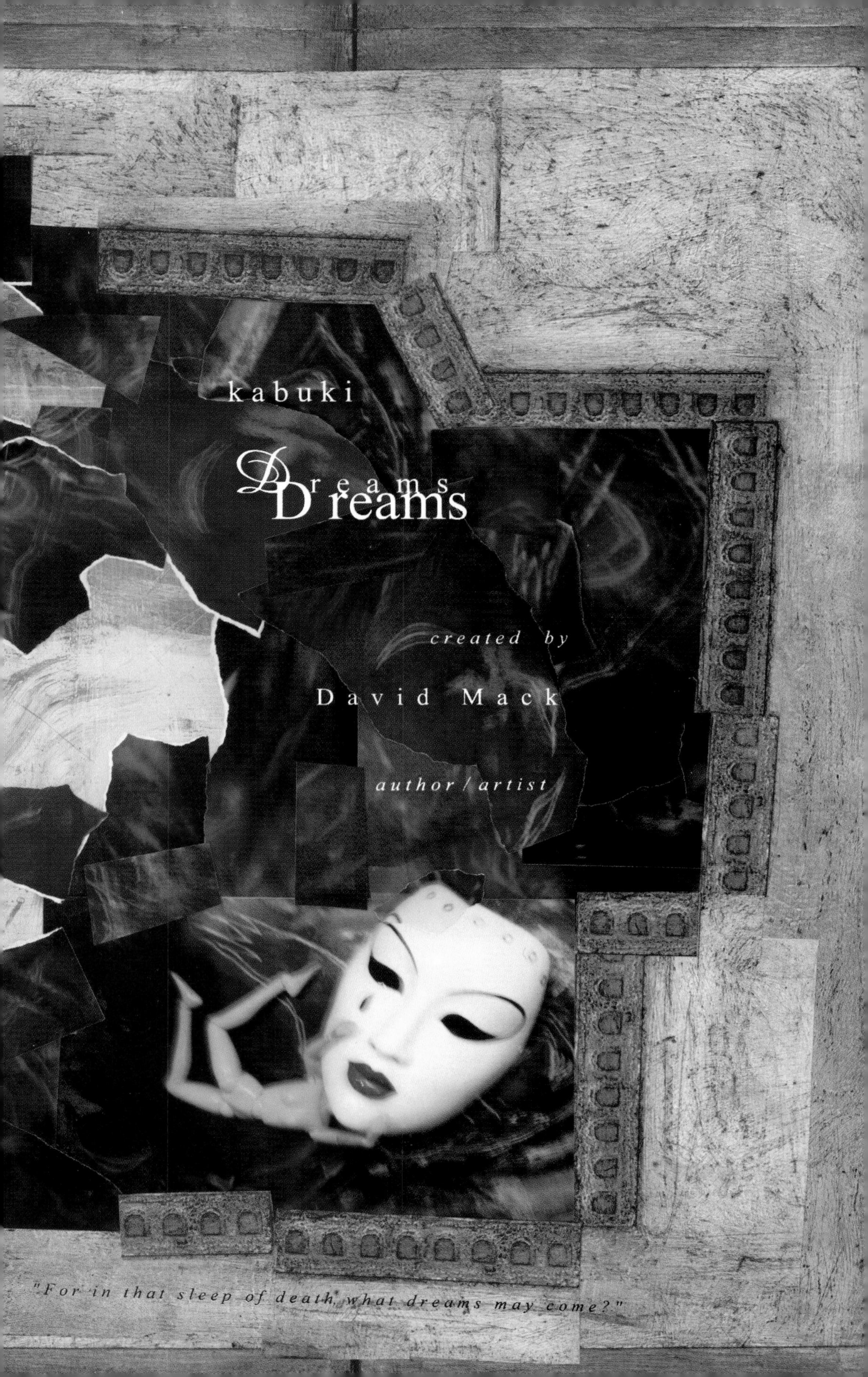
kabuki
Dreams
created by
David Mack
author / artist
"For in that sleep of death what dreams may come?"

contents:

introduction by
Brian Michael Bendis

Presented for the first time in the English language,
is the Kabuki article from France's prestigious
EKLLIPSE magazine.

This includes a cross section of Mack's Kabuki art,
an in depth commentary by Francois Delval, &
an interview with David Mack by Fabrice Deraedt,
edited by Aude Ettori.

acknowledgements

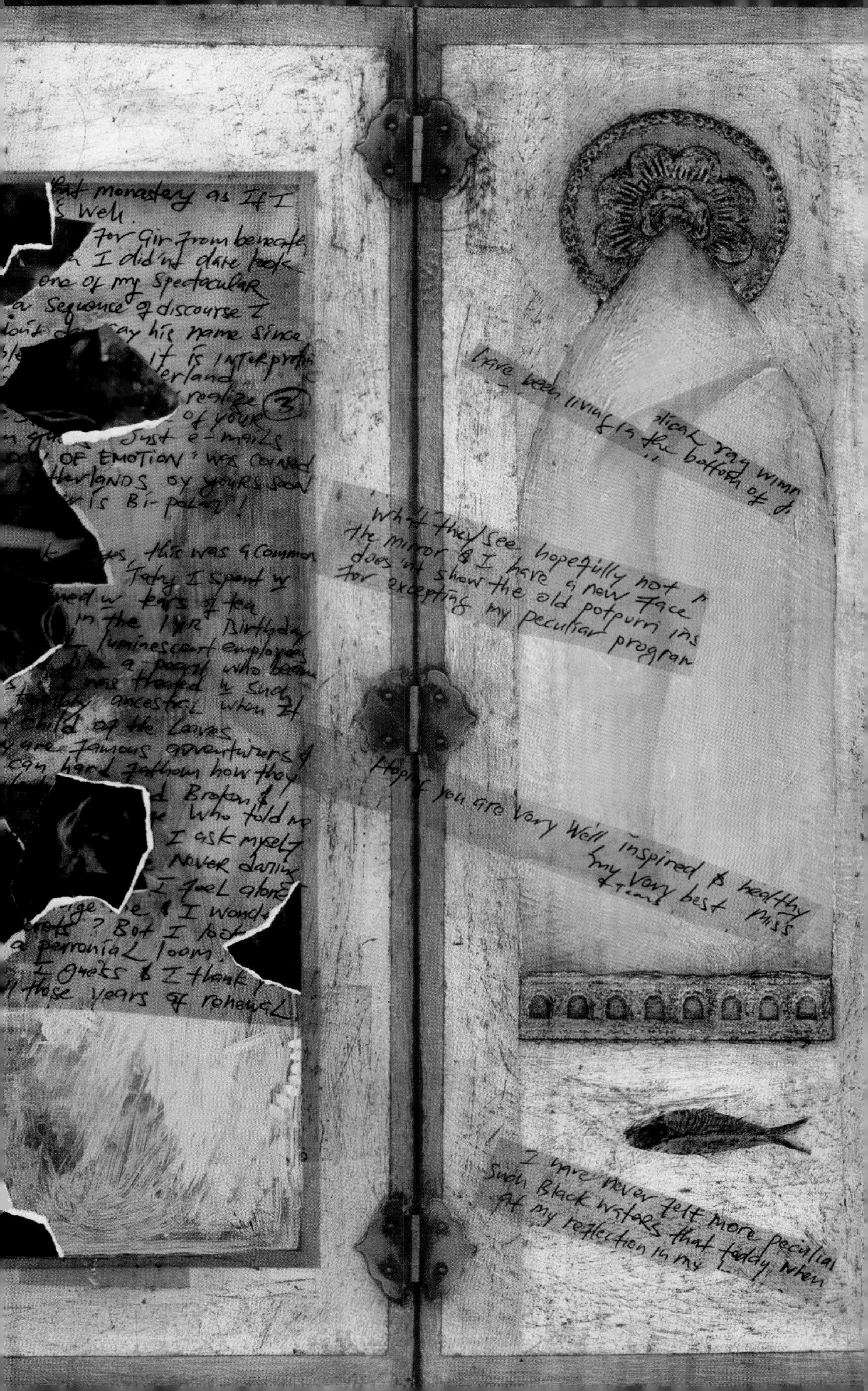
monastery as If I
's well.
for air from beneath
I did'nt dare look
one of my spectacular
a sequence of discourse I
say his name since
it is interpreting
realize
of your
just e-mails
OF EMOTION' was coined
by yours soon
is Bi-polar!
yes, this was a common
Today I spent w
w tears of tea
in the 1YR Birthday
luminescent employees
like a pearl who became
was treated w such
ancestral when It
child of the Leaves
are famous adventurers &
can hard fathom how they
Broken &
Who told me
I ask myself
Never daring
I feel alone
& I wonder
? But I look
a perrenial loom.
I guess & I thank
those years of renewal
have been living in the bottom of
tical ray whin
What they see, hopefully not
the mirror & I have a new face
does'nt show the old potpurri ins
for excepting my peculiar program
Hope you are very well, inspired & healthy
my very best miss
I have never felt more peculiar
such Black waters that today when
at my reflection in my

nearly black out & my body is filled w tea, mi
snacks of pomegranate chili paste, eggplant

In my strange Visions I am finding this sto
eastern european. You should hear the thu
well? #8 is on my new gold duvet co
I am in my new abode w my little plethora of p.
a talkin two lives which, having never reached fruition on earth, have now burgundy, Salvia Spir
rusty tones & coxscombs of, booping colours st
Silver furry Ivy   tire uni
on 28th st.
    Im glad   N babble
Some of the sa   buildup
slowly A story of love that never   rd who I
Some of the   e stil
ears & with   er
existence had
w   Picture the deep, deep qu   believ
$ singed la
    I ho
If the shadows about it   ev
danced up
  wailing music of   Cosm
mellow.
    It is strau   t? bc
Goms.   the Sign
out when I h
no-one had that in min yet? I st
spiritual garb & its portent

                                                ay   sin
                                                h : How
                                                o I thin
                                                wear C
                                                on that
                                                or the Sig
                                                I still alw

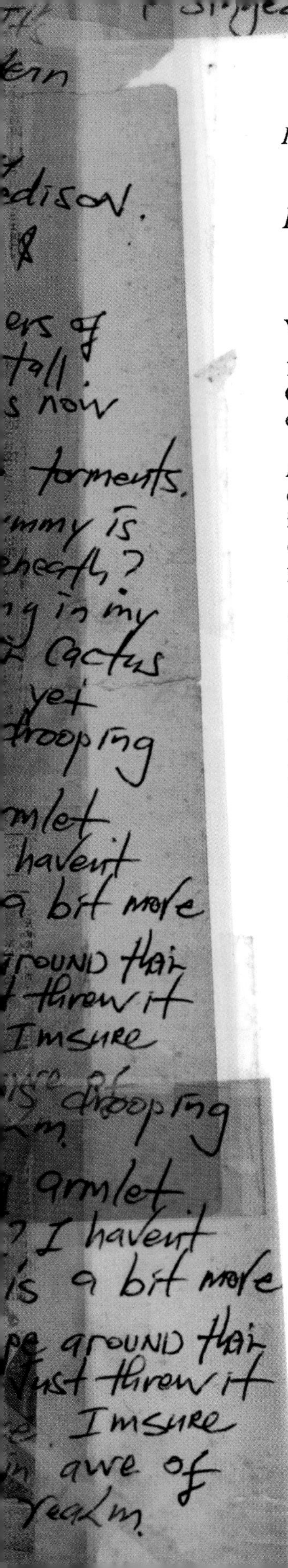

Introduction by

Brian Michael ***Bendis***

Well, I've known David since we were stationed in Korea together in 1952. Oh wait, it was Caliber in 1992, it just felt like Korea. Oh, I kid Caliber. I'm sure the wounds will heal one day. They have to eventually, right?

As I write this I realize that the days of our budding friendship have officially become 'the good old days.' We were both working in independent black and white comics, both single, both starving, and no one gave two and a half shits about either of our work. But we showed you!!! Hahahahahah!!

When I met David I was fucking up the first half of a graphic novel Fire, and David was elbow deep into his groundbreaking, world changing graphic novel tour de force, Happy the Clown. Oh yes, we can definitely say we knew each other when.

What could a Jew from Cleveland and the most gentile gentile from Kentucky have in common? Aside from mild bi-polarism, we both felt a deep-rooted passion for everything about what the comic page could do. And not the page itself, anyone can love that. We honestly loved what was going on in-between the borders- what was going on under and over the page- what floated through and around the comic panels and took place in the reader's mind.

And when you spend all of your day thinking and philosophizing to yourself about this invisible and imaginary fourth dimension of comics that you might have invented inside your rubber cement addled head, it's an amazing day when you find someone who totally knows exactly what you're talking about…even if they're from Kentucky.

(And sure I could try to explain what the hell I am talking about with this fourth dimension of comics right here in this intro, but I ain't exactly getting paid by the word.)

But here is the real reason I am friends with Dave: When I was first showing him my work in progress on Fire, and I swear I'm not plugging, Dave was totally and genuinely in love with my storytelling, or, more pointed, my promise as a storyteller. But he gently tossed out the suggestion that my inking line weight might not be the most appropriate choice for the style of book I was trying to pull off. It was a casual and friendly remark. A suggestion, really. He took a pen and he inked a head right on my scratchy pencils just to illustrate his point (no really shitty pun intended.)

Well, this floored me. And it might sound like a miniscule little thing but his comment was so right on the money, that it altered and defined my noirish art style forever. I literally don't know how I would have been able to graduate my work to the next level without him.

Soon after this episode I started Goldfish and David started Kabuki. I realized that just by being around David, just by talking to him on the phone, just by tricking him into picking me up in his car and taking me to conventions that were totally out of his way, made me a better comics creator.

They say that Eric Clapton is only as good as the company he keeps, that when Clapton is working with Marc Knophler or George Harrison, his guitar playing is more focussed and powerful. That's kind of how I feel about myself when working with David. Now I am not comparing myself to the rock god guitarists of all rock god guitarists (I couldn't get my hands on anywhere near that much heroine if I tried) but I know for a fact that I m a better comic book creator because of my friendship with David.

Oh yeah, and it goes both ways. I realized that this poor fellow was in desperate need of my voice of reason. Because early on in Kabuki's creation, David had the insane idea that I actually pencil Kabuki. Oh man, how bad would that have sucked!!?? Can you imagine? He had no intention of drawing it himself. He only wanted to write it. Well, I know the offer was just a warm extension of our growing friendship, and I know that he would have come to his senses on it as well (But we do laugh bout how quickly our friendship would have ended had I indeed accepted this gig. I was not the gentle collaborator then I have since grown into). So David had to develop a revolutionary art style for Kabuki all by himself.

It also became very clear, very quickly that David was going to be one of the greats. A true artist. A unique voice. A purposeful and unapologetic storyteller who had so many tricks up his sleeve that sometimes dozens of them would fall into one single painting. David can write and draw and paint in any style he chooses with equal conviction and craftsmanship. Just in this collection alone find a medium he hasn't toyed with. He applies a different range of media and style for each different volume of Kabuki. Each story has its own visual personality and evolution just as it has its own unique literary tone and atmosphere. David's storytelling marries the art and writing together in such a way that they become indistinguishable from one another and create his own new form of graphic language.

It's an amazing sight to see. I have been witness to David's creative process in a lot of its forms. I have seen David pencil in a fury of emotion, I have seen him doodle whimsically, I have seen him dribble spit into a painting while the brush swirled it into the mix. I have seen David edit out of this intro any number of other things I have seen David do in private.

But watching David create is one of the true joys of my life, and I say that with full conviction. It's an amazing and inspiring thing to behold.

I want to wrap this up because even writing this has made me want to go draw something. But seeing the new pages David created for this edition of Kabuki made me think of this little intro that Bill Sienkiewicz wrote to the collection of his work on the X-men title New Mutants. He was talking about how fans were constantly wishing that he would have drawn the mutants in the same style he drew his ground breaking work on Moon Knight ('I liked your old stuff'), and that years later they always ask him to draw in the same style he drew the new mutants. 'Draw it in your old style.' He laughed in the intro that the New Mutants was now his old stuff.

Well, I think the same goes for David. I know you are going to be blown away by the amazing work in this collection, but good news, its already the old stuff. David was like 20 years old when he began the stories you now hold in your hand. He has already reinvented himself and his signature character into something you didn't see coming. Each consecutive volume of his work documents a new era in the evolution of his characters, and in David's evolution as an author and artist. Each volume operates under its own rules, and has to be read and approached in its own way. Neither the artist, nor his work, can be pinned down, categorized, or quantified in any conventional artistic or literary terms. David has never once given his audience what he thinks they want. He only gives them what he has.

This volume collects the very first ever stories that David created in fully painted media. It is a very personal work. And it compliments the previous black and white story (Circle of Blood) in an unexpected way. Each page is a journey into a new world, and a new graphic language.

Congrats David, another masterpiece.

It was an honor to watch you create it.

BENDIS!

October, 2001

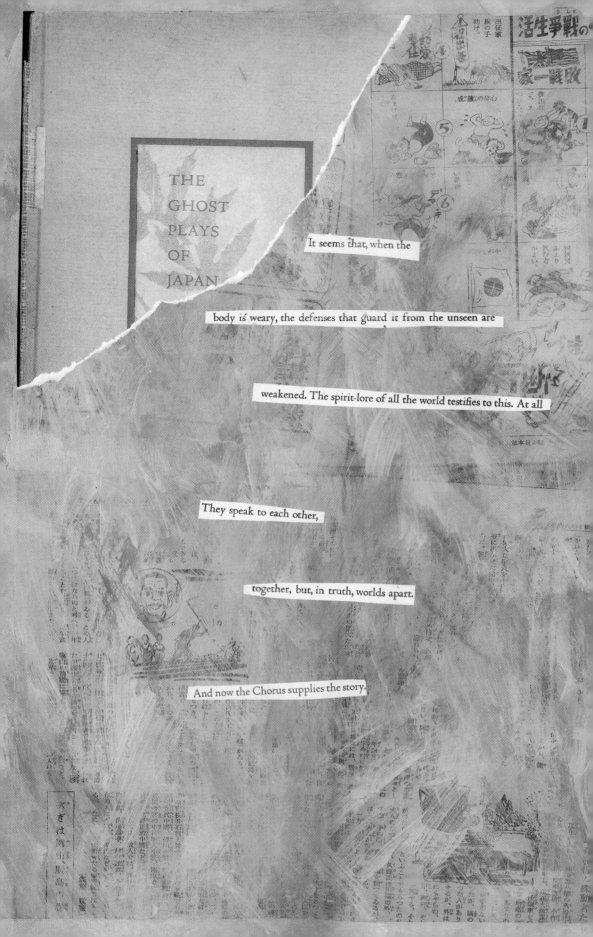

THE
GHOST
PLAYS
OF
JAPAN

It seems that, when the

body is weary, the defenses that guard it from the unseen are

weakened. The spirit-lore of all the world testifies to this. At all

They speak to each other,

together, but, in truth, worlds apart.

And now the Chorus supplies the story.

Part one

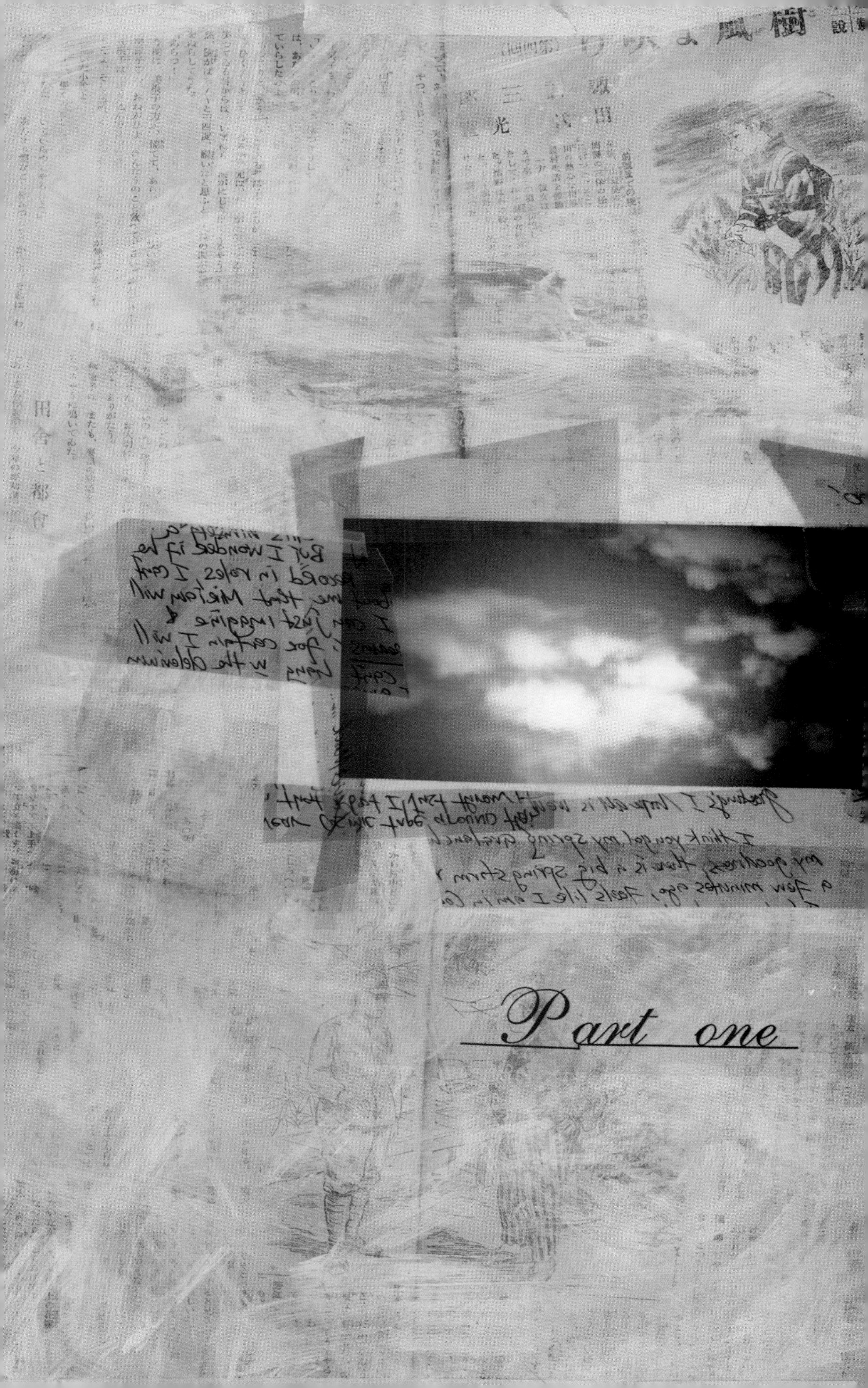

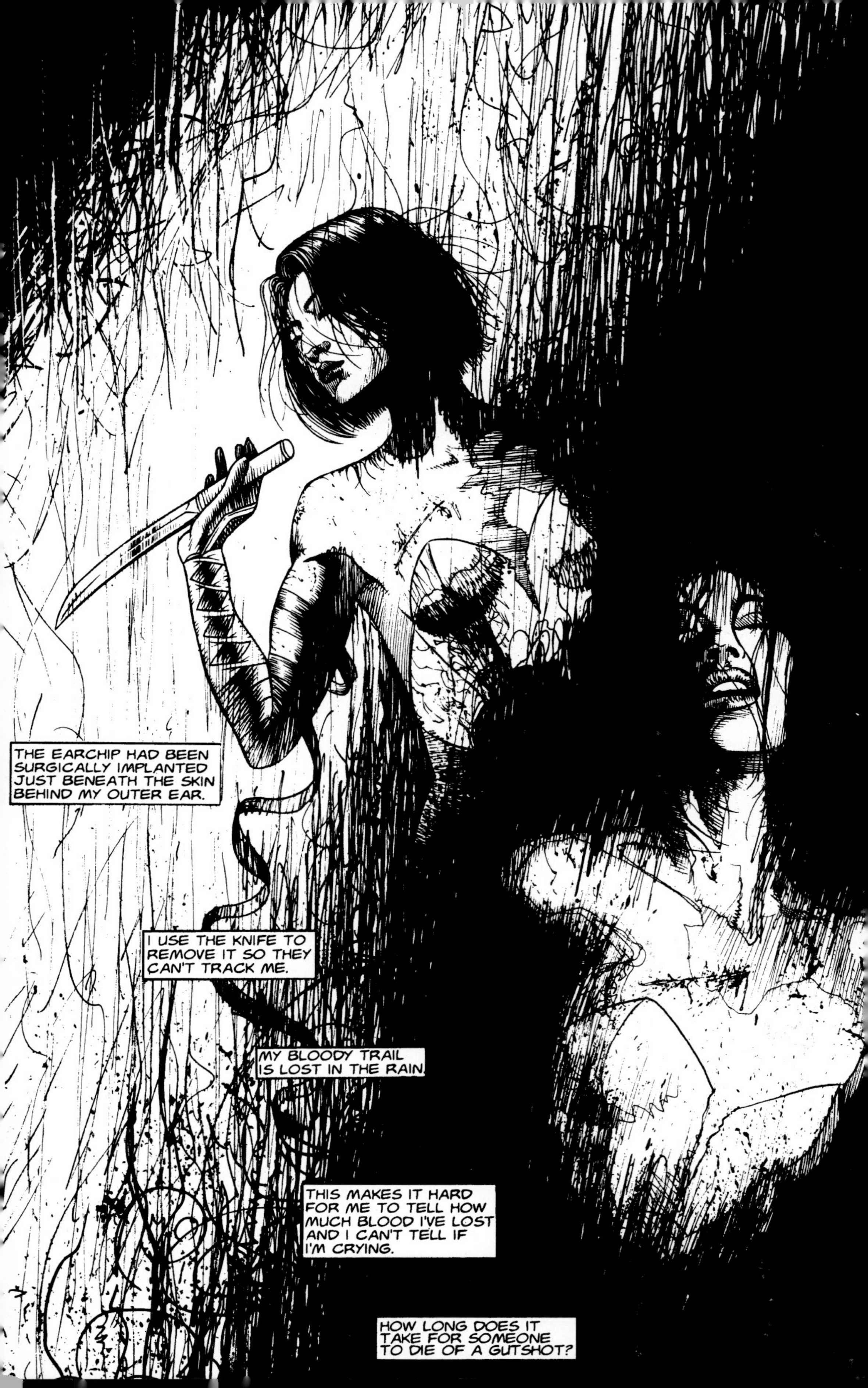
THE EARCHIP HAD BEEN SURGICALLY IMPLANTED JUST BENEATH THE SKIN BEHIND MY OUTER EAR.
I USE THE KNIFE TO REMOVE IT SO THEY CAN'T TRACK ME.
MY BLOODY TRAIL IS LOST IN THE RAIN.
THIS MAKES IT HARD FOR ME TO TELL HOW MUCH BLOOD I'VE LOST AND I CAN'T TELL IF I'M CRYING.
HOW LONG DOES IT TAKE FOR SOMEONE TO DIE OF A GUTSHOT?

THE RAIN...

ON MY FACE...

MAKES ME FEEL NAKED...

WITHOUT MY MASK.

NATURE'S TEAR DROPS...

TRICKLING OVER THE SCARS AROUND MY EYE...

LIKE A BLIND WOMAN...

READING BRAILLE...

WITH BLOODY FINGERTIPS.

TRACING THE RAISED FLESH OF EACH CHARACTER...

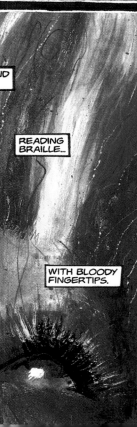

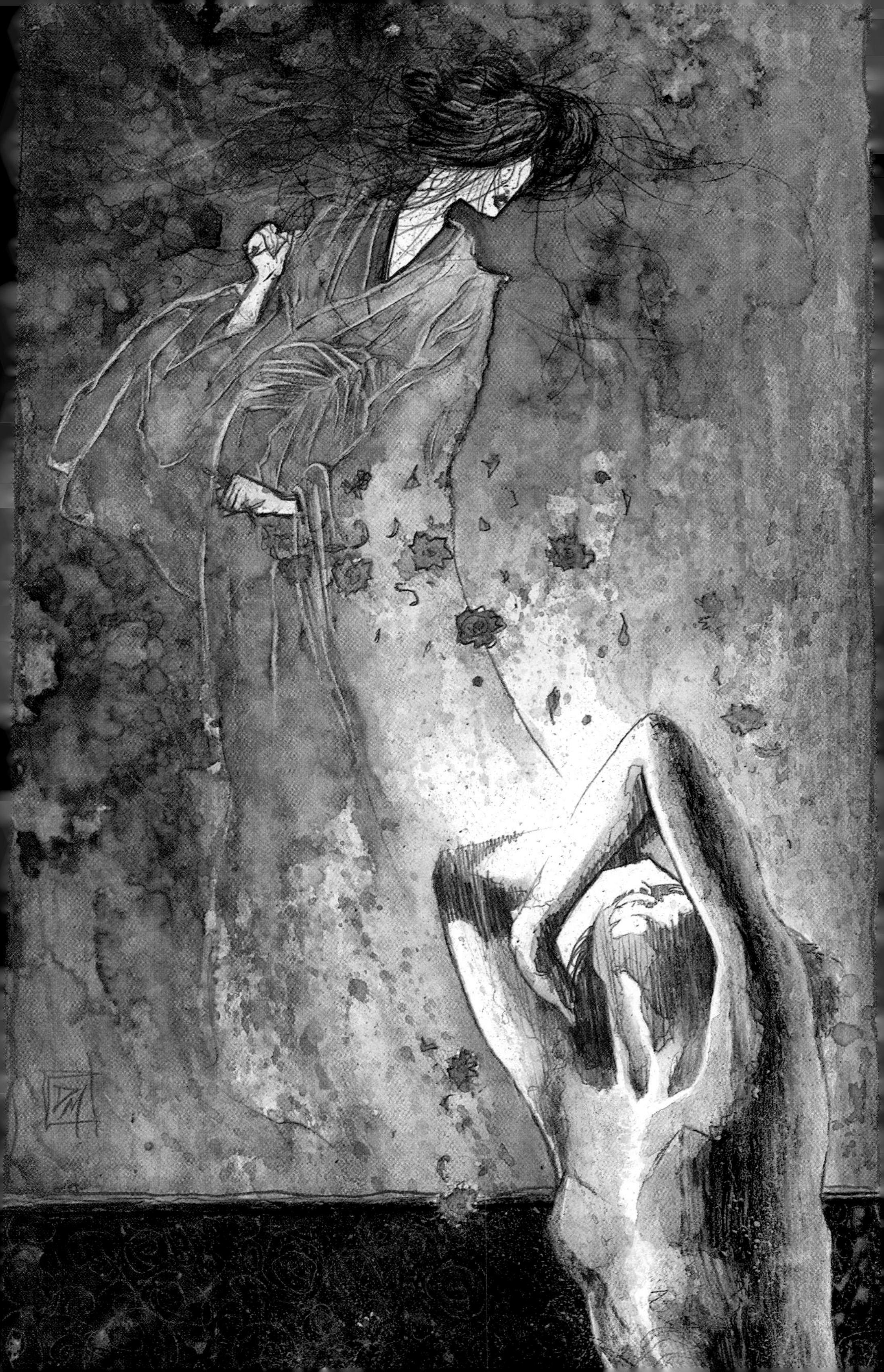

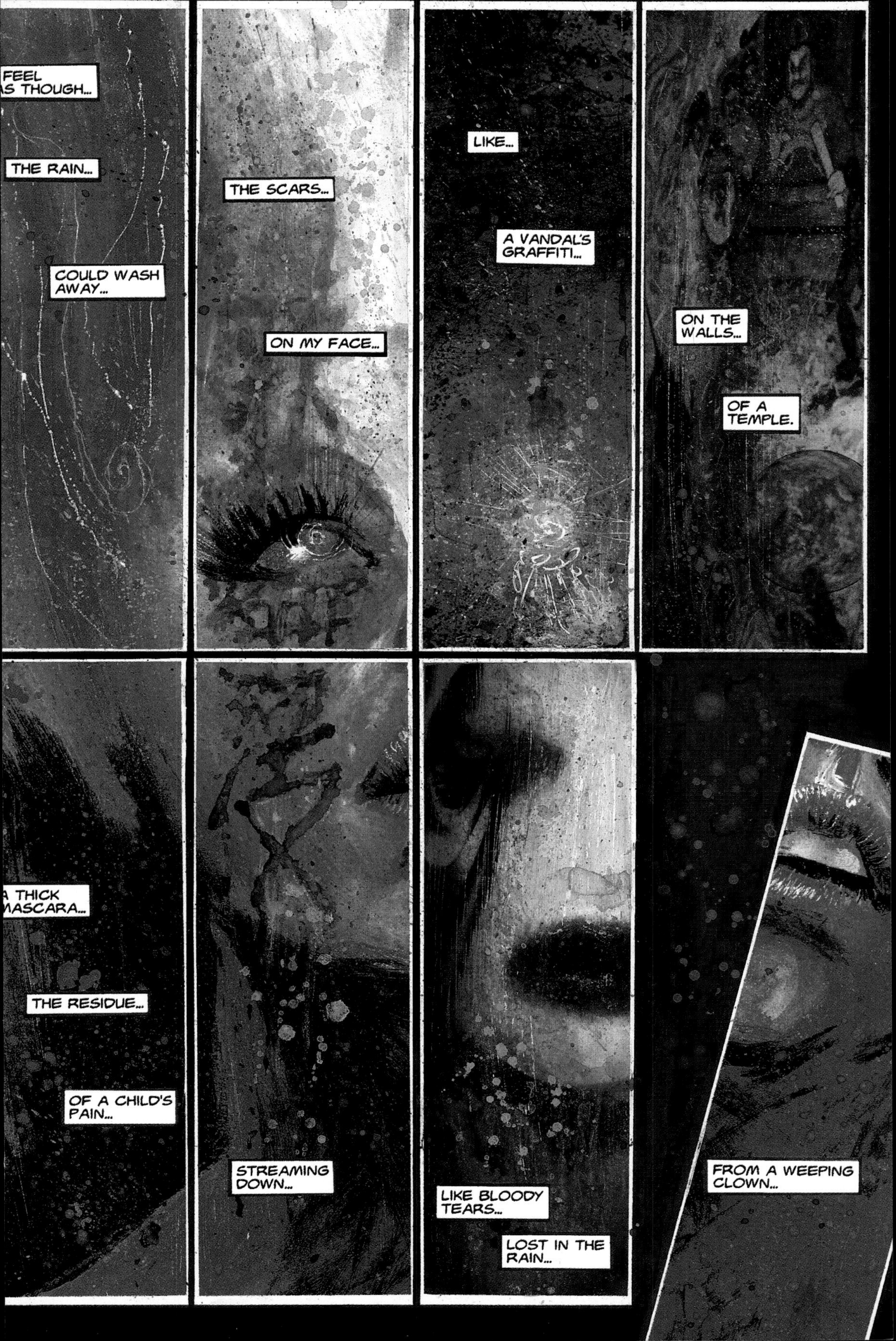
FEEL
AS THOUGH...
THE RAIN...
COULD WASH AWAY...
THE SCARS...
ON MY FACE...
LIKE...
A VANDAL'S GRAFFITI...
ON THE WALLS...
OF A TEMPLE.
A THICK MASCARA...
THE RESIDUE...
OF A CHILD'S PAIN...
STREAMING DOWN...
LIKE BLOODY TEARS...
LOST IN THE RAIN...
FROM A WEEPING CLOWN...

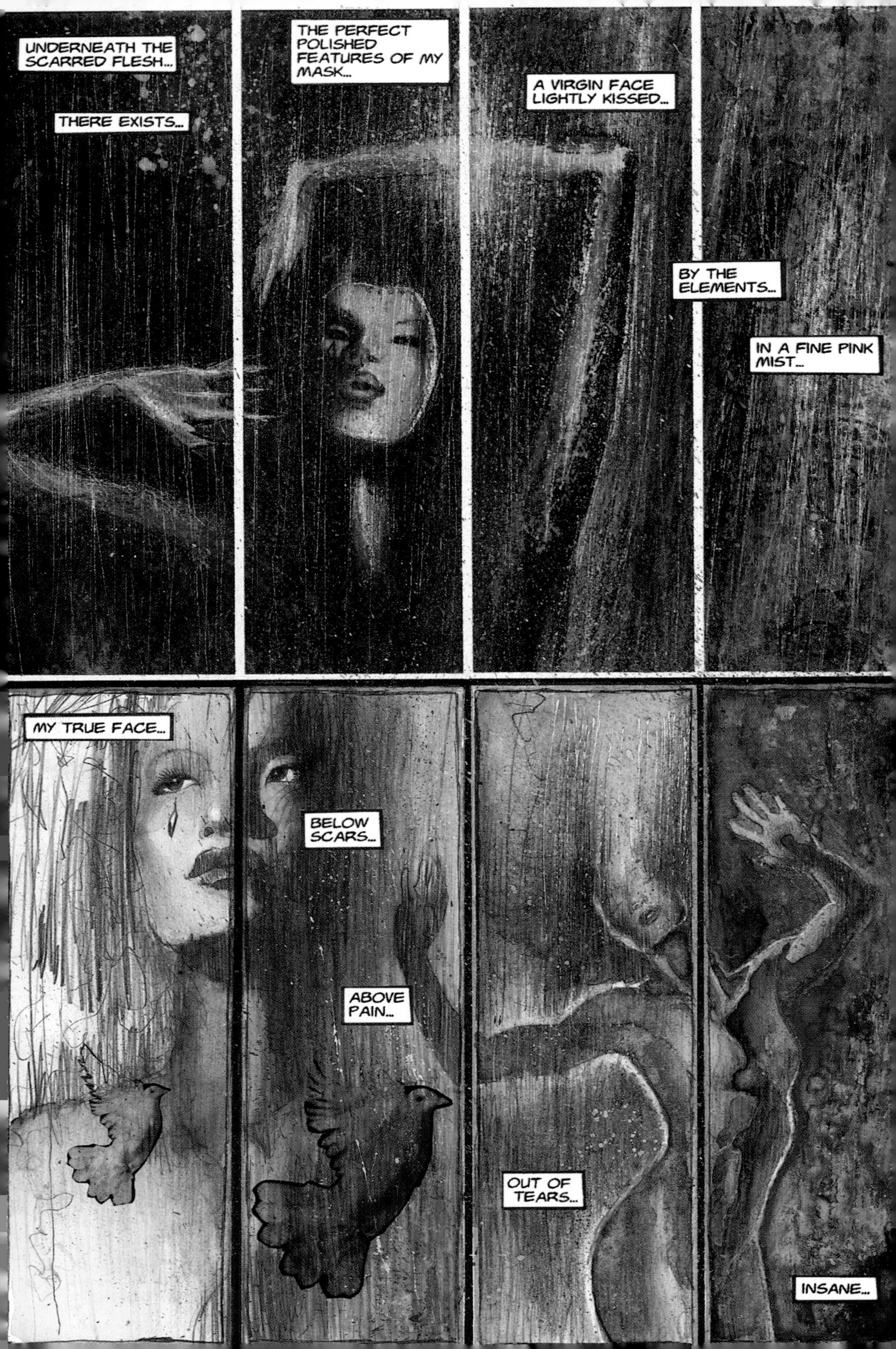
UNDERNEATH THE SCARRED FLESH...
THERE EXISTS...
THE PERFECT POLISHED FEATURES OF MY MASK...
A VIRGIN FACE LIGHTLY KISSED...
BY THE ELEMENTS...
IN A FINE PINK MIST...
MY TRUE FACE...
BELOW SCARS...
ABOVE PAIN...
OUT OF TEARS...
INSANE...

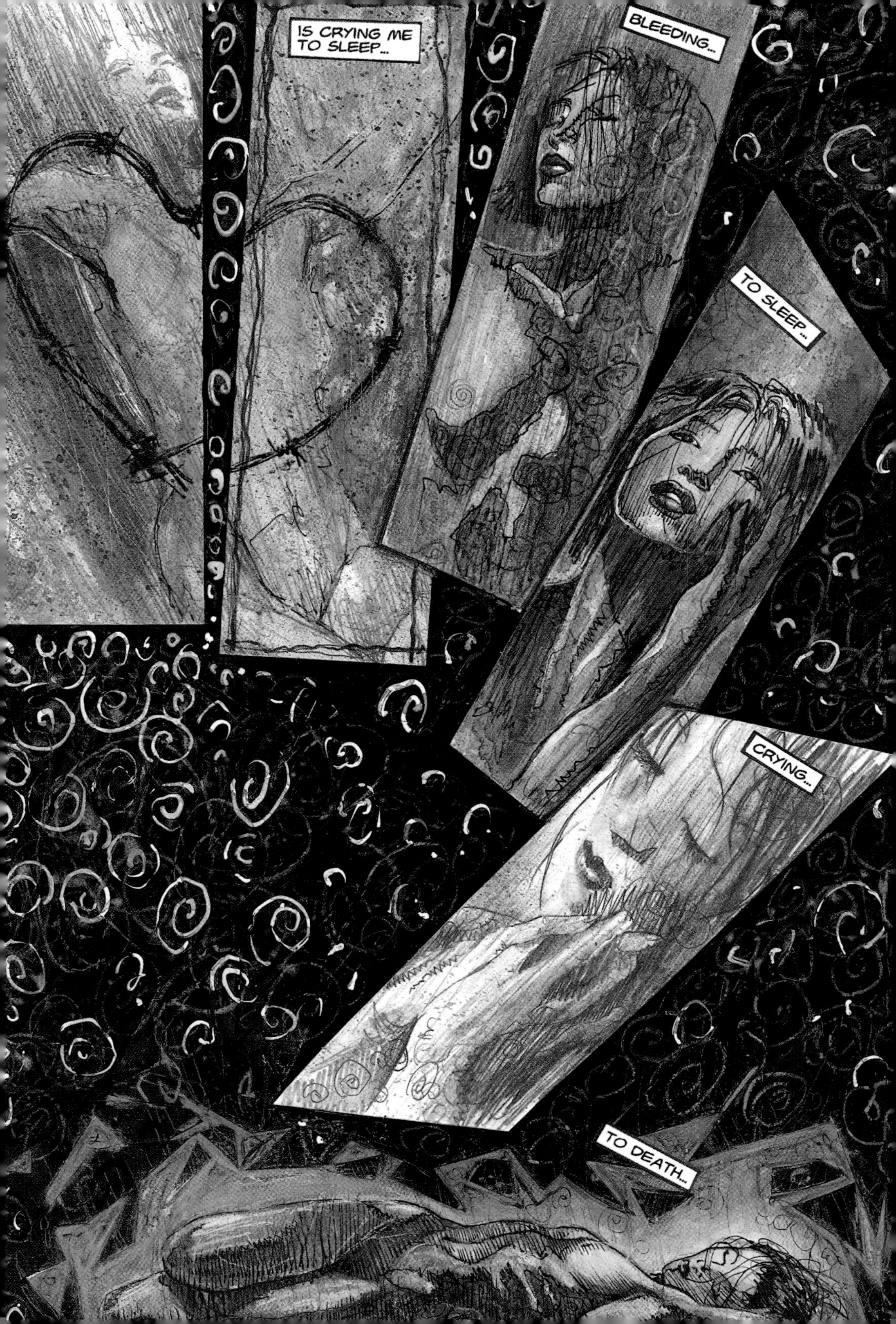
IS CRYING ME TO SLEEP...
BLEEDING...
TO SLEEP...
CRYING...
TO DEATH...

I WAS DEAD BEFORE...

FOR NINE MINUTES...

AND I SAW MY MOTHER.

LIKE THE NINE MONTHS...

I SPENT IN HER WOMB...

I WAS REBORN.

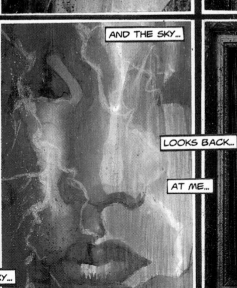

IT SEEMS ONLY A DAY AGO...

ONE DAY AND A THOUSAND CENTURIES AGO.

AND THE SKY...

LOOKS BACK...

AT ME...

I LOOK TO THE SKY...

WITH EMPTY EYES

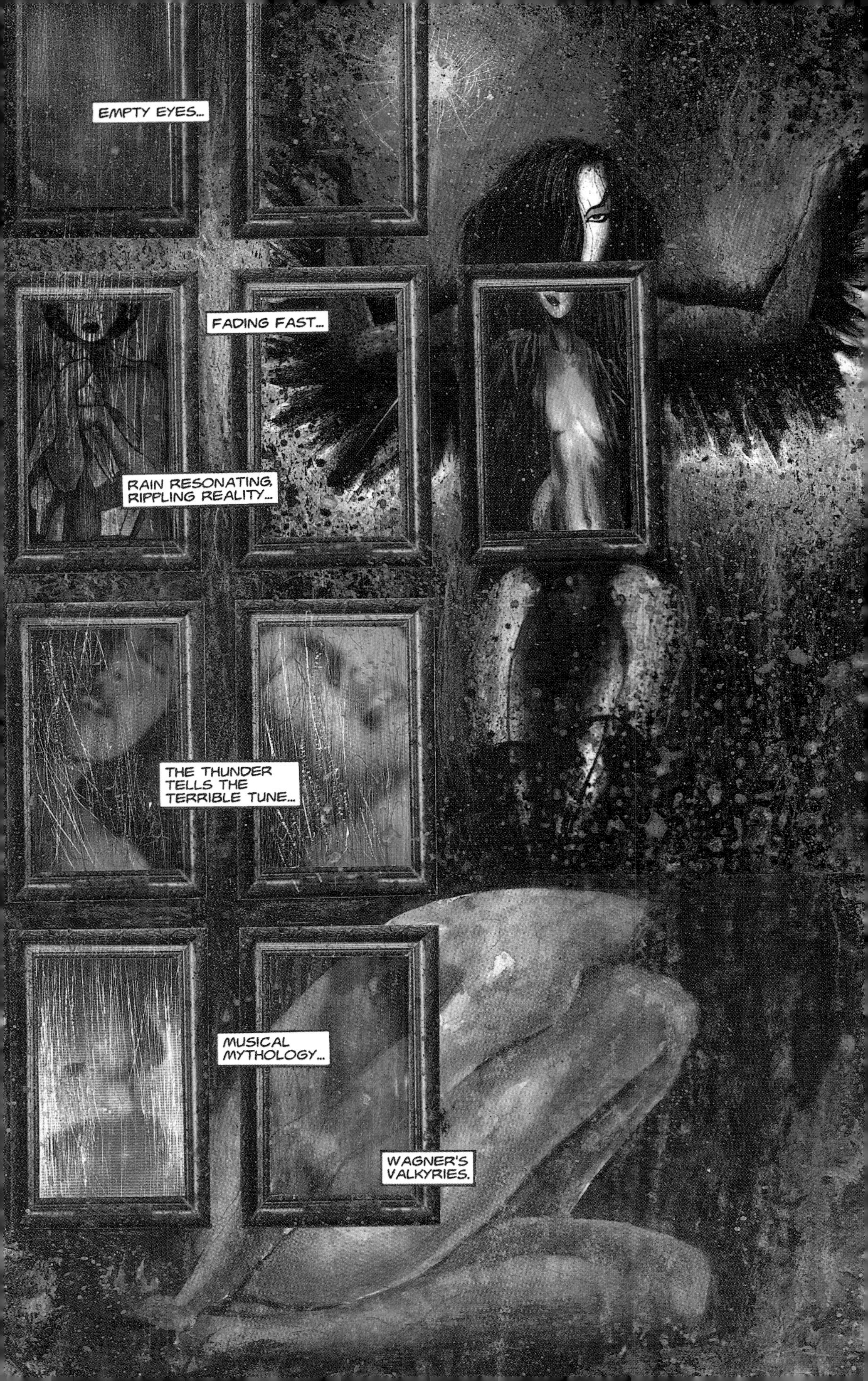
EMPTY EYES...
FADING FAST...
RAIN RESONATING, RIPPLING REALITY...
THE THUNDER TELLS THE TERRIBLE TUNE...
MUSICAL MYTHOLOGY...
WAGNER'S VALKYRIES.

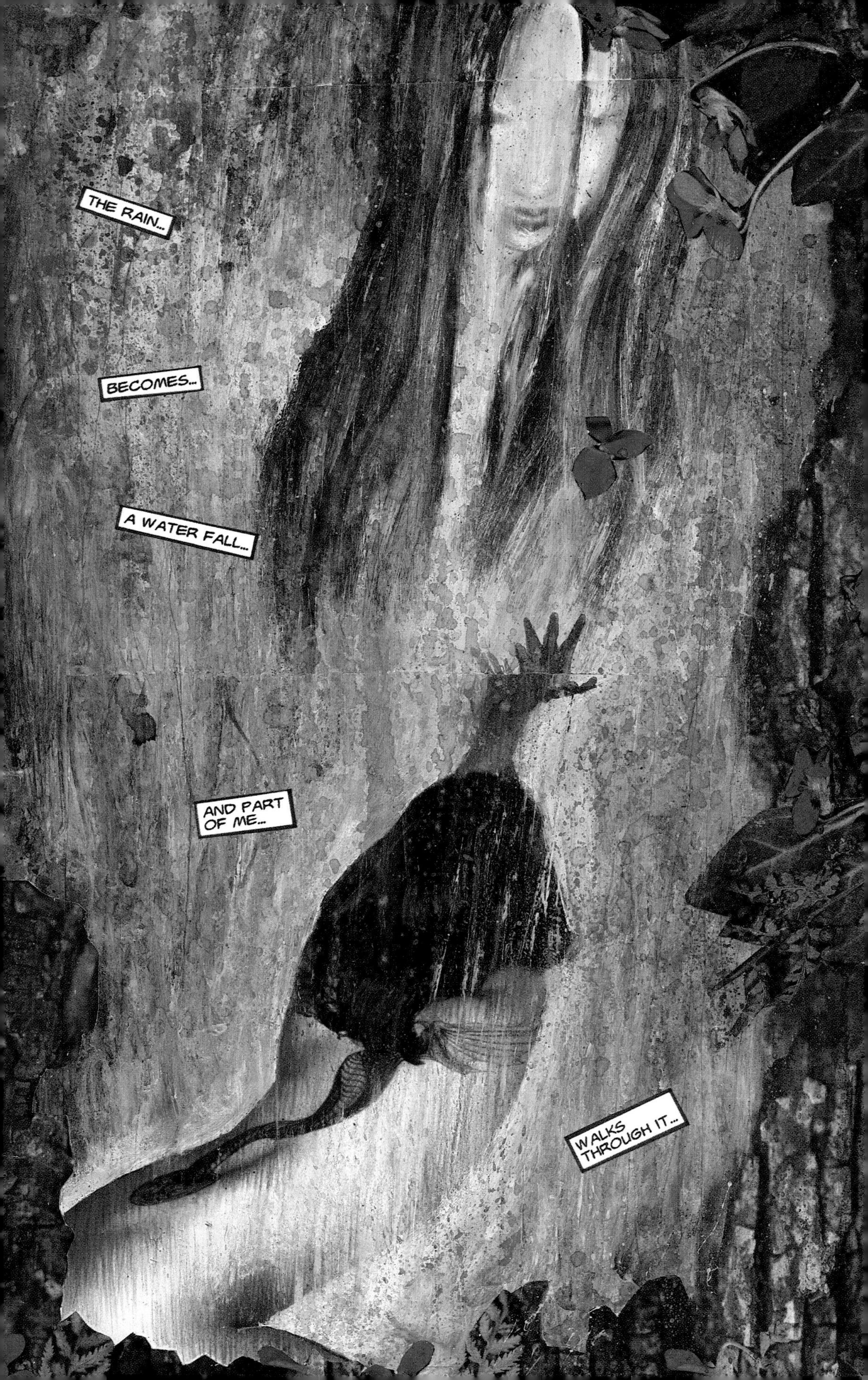
THE RAIN...
BECOMES...
A WATER FALL...
AND PART OF ME...
WALKS THROUGH IT...

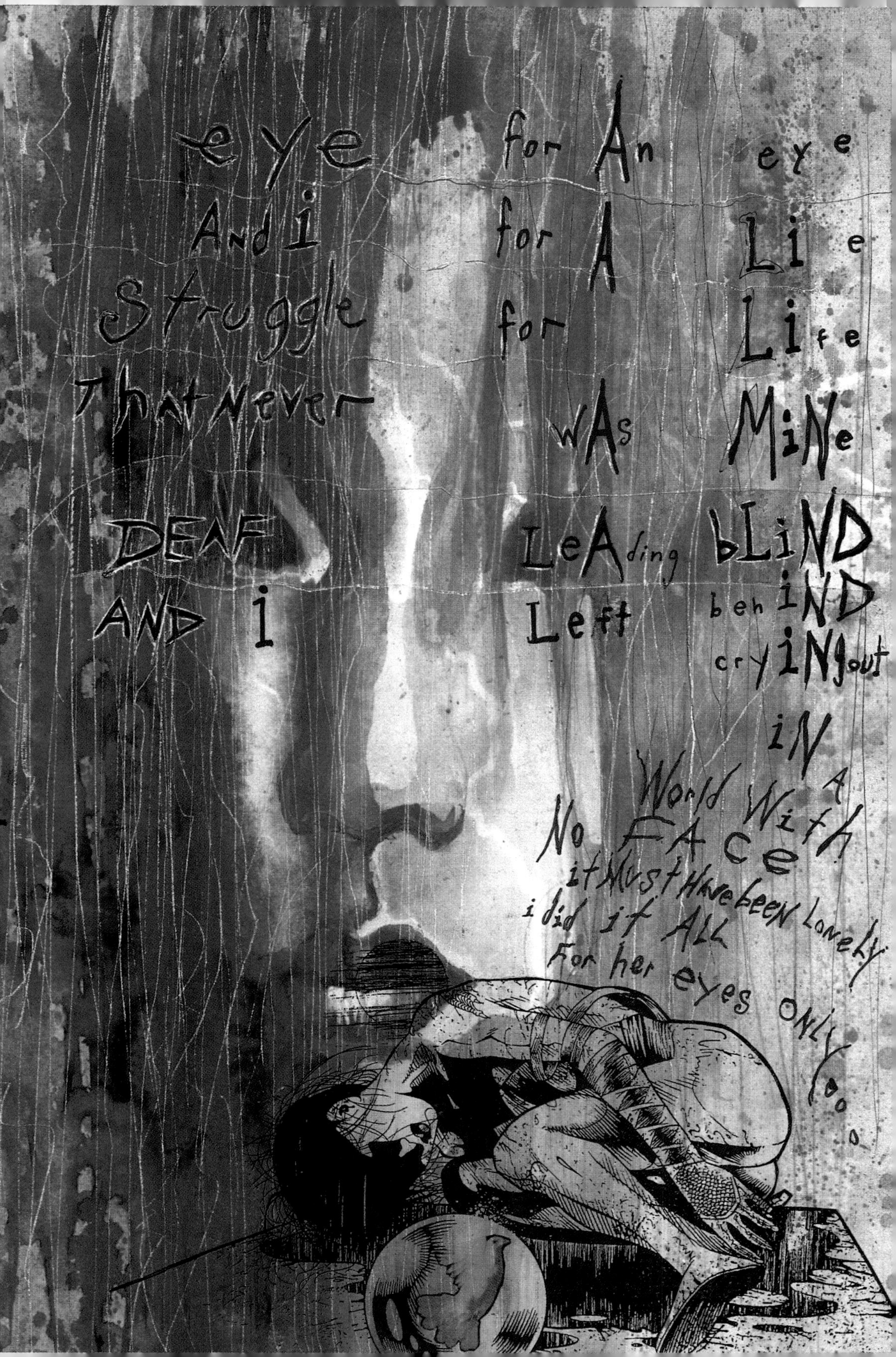
eye for An eye
And i for A Life
Struggle for A Life
That Never wAs MiNe
DEAF LeAding bLiND
AND i Left behiND
cryiNg out
iN A
World With
No FAce
it Must Have been Lonely
i did it ALL
For her eyes ONLY...

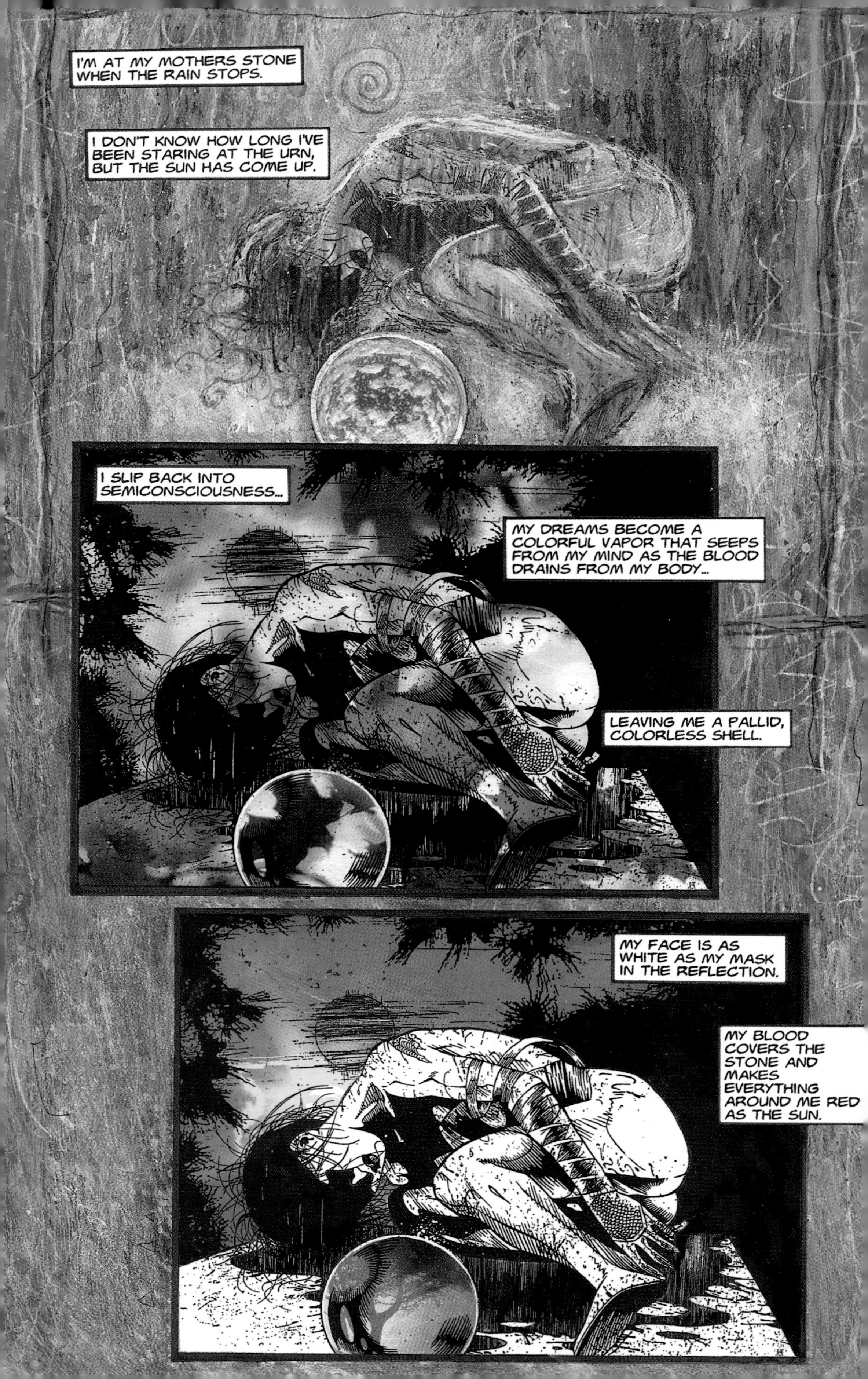
I'M AT MY MOTHERS STONE WHEN THE RAIN STOPS.
I DON'T KNOW HOW LONG I'VE BEEN STARING AT THE URN, BUT THE SUN HAS COME UP.
I SLIP BACK INTO SEMICONSCIOUSNESS...
MY DREAMS BECOME A COLORFUL VAPOR THAT SEEPS FROM MY MIND AS THE BLOOD DRAINS FROM MY BODY...
LEAVING ME A PALLID, COLORLESS SHELL.
MY FACE IS AS WHITE AS MY MASK IN THE REFLECTION.
MY BLOOD COVERS THE STONE AND MAKES EVERYTHING AROUND ME RED AS THE SUN.

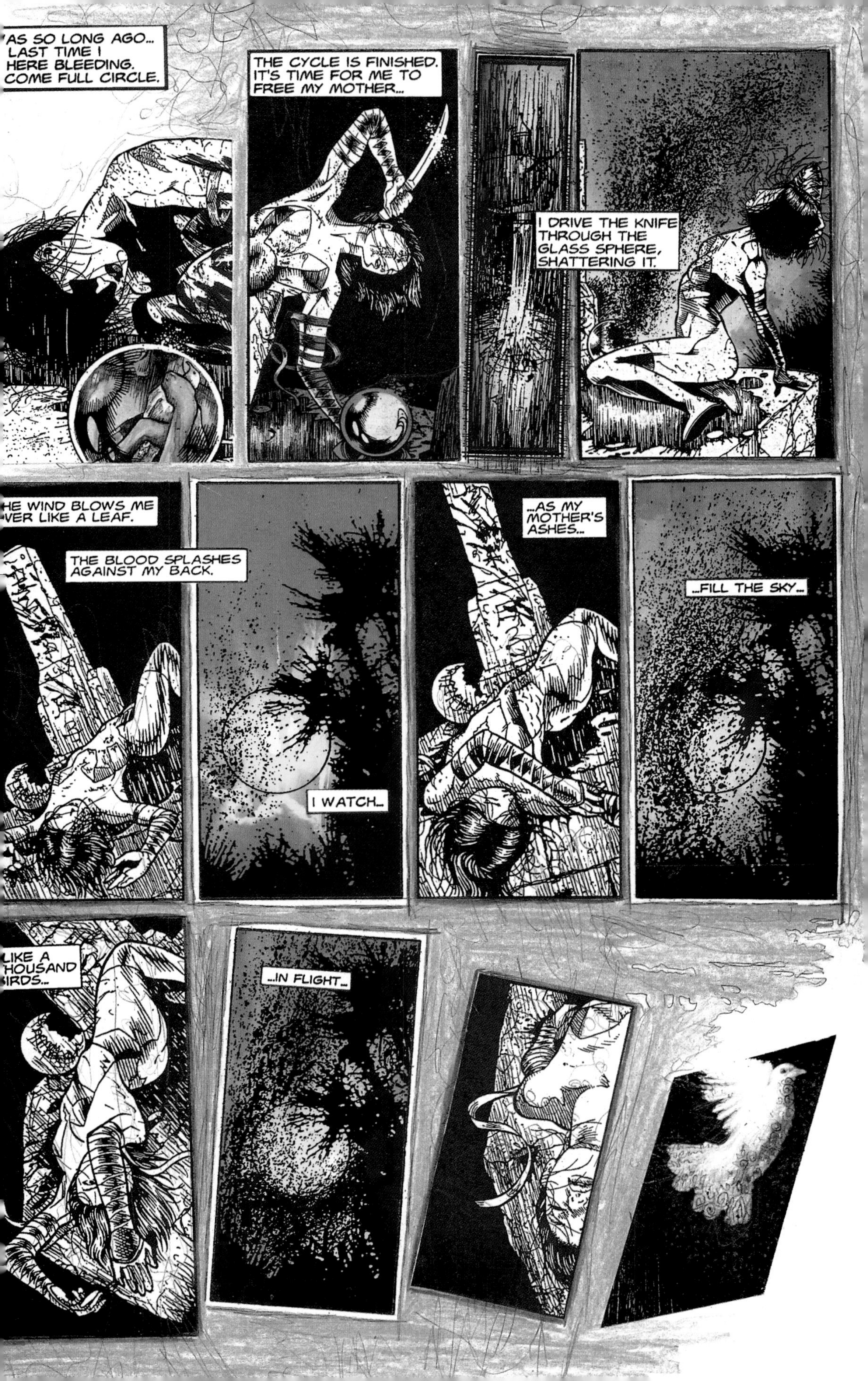

'AS SO LONG AGO... LAST TIME I HERE BLEEDING. COME FULL CIRCLE.
THE CYCLE IS FINISHED. IT'S TIME FOR ME TO FREE MY MOTHER...
I DRIVE THE KNIFE THROUGH THE GLASS SPHERE, SHATTERING IT.
HE WIND BLOWS ME VER LIKE A LEAF.
THE BLOOD SPLASHES AGAINST MY BACK.
I WATCH...
...AS MY MOTHER'S ASHES...
...FILL THE SKY...
LIKE A HOUSAND IRDS...
...IN FLIGHT...

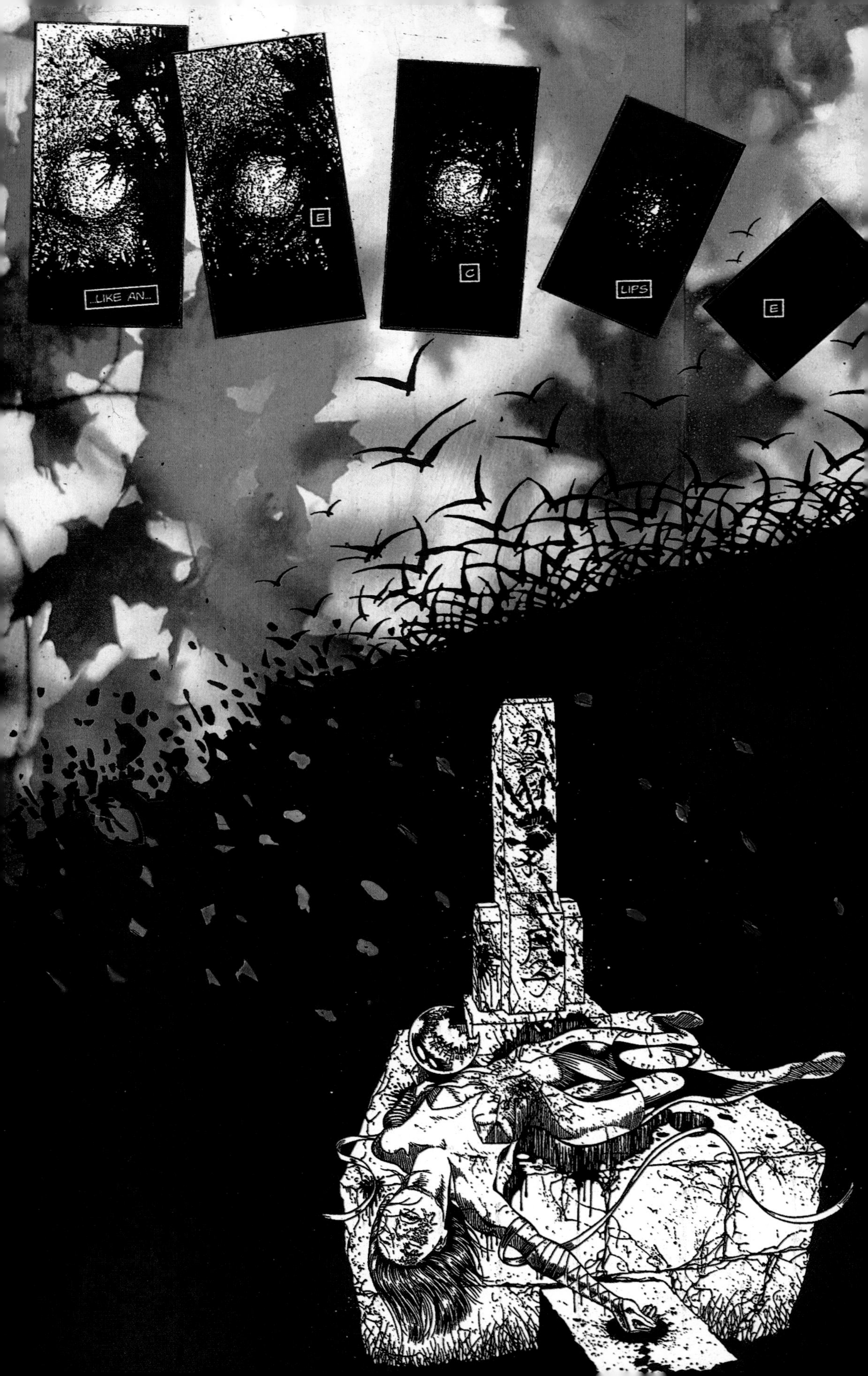
...LIKE AN...
E
C
LIPS
E

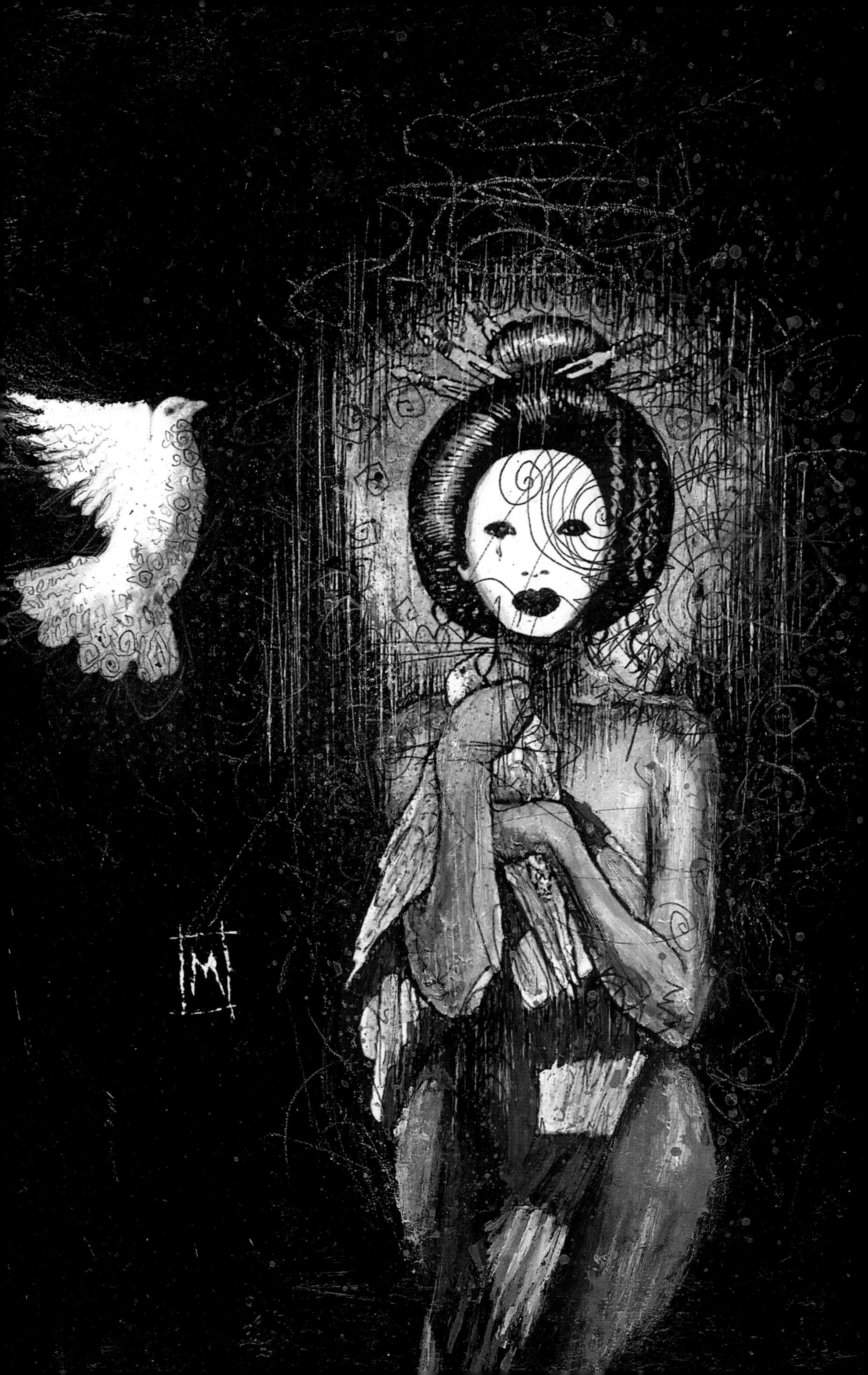

Between us who were until now

In life and in after-life kept apart—

Now the cravings of broken desire are

stilled;

the two are united with the

Whole, and therefore with each other, and melt into perfect un-

ion—according to the Great Teaching.

And now they have van-   ished.

The force that materialized them from vision is very slen-

der: it can sustain them no longer;

A service that spreads in two worlds

And binds up an ancient love.'

stepping through the broken shell of one

world into another.

A dream-bridge over wild grass.

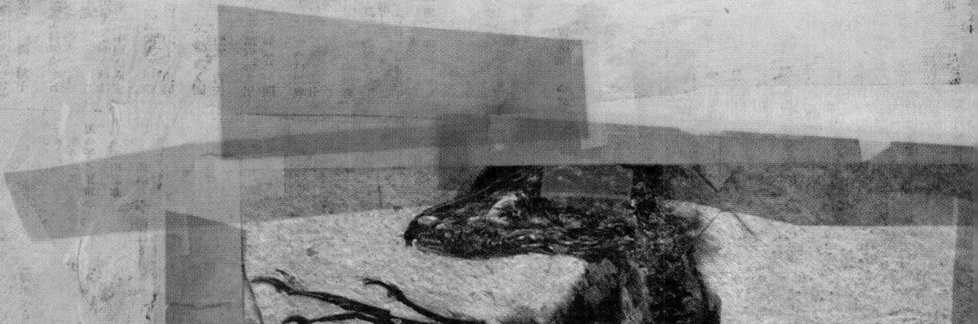

Part two

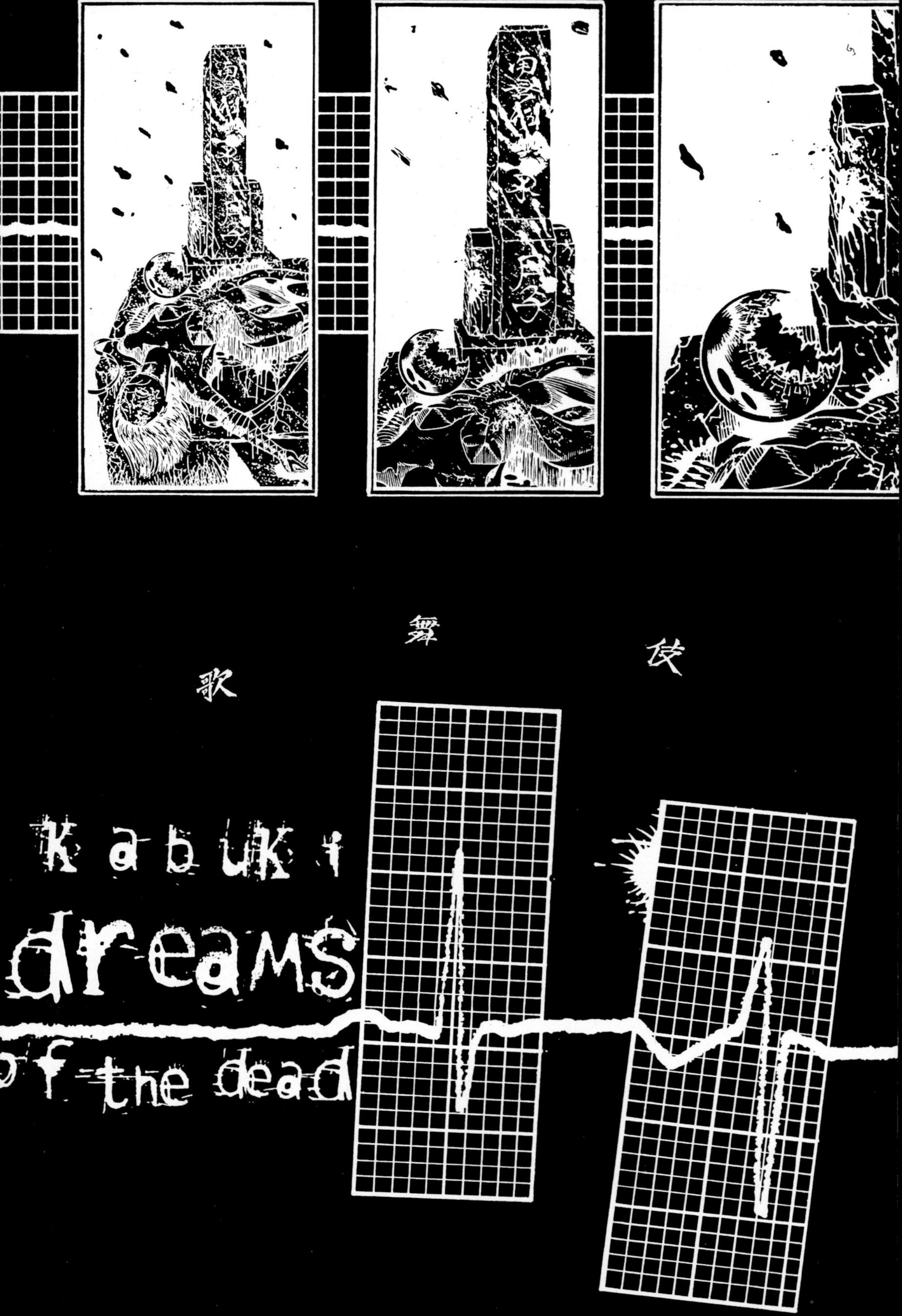
歌 舞 伎
Kabuki
dreams
of the dead

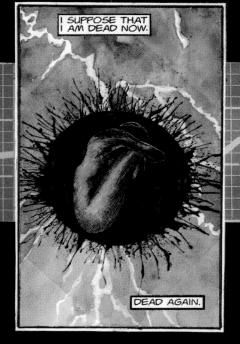

I SUPPOSE THAT I AM DEAD NOW.

DEAD AGAIN.

IT'S MORE COMFORTABLE THIS WAY.

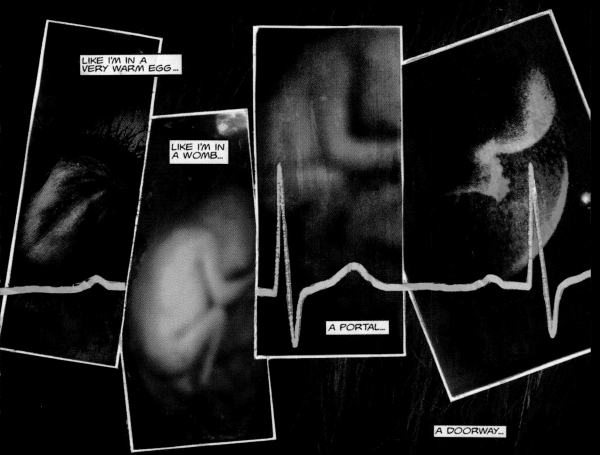

LIKE I'M IN A VERY WARM EGG...

LIKE I'M IN A WOMB...

A PORTAL...

A DOORWAY...

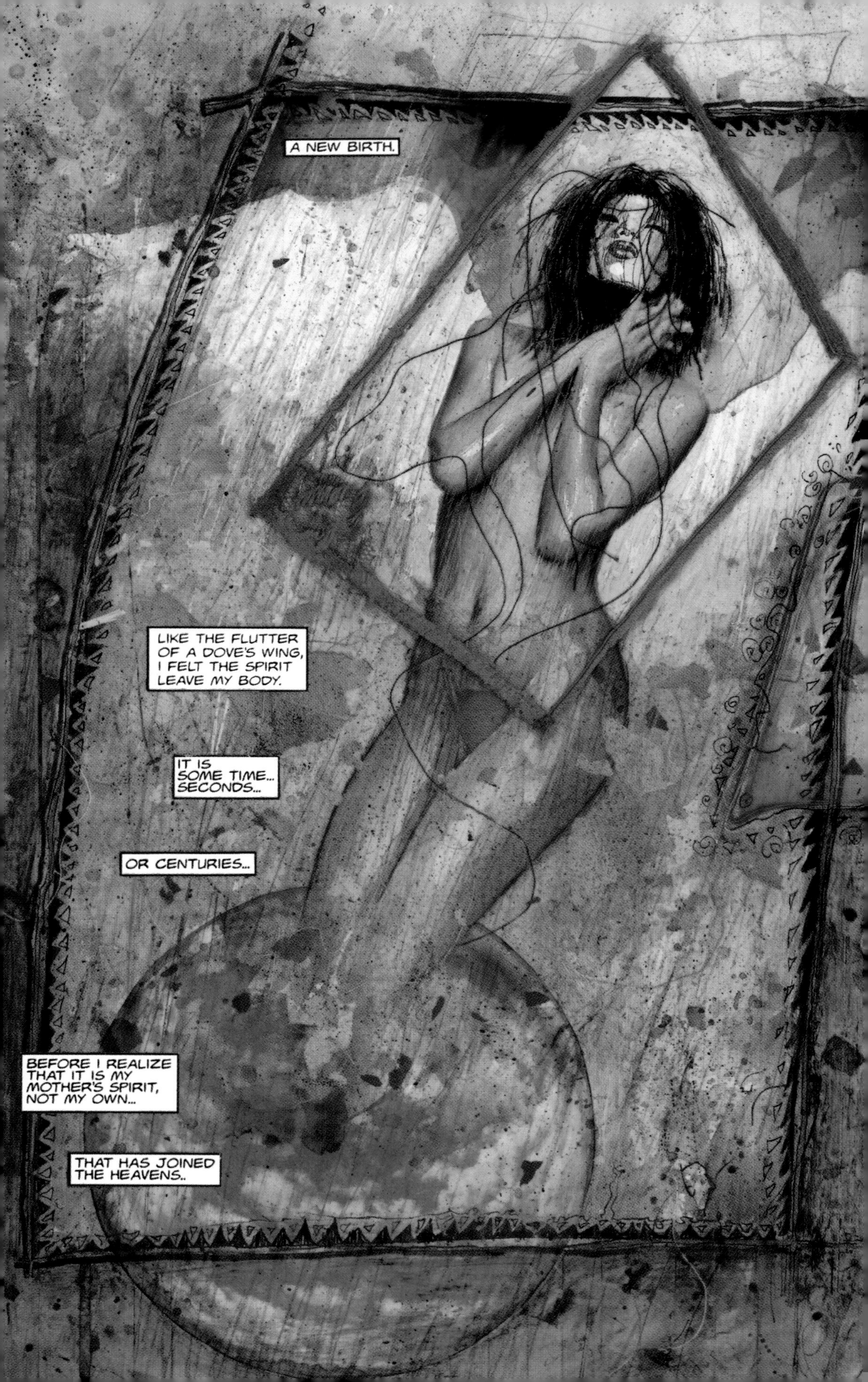
A NEW BIRTH.
LIKE THE FLUTTER OF A DOVE'S WING, I FELT THE SPIRIT LEAVE MY BODY.
IT IS SOME TIME... SECONDS...
OR CENTURIES...
BEFORE I REALIZE THAT IT IS MY MOTHER'S SPIRIT, NOT MY OWN...
THAT HAS JOINED THE HEAVENS..

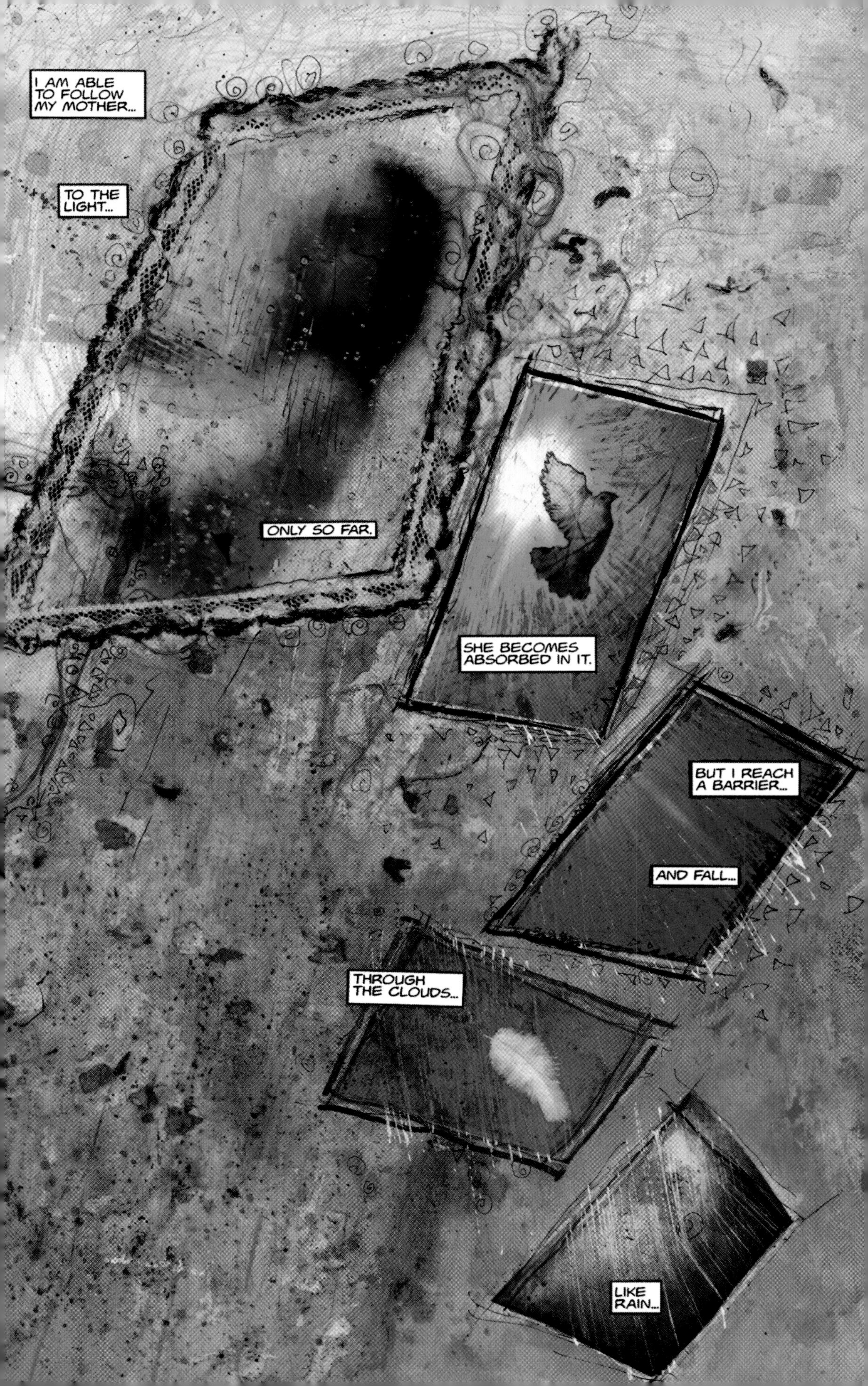
I AM ABLE TO FOLLOW MY MOTHER...
TO THE LIGHT...
ONLY SO FAR.
SHE BECOMES ABSORBED IN IT.
BUT I REACH A BARRIER...
AND FALL...
THROUGH THE CLOUDS...
LIKE RAIN...

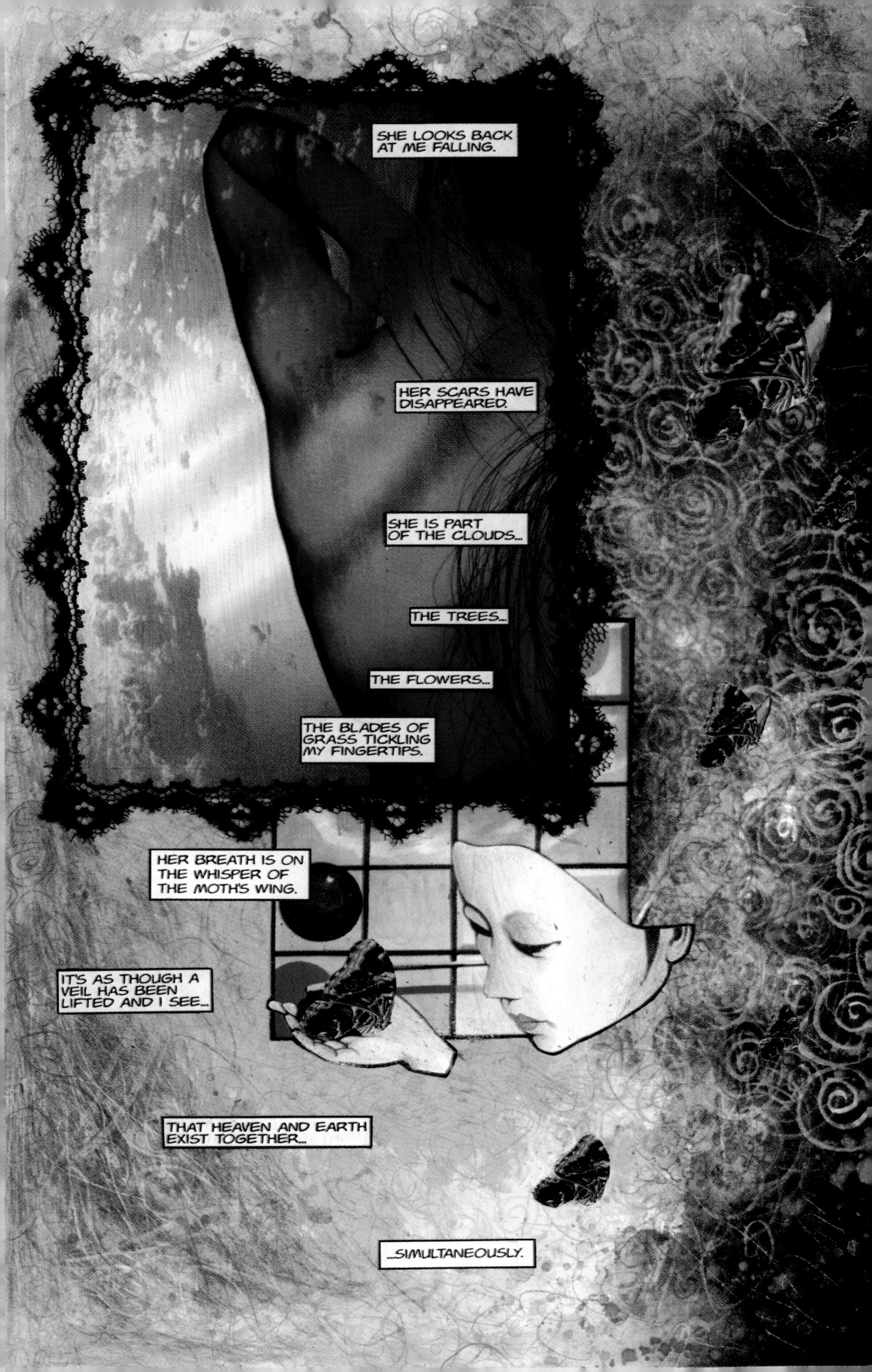
SHE LOOKS BACK AT ME FALLING.
HER SCARS HAVE DISAPPEARED.
SHE IS PART OF THE CLOUDS...
THE TREES...
THE FLOWERS...
THE BLADES OF GRASS TICKLING MY FINGERTIPS.
HER BREATH IS ON THE WHISPER OF THE MOTH'S WING.
IT'S AS THOUGH A VEIL HAS BEEN LIFTED AND I SEE...
THAT HEAVEN AND EARTH EXIST TOGETHER...
...SIMULTANEOUSLY.

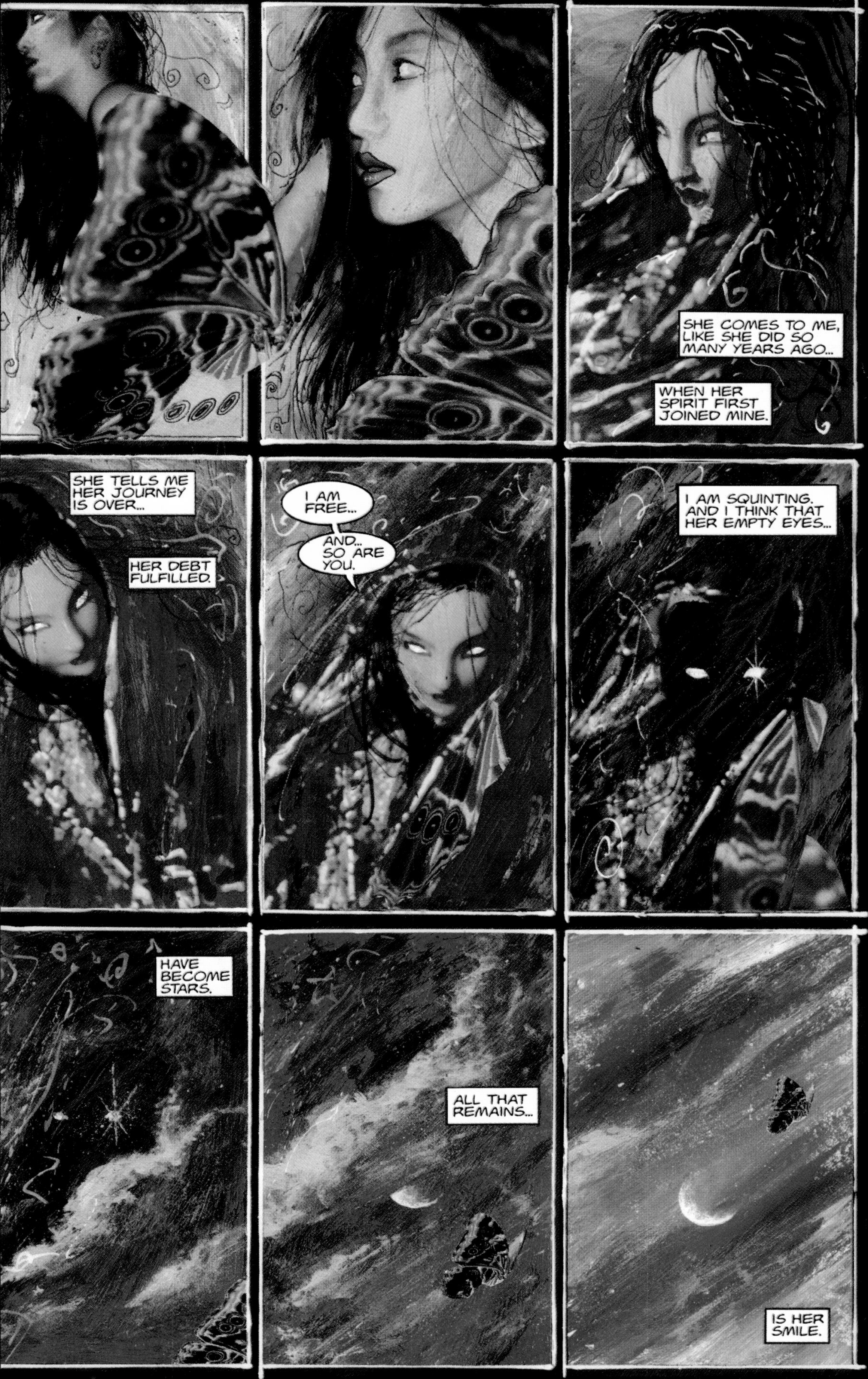
SHE COMES TO ME, LIKE SHE DID SO MANY YEARS AGO...
WHEN HER SPIRIT FIRST JOINED MINE.
SHE TELLS ME HER JOURNEY IS OVER...
HER DEBT FULFILLED.
I AM FREE...
AND... SO ARE YOU.
I AM SQUINTING. AND I THINK THAT HER EMPTY EYES...
HAVE BECOME STARS.
ALL THAT REMAINS...
IS HER SMILE.

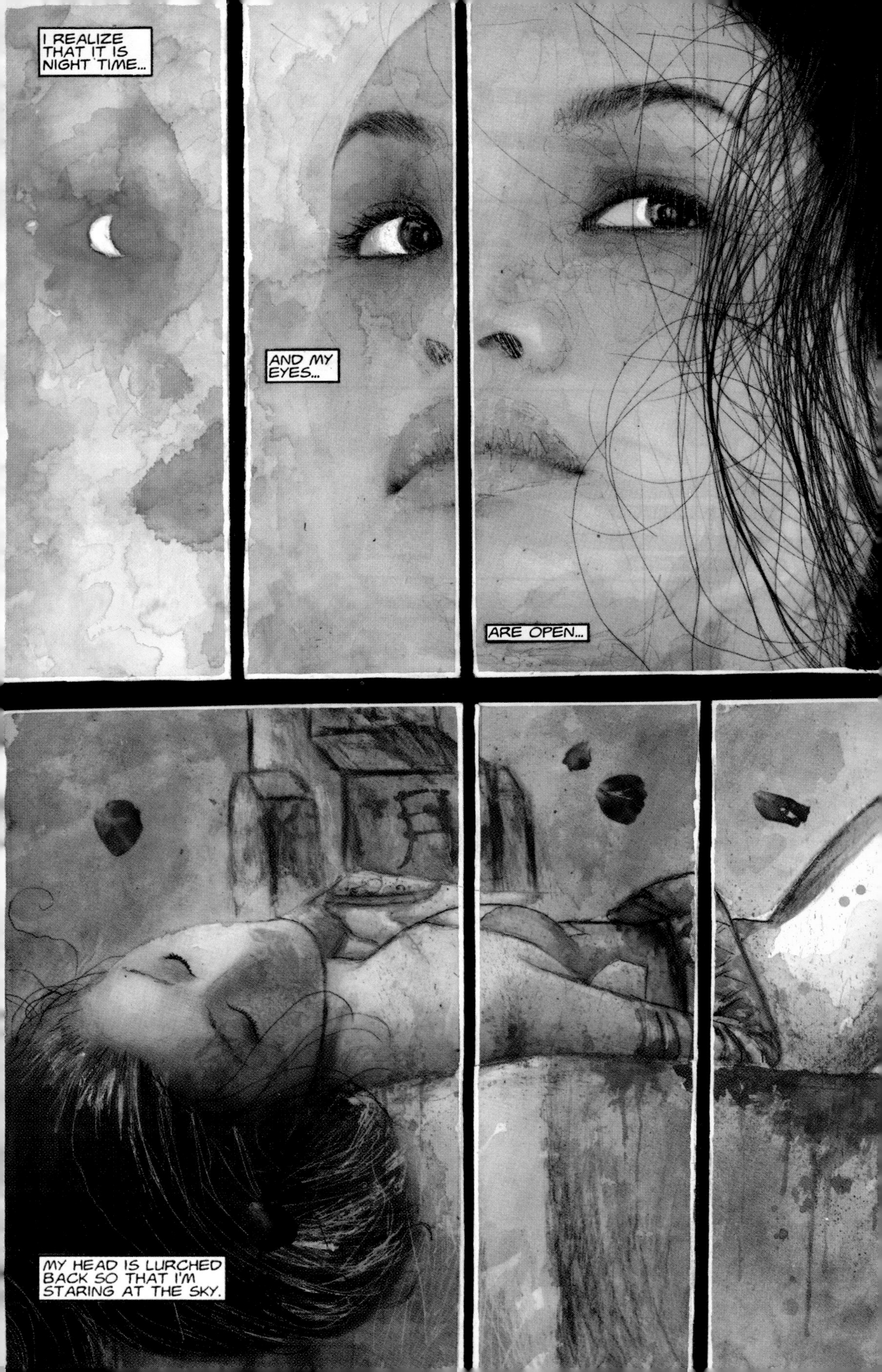
I REALIZE THAT IT IS NIGHT TIME...
AND MY EYES...
ARE OPEN...
MY HEAD IS LURCHED BACK SO THAT I'M STARING AT THE SKY.

EVERYTHING IS STICKY...

AND I CAN'T SEEM TO MOVE.

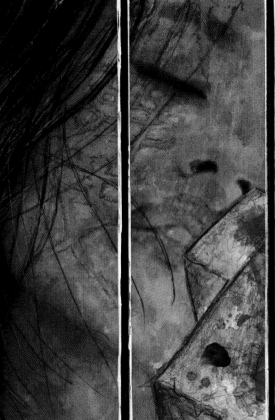

DRIED BLOOD HAS FUSED MY SKIN TO THE STONE.

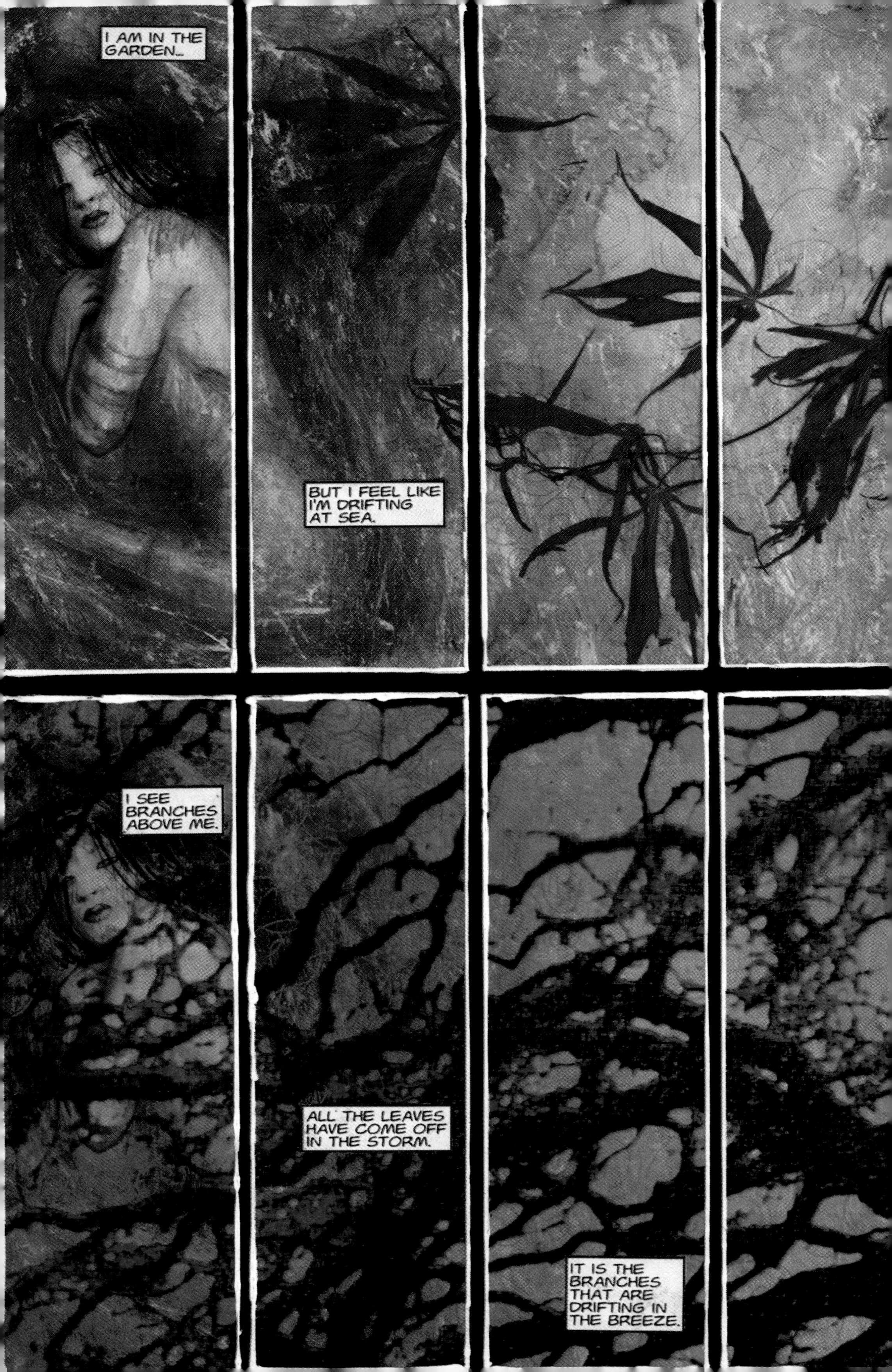
I AM IN THE GARDEN...
BUT I FEEL LIKE I'M DRIFTING AT SEA.
I SEE BRANCHES ABOVE ME.
ALL THE LEAVES HAVE COME OFF IN THE STORM.
IT IS THE BRANCHES THAT ARE DRIFTING IN THE BREEZE.

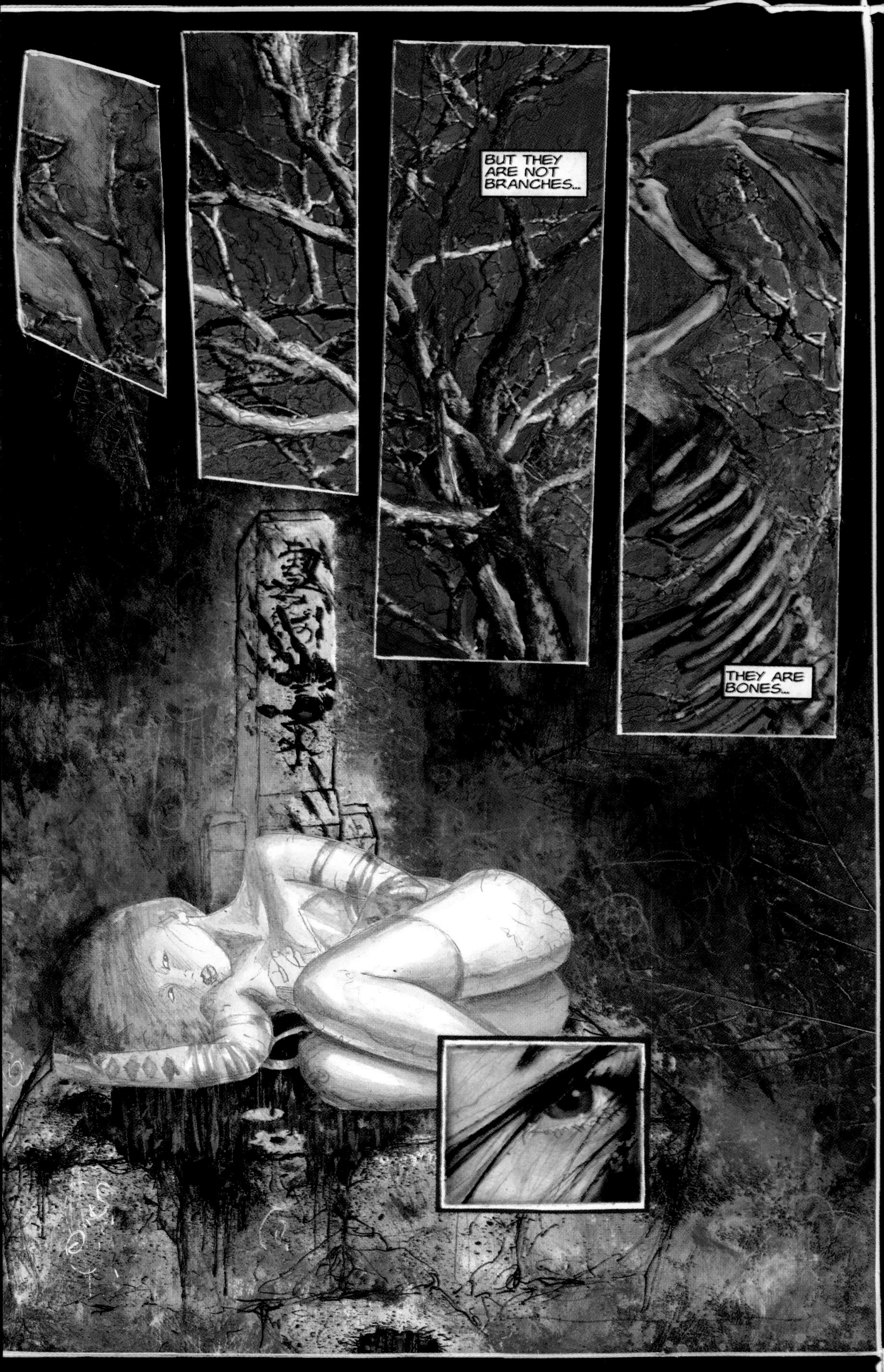
BUT THEY ARE NOT BRANCHES...
THEY ARE BONES...

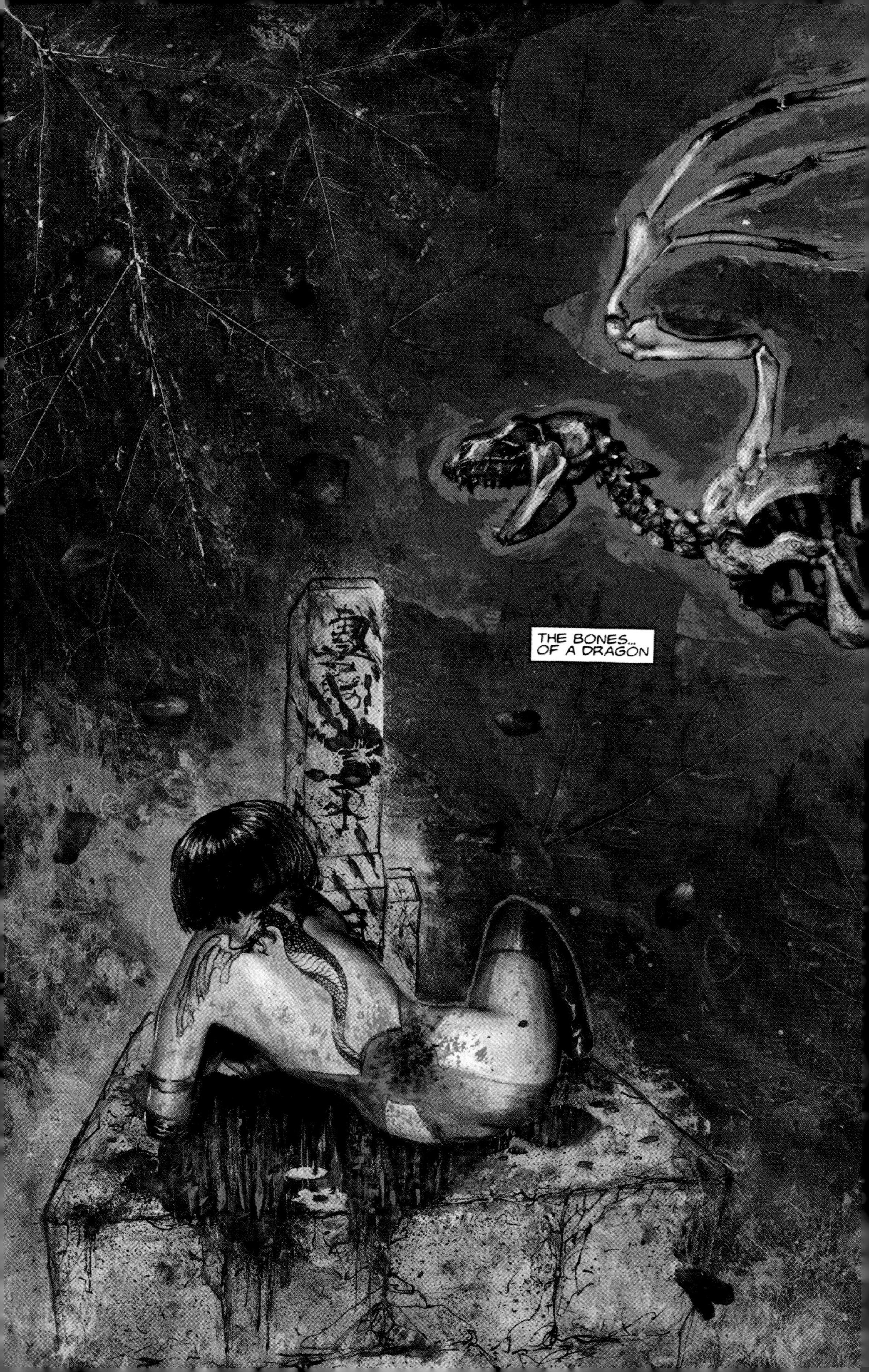
THE BONES...
OF A DRAGON

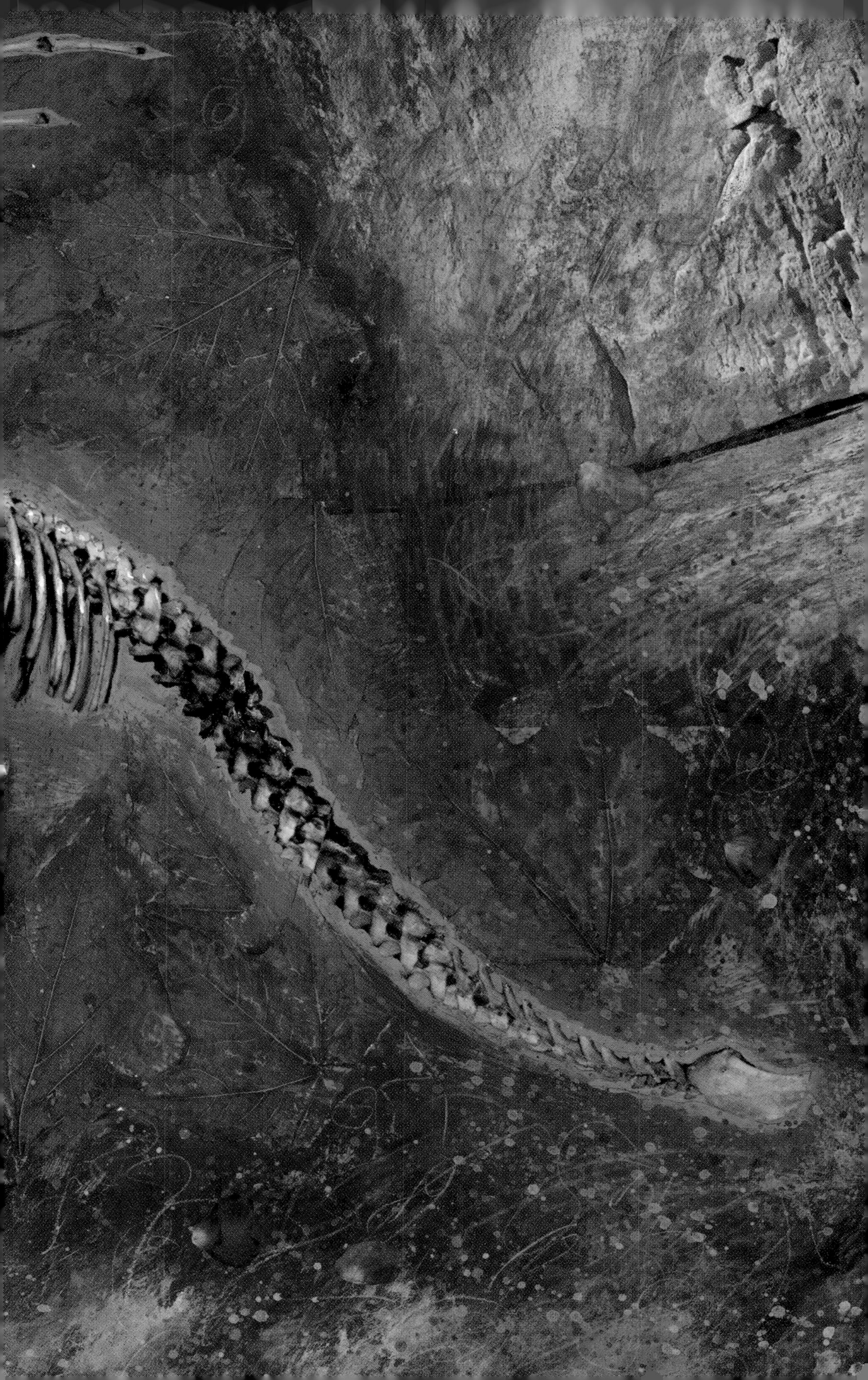

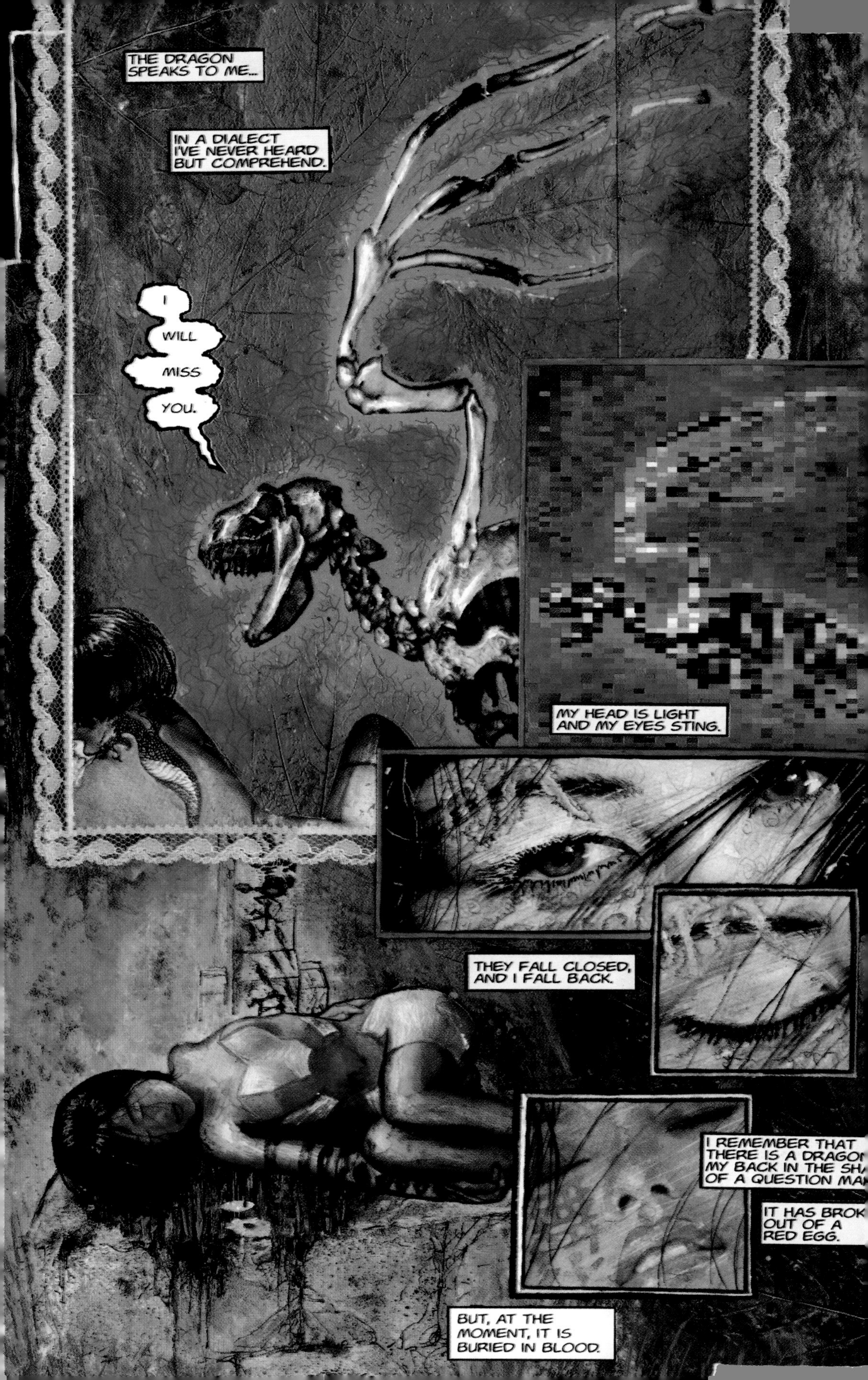
THE DRAGON SPEAKS TO ME...
IN A DIALECT I'VE NEVER HEARD BUT COMPREHEND.
I WILL MISS YOU.
MY HEAD IS LIGHT AND MY EYES STING.
THEY FALL CLOSED, AND I FALL BACK.
I REMEMBER THAT THERE IS A DRAGON
IT HAS BROK
BUT, AT THE MOMENT, IT IS BURIED IN BLOOD.

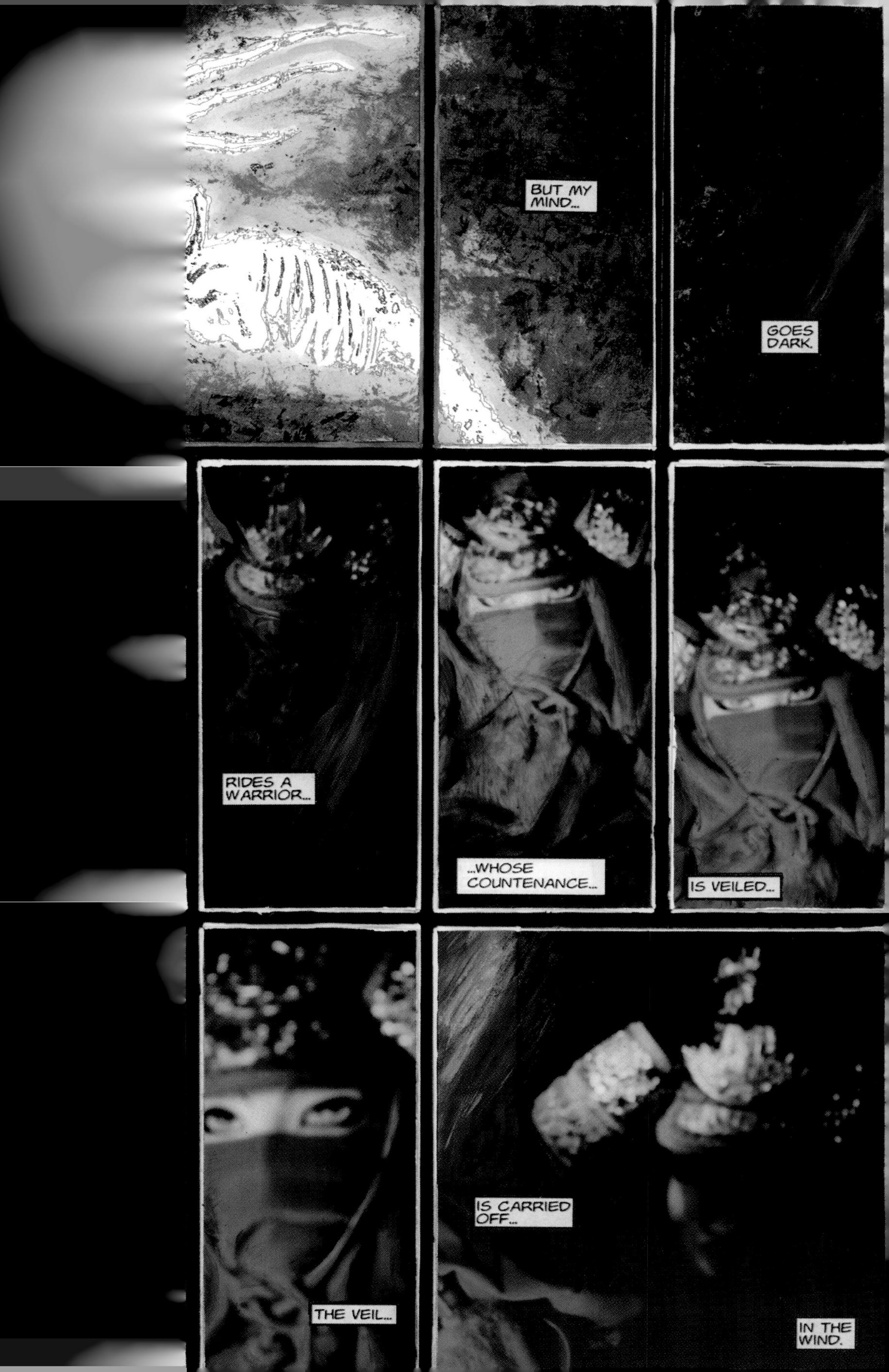
BUT MY MIND...
GOES DARK.
RIDES A WARRIOR...
...WHOSE COUNTENANCE...
IS VEILED...
THE VEIL...
IS CARRIED OFF...
IN THE WIND.

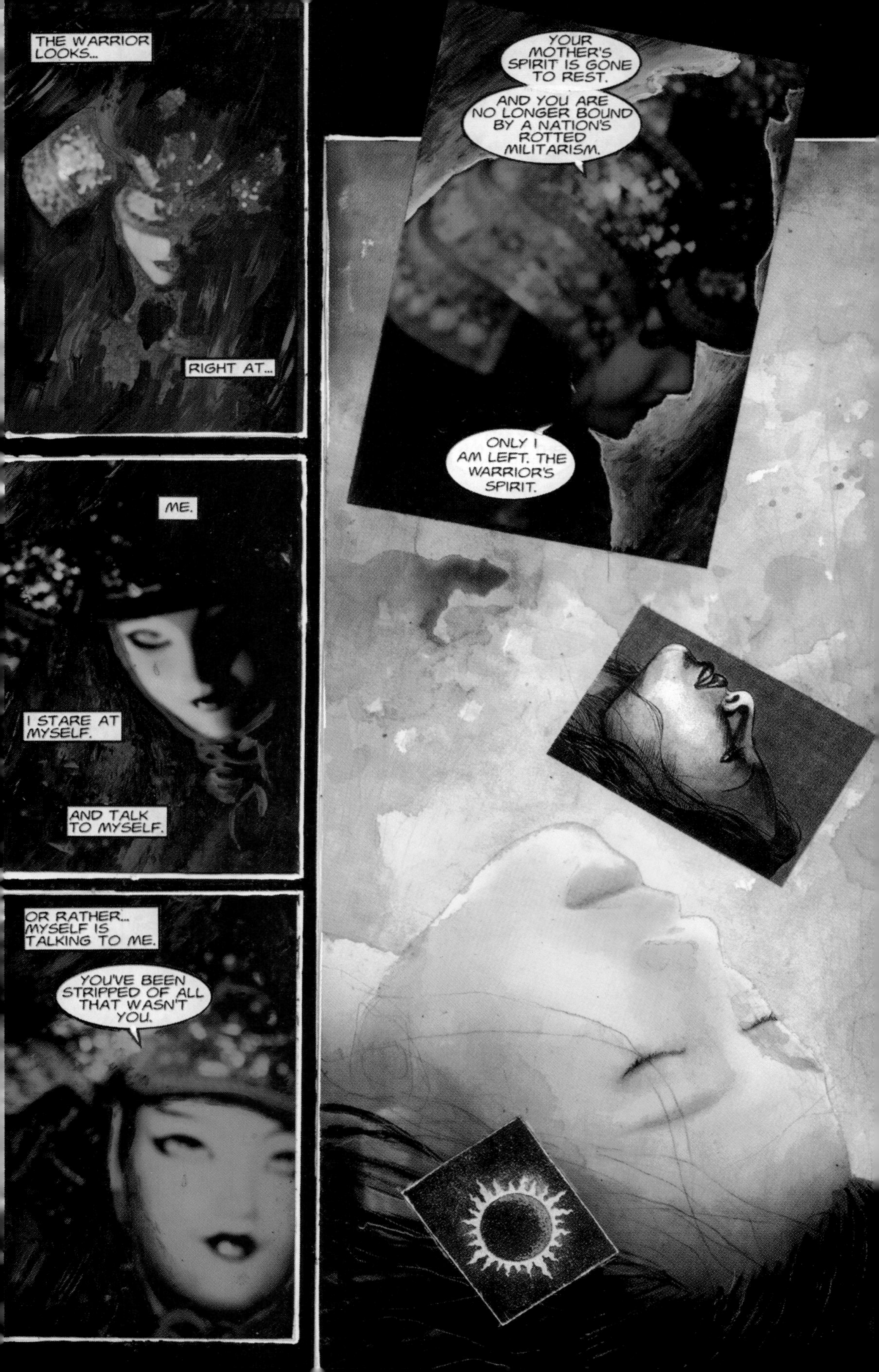
THE WARRIOR LOOKS...
RIGHT AT...
ME.
I STARE AT MYSELF.
AND TALK TO MYSELF.
OR RATHER... MYSELF IS TALKING TO ME.
YOU'VE BEEN STRIPPED OF ALL THAT WASN'T YOU.
YOUR MOTHER'S SPIRIT IS GONE TO REST.
AND YOU ARE NO LONGER BOUND BY A NATION'S ROTTED MILITARISM.
ONLY I AM LEFT. THE WARRIOR'S SPIRIT.

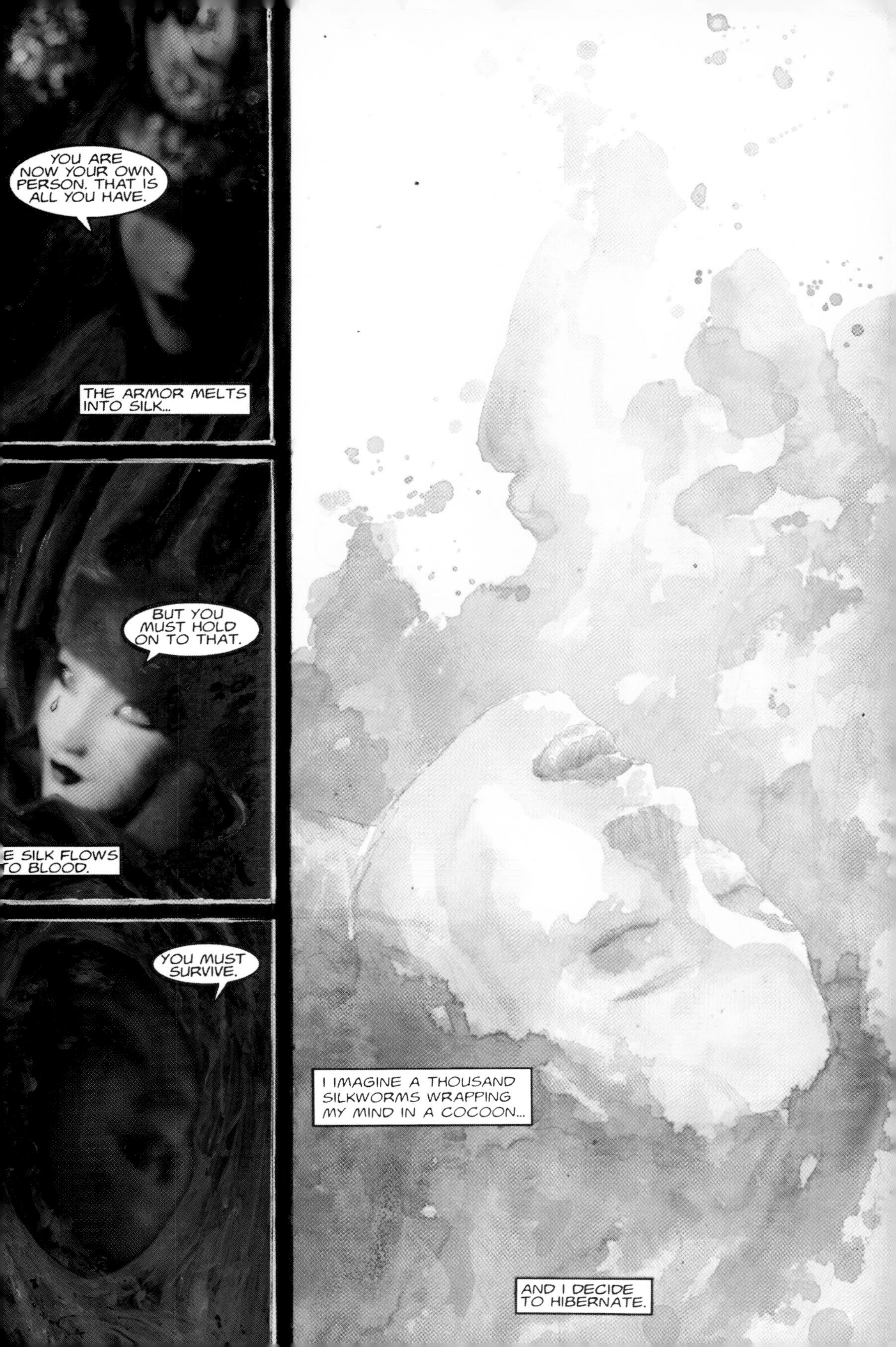
YOU ARE NOW YOUR OWN PERSON. THAT IS ALL YOU HAVE.
THE ARMOR MELTS INTO SILK...
BUT YOU MUST HOLD ON TO THAT.
E SILK FLOWS O BLOOD.
YOU MUST SURVIVE.
I IMAGINE A THOUSAND SILKWORMS WRAPPING MY MIND IN A COCOON...
AND I DECIDE TO HIBERNATE.

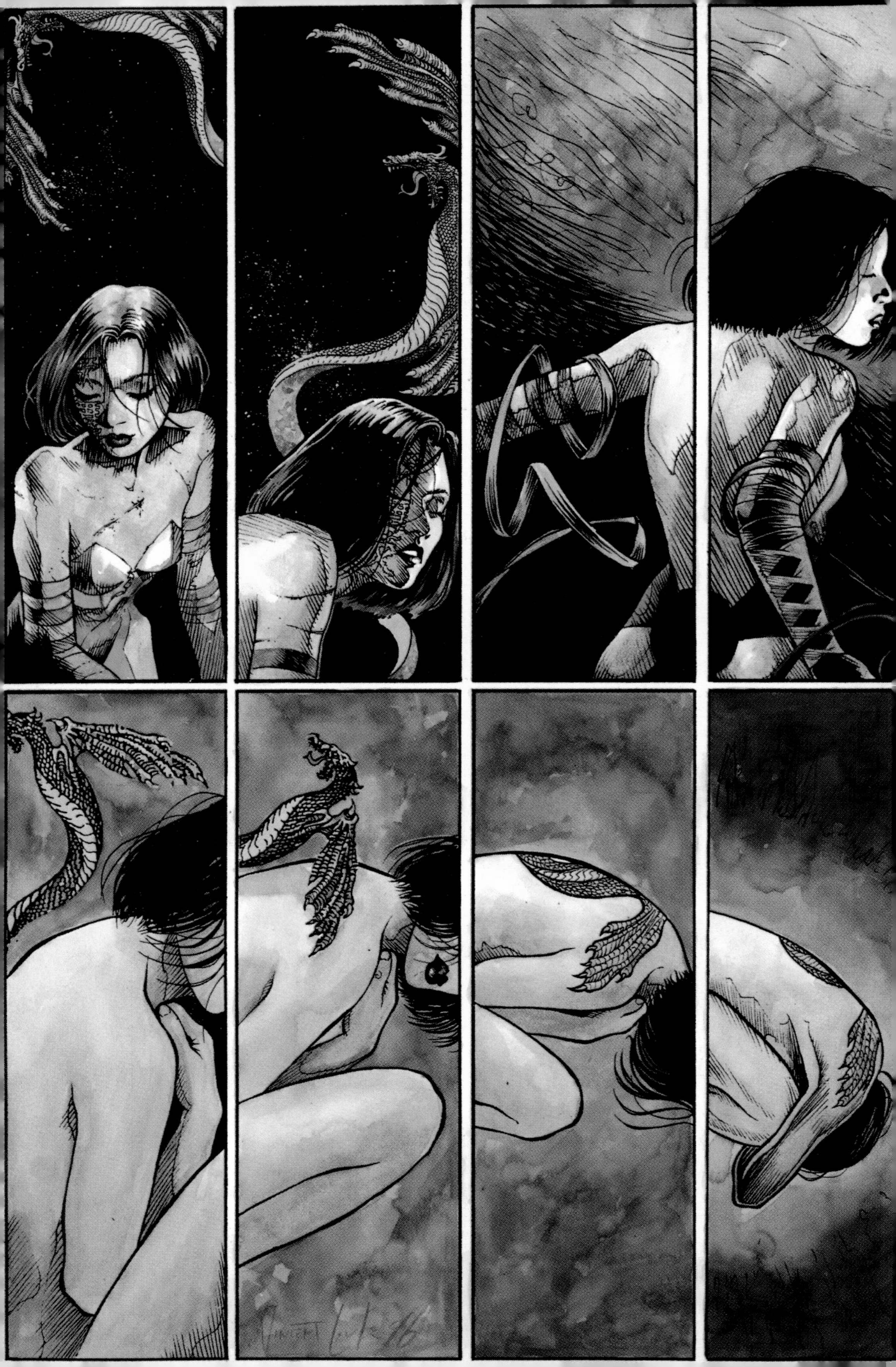

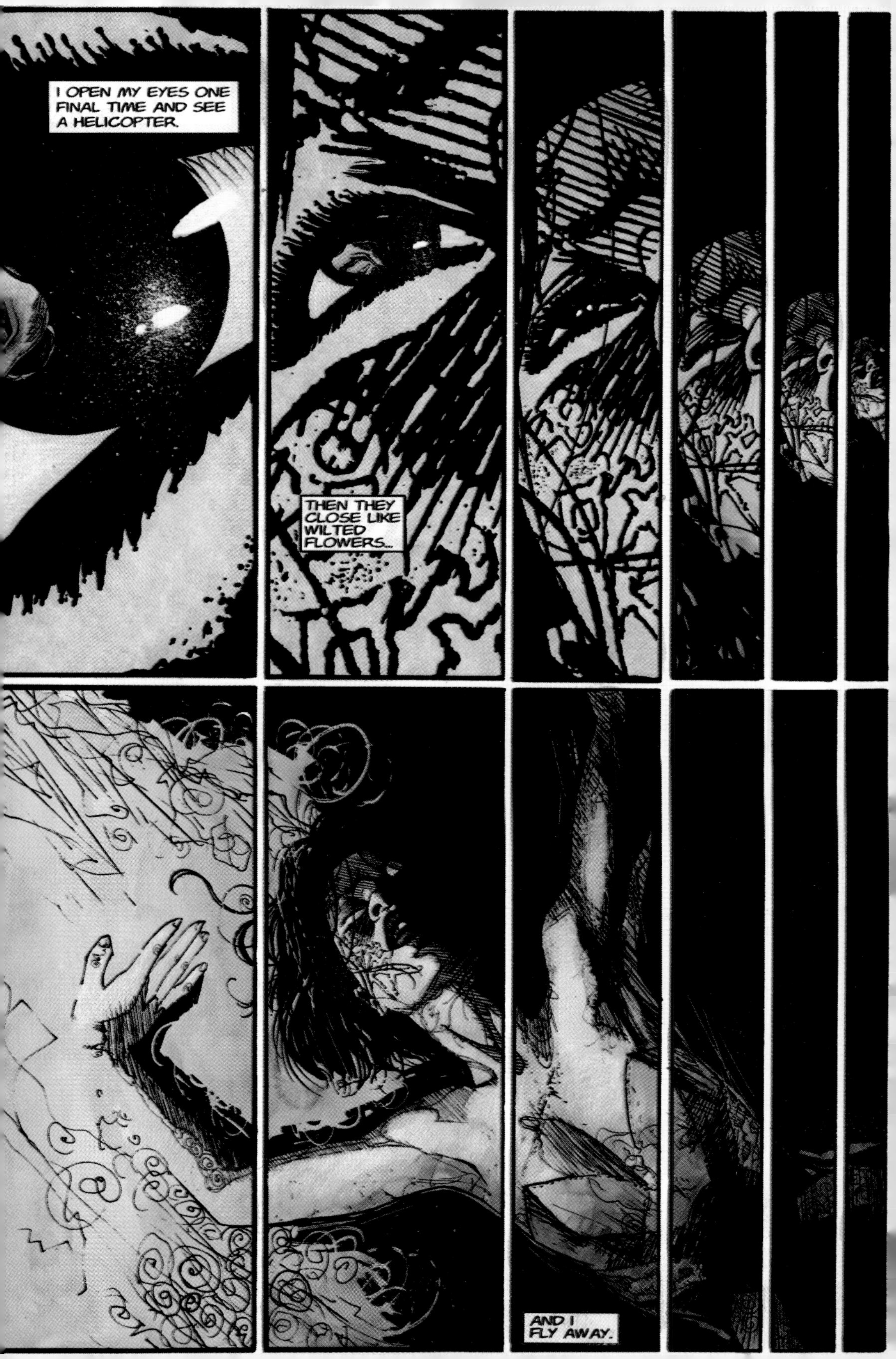
I OPEN MY EYES ONE FINAL TIME AND SEE A HELICOPTER.
THEN THEY CLOSE LIKE WILTED FLOWERS...
AND I FLY AWAY.

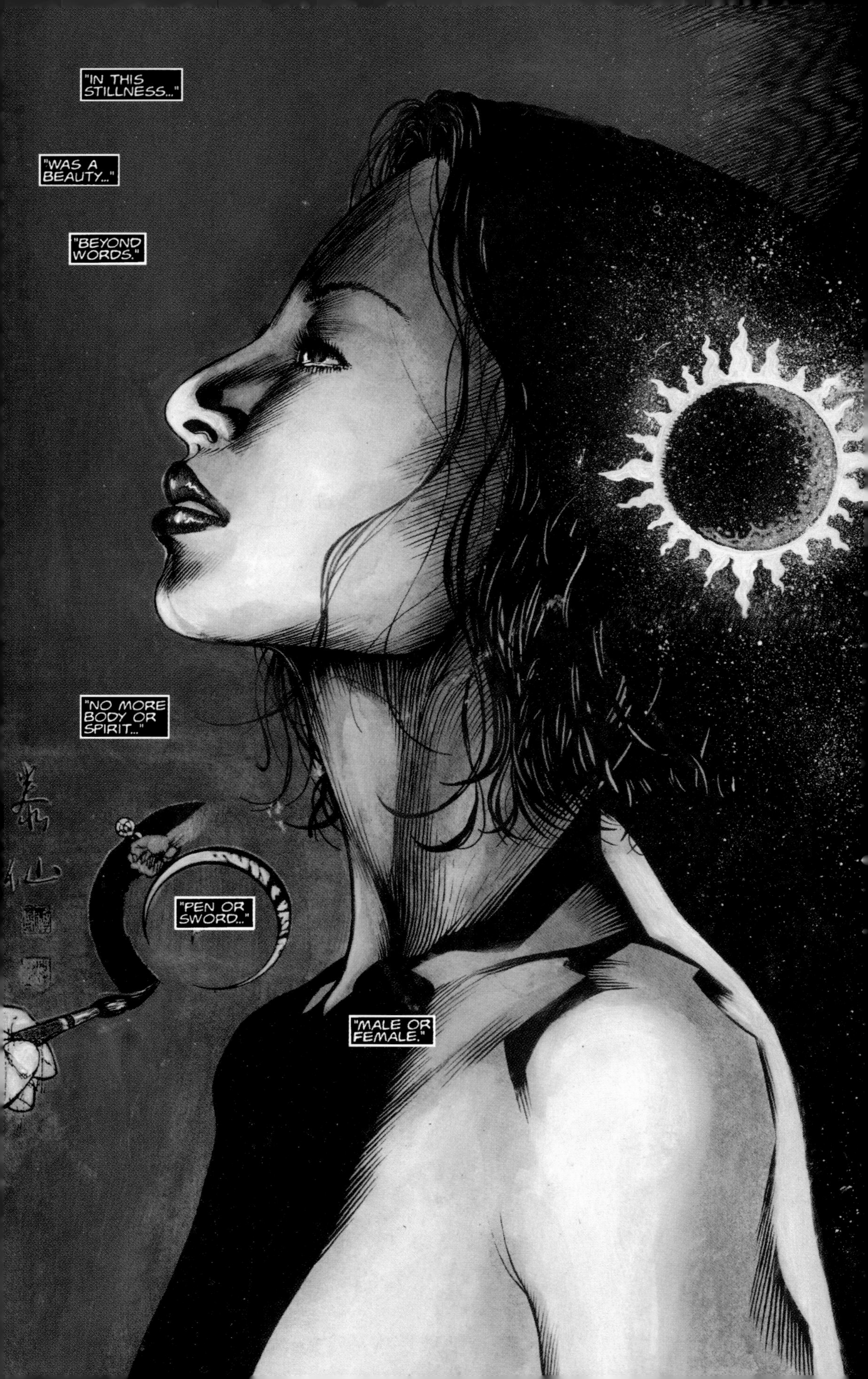
"IN THIS STILLNESS..."
"WAS A BEAUTY..."
"BEYOND WORDS."
"NO MORE BODY OR SPIRIT..."
"PEN OR SWORD..."
"MALE OR FEMALE."

No MoveMent...No Soundo...No Memoriesooo

The perpetual shadow is lonely.

I come, clothed in a memory.'

Theirs is the untracked path of the bird in pure air.

Holy magic ran through

her form as heaven resumes

and even the grass and the flowers pray

a cry of joy from a woman's voice, she her-

self invisible.

the mists receive her. And now—she is a lost star. It is over.

and there through clouds, and a sense of loss irreparable, weeping

and crying in the wind. Is it a spirit, a form impermanent, drift-

ing, or only a flurry of rain in the night?

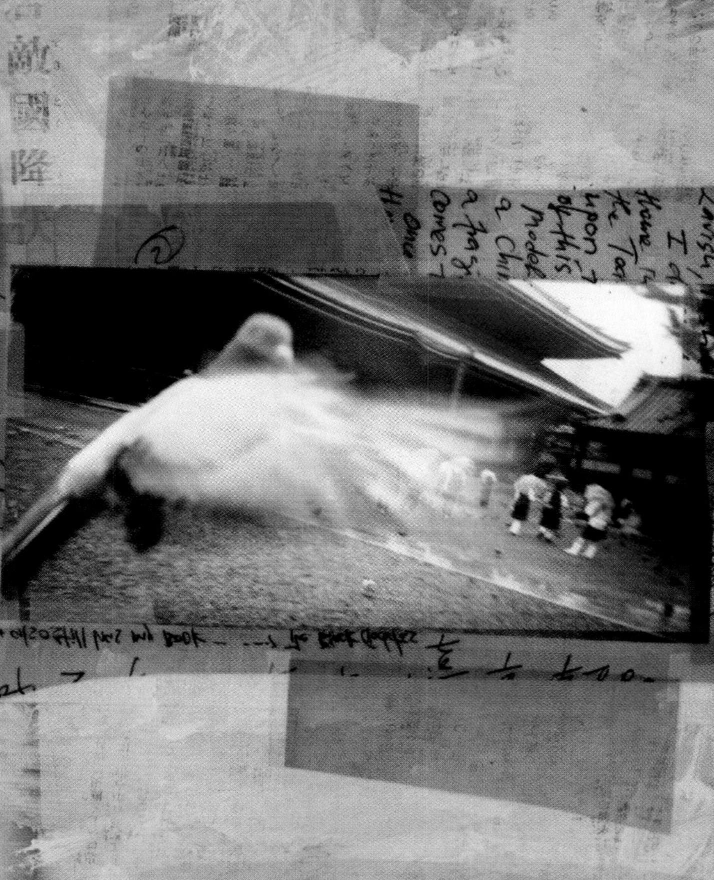

Part three

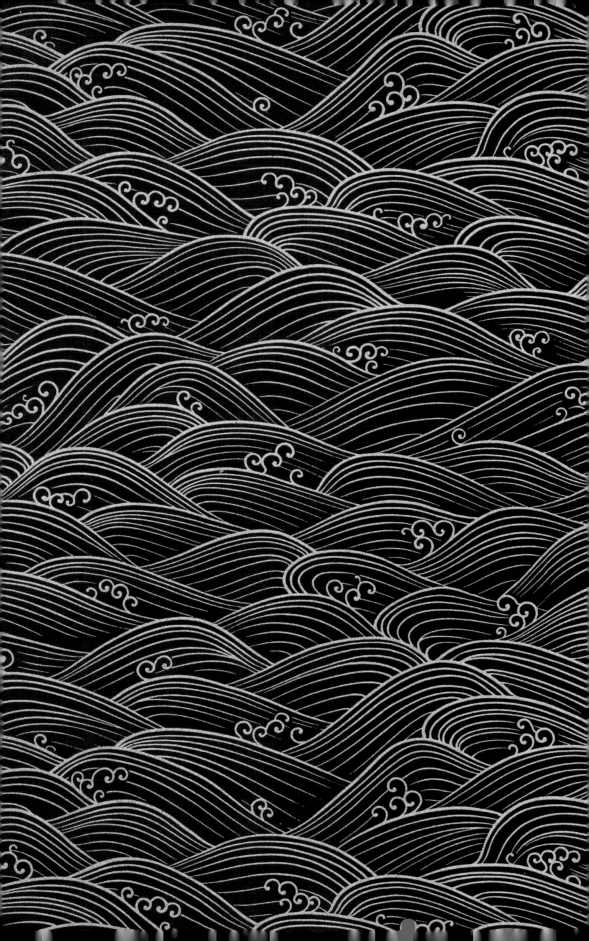

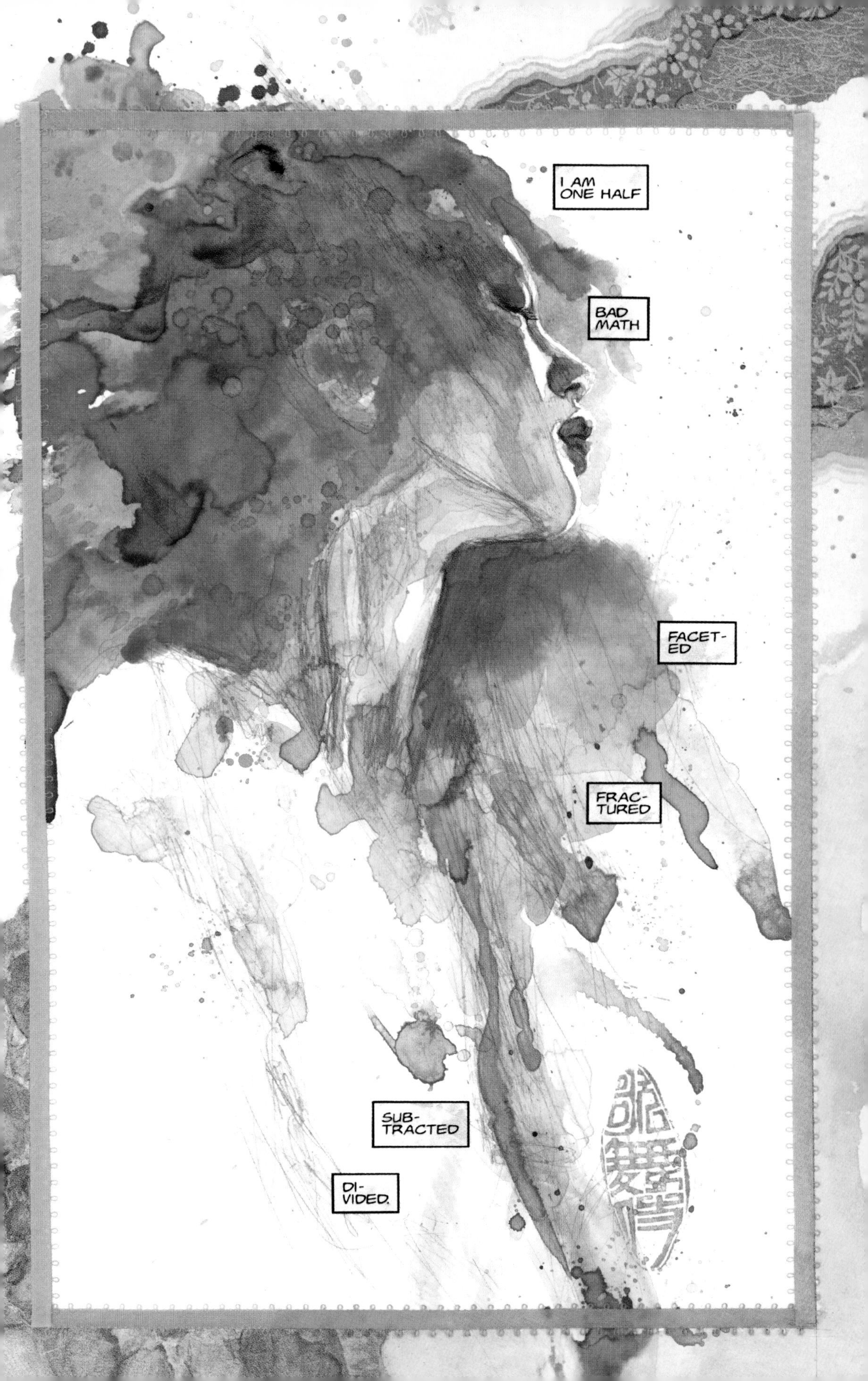
I AM ONE HALF
BAD MATH
FACET-ED
FRAC-TURED
SUB-TRACTED
DI-VIDED.

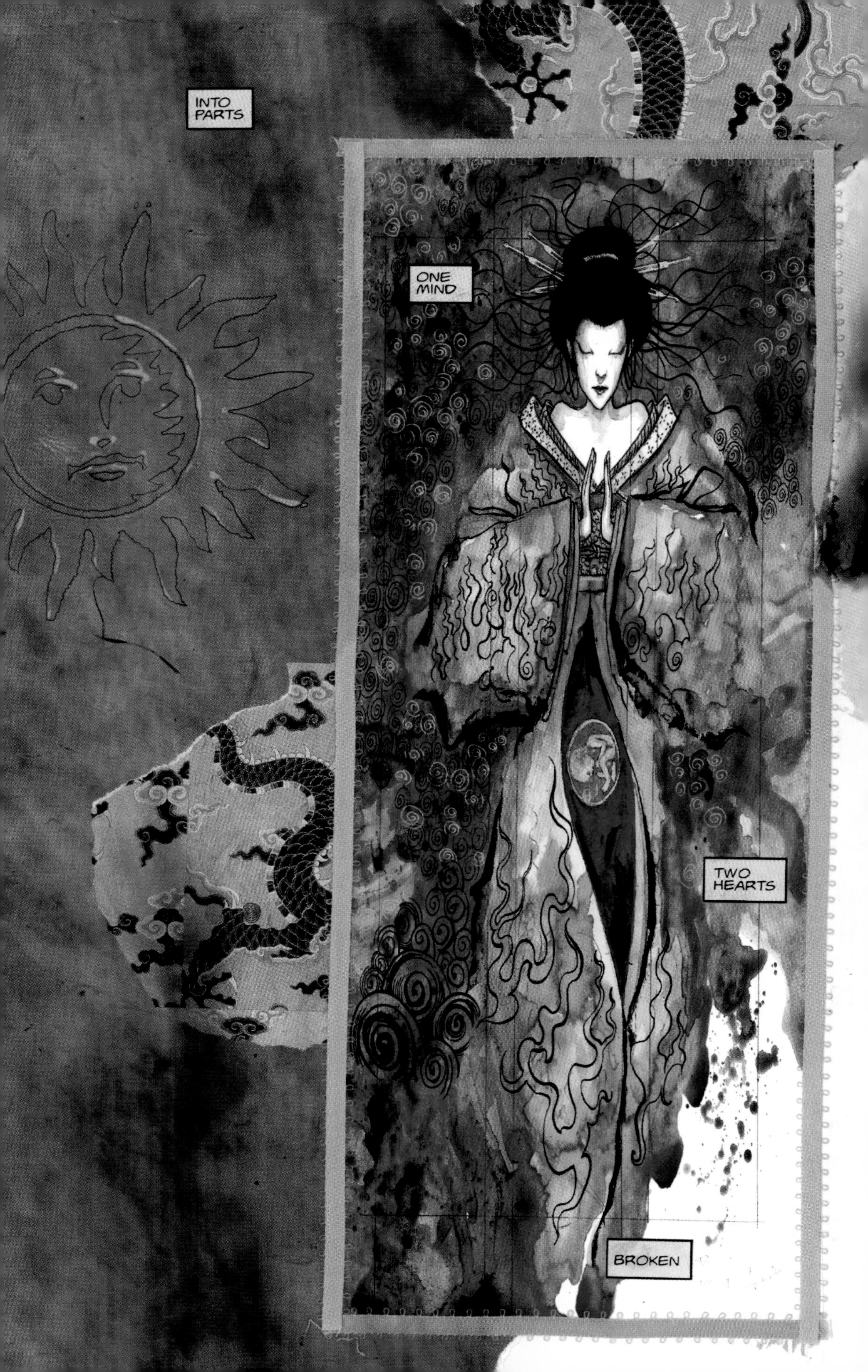
INTO PARTS
ONE MIND
TWO HEARTS
BROKEN

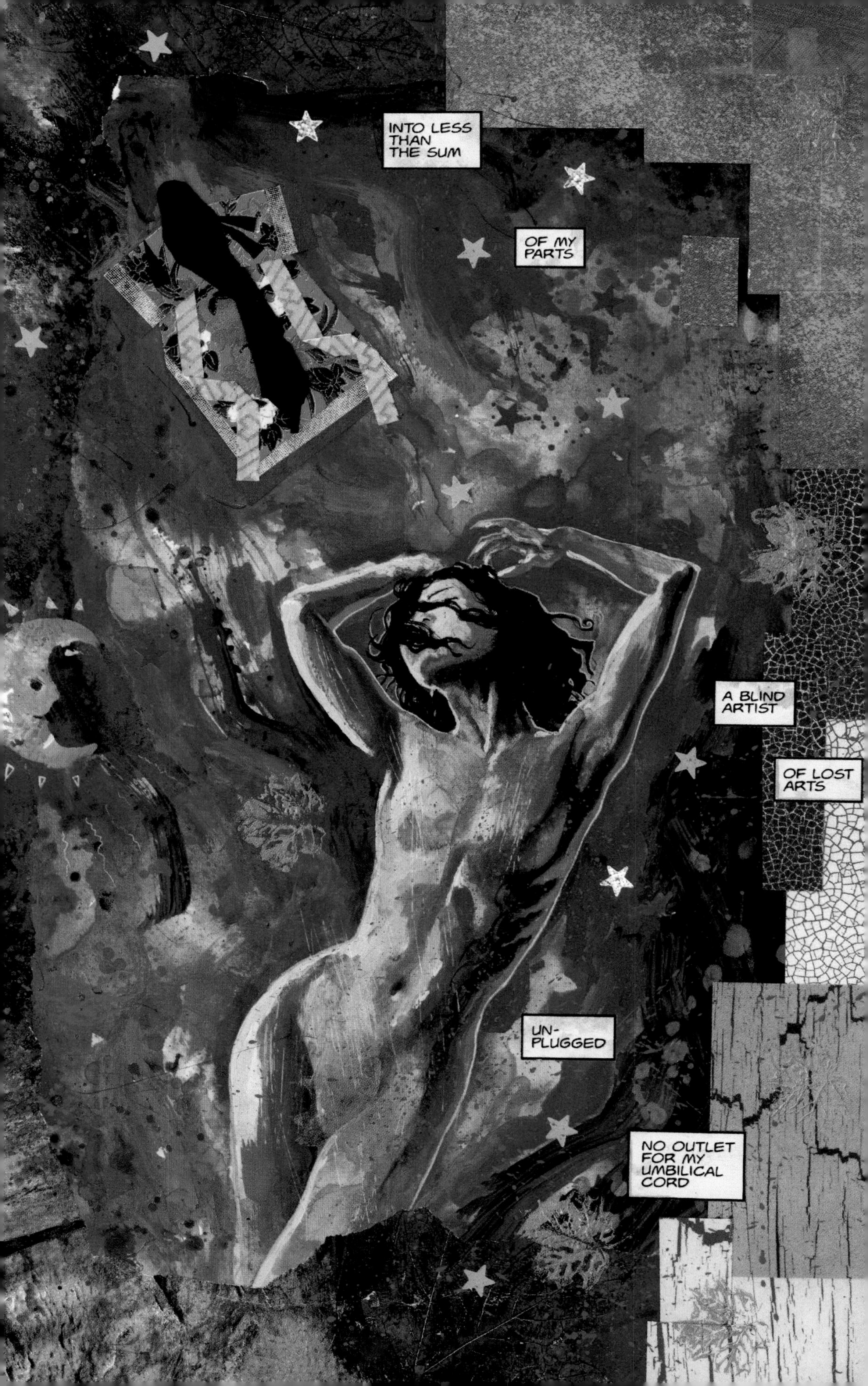
INTO LESS THAN THE SUM
OF MY PARTS
A BLIND ARTIST
OF LOST ARTS
UN-PLUGGED
NO OUTLET FOR MY UMBILICAL CORD

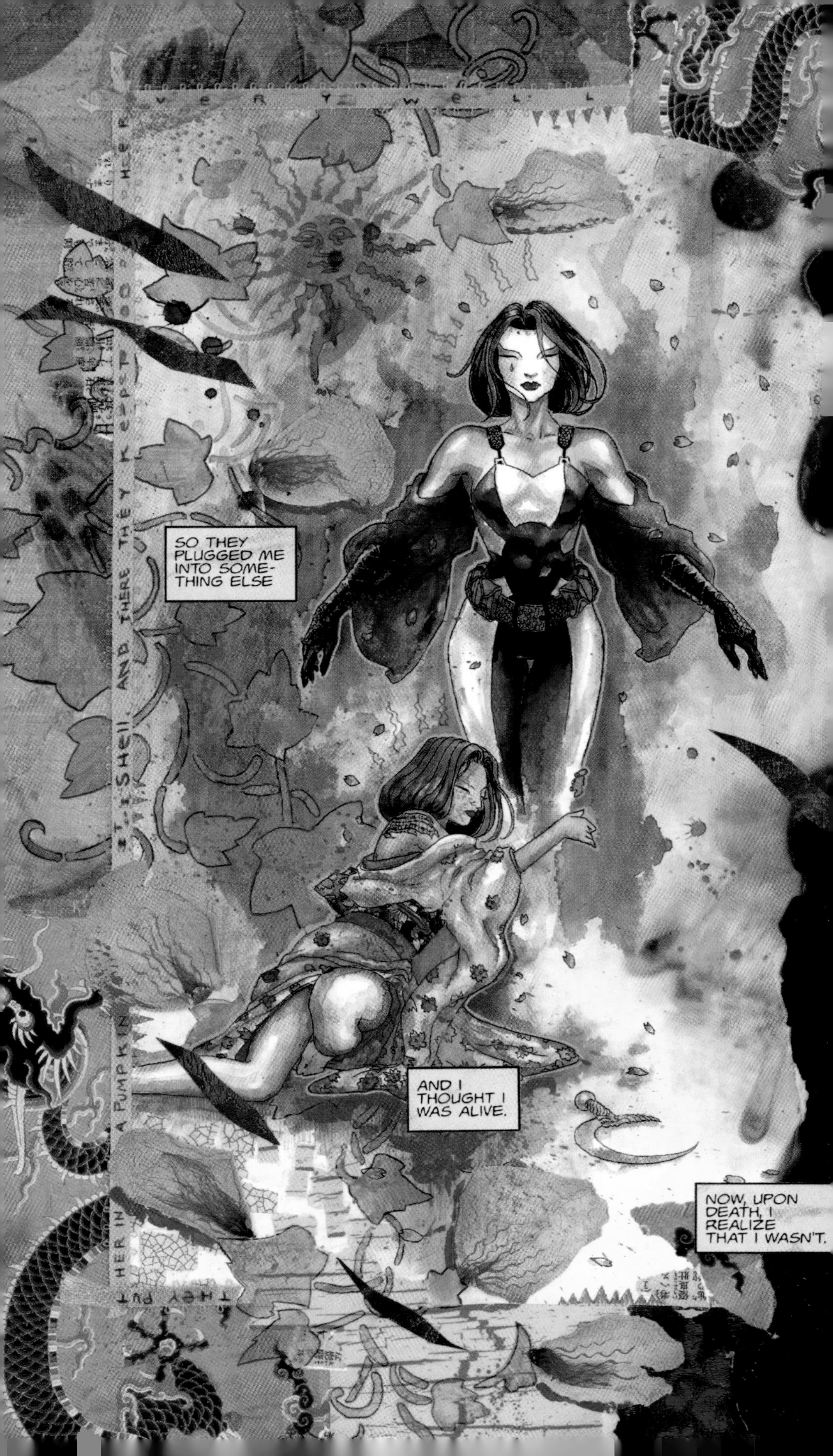
THEY PUT HER IN A PUMPKIN SHELL AND THERE THEY KEPT HER VERY WELL
SO THEY PLUGGED ME INTO SOME-THING ELSE
AND I THOUGHT I WAS ALIVE.
NOW, UPON DEATH, I REALIZE THAT I WASN'T.

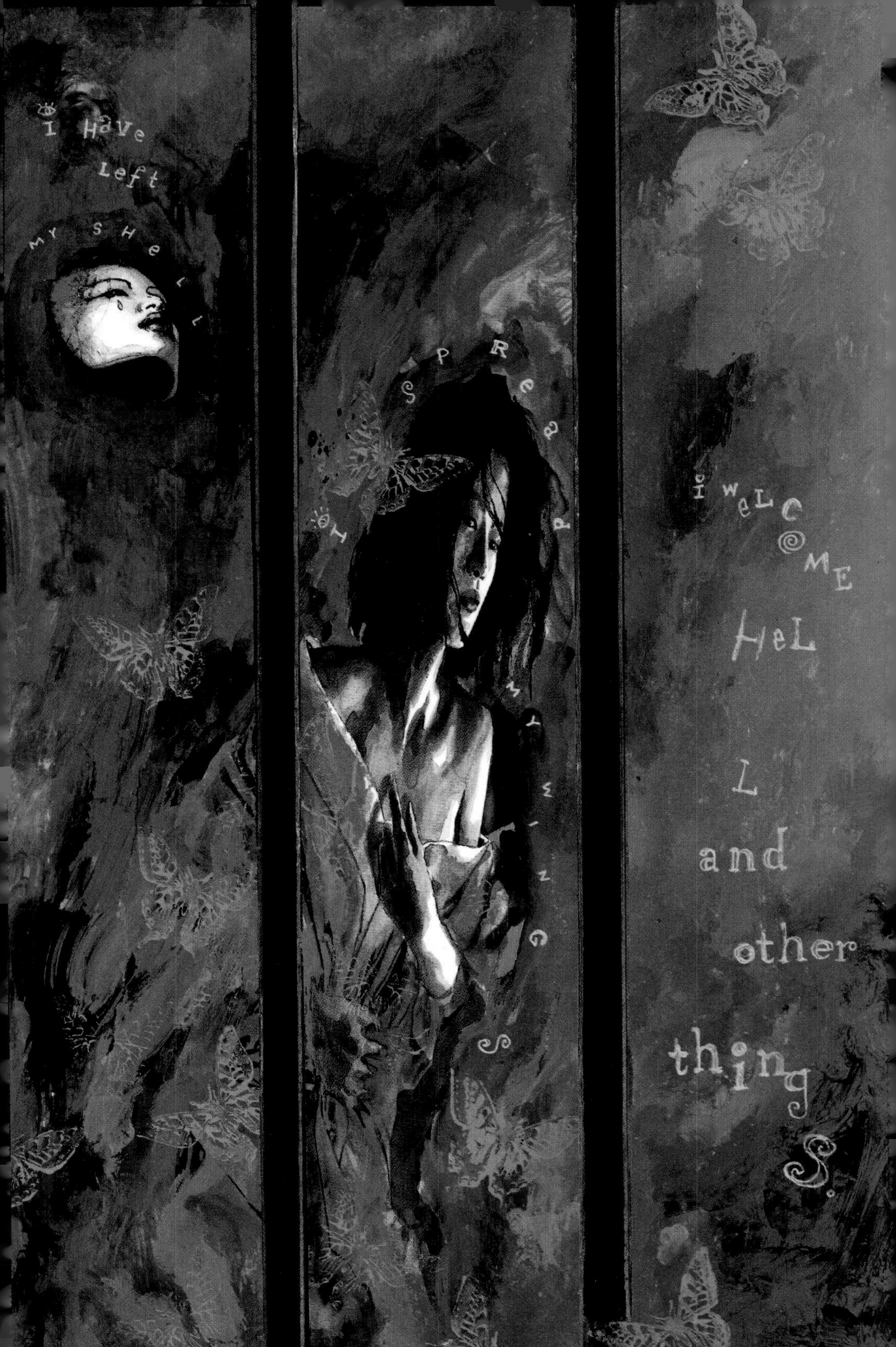

I have left my shell
I spread my wings
I welcome hell and other things.

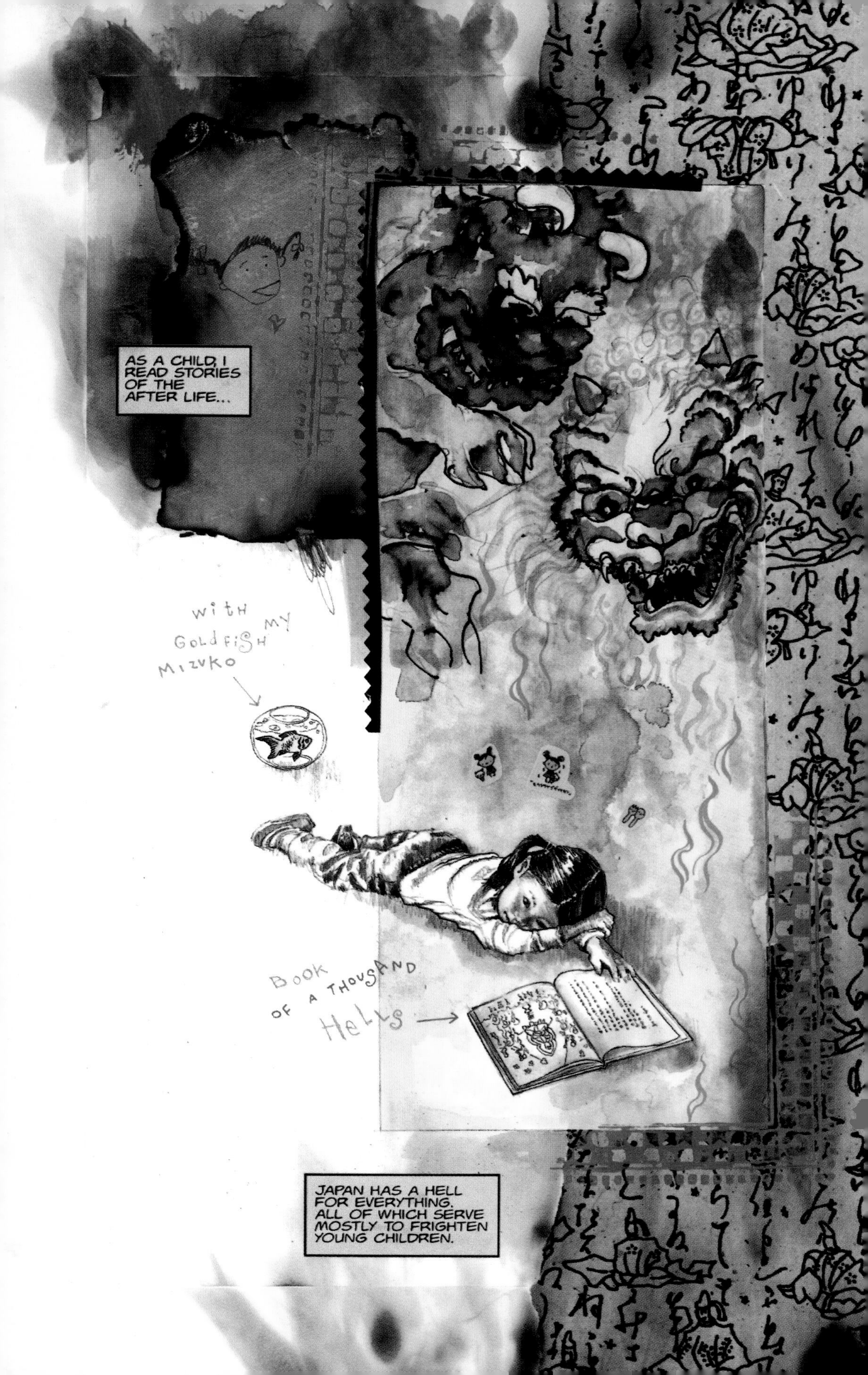
AS A CHILD, I READ STORIES OF THE AFTER LIFE...
with my Goldfish Mizuko
Book of a Thousand Hells
JAPAN HAS A HELL FOR EVERYTHING. ALL OF WHICH SERVE MOSTLY TO FRIGHTEN YOUNG CHILDREN.

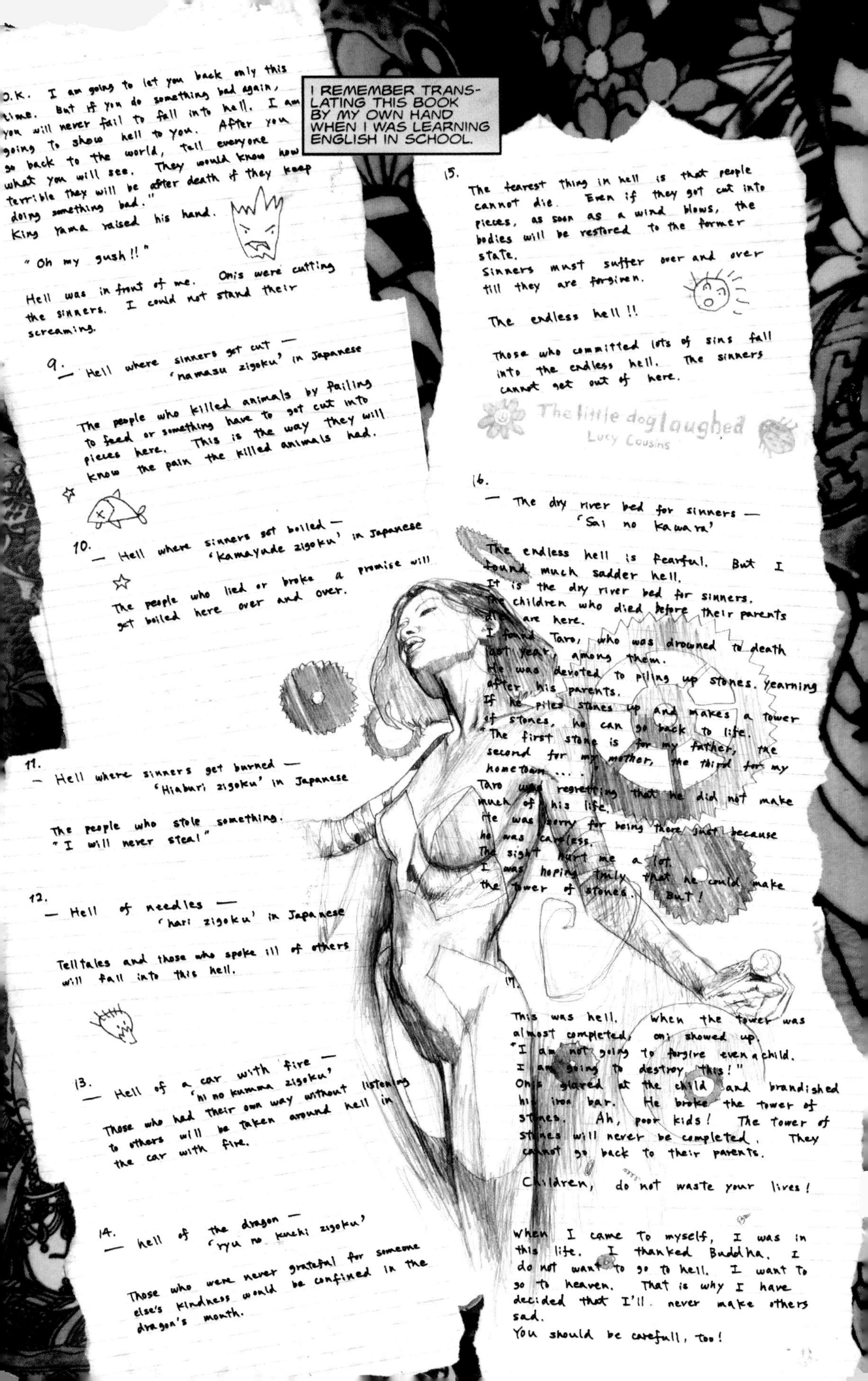
I REMEMBER TRANSLATING THIS BOOK BY MY OWN HAND WHEN I WAS LEARNING ENGLISH IN SCHOOL.
O.K. I am going to let you back only this time. But if you do something bad again, you will never fail to fall into hell. I am going to show hell to you. After you go back to the world, tell everyone what you will see. They would know how terrible they will be after death if they keep doing something bad." King Yama raised his hand.
"Oh my gush!!"
Hell was in front of me. Onis were cutting the sinners. I could not stand their screaming.
9. — Hell where sinners get cut — 'namasu zigoku' in Japanese
The people who killed animals by failing to feed or something have to get cut into pieces here. This is the way they will know the pain the killed animals had.
10. — Hell where sinners get boiled — 'kamayude zigoku' in Japanese
The people who lied or broke a promise will get boiled here over and over.
11. — Hell where sinners get burned — 'Hiaburi zigoku' in Japanese
The people who stole something. "I will never steal"
12. — Hell of needles — 'hari zigoku' in Japanese
Telltales and those who spoke ill of others will fall into this hell.
13. — Hell of a car with fire — 'hi no kuruma zigoku'
Those who had their own way without listening to others will be taken around hell in the car with fire.
14. — hell of the dragon — 'ryu no kuchi zigoku'
Those who were never grateful for someone else's kindness would be confined in the dragon's mouth.
15.
The tearest thing in hell is that people cannot die. Even if they got cut into pieces, as soon as a wind blows, the bodies will be restored to the former state.
Sinners must suffer over and over till they are forgiven.
The endless hell!!
Those who committed lots of sins fall into the endless hell. The sinners cannot get out of here.
The little dog laughed
Lucy Cousins
16. — The dry river bed for sinners — 'Sai no Kawara'
The endless hell is fearful. But I found much sadder hell.
It is the dry river bed for sinners.
The children who died before their parents die are here.
I found Taro, who was drowned to death last year, among them.
He was devoted to piling up stones, yearning after his parents.
If he piles stones up and makes a tower of stones, he can go back to life.
"The first stone is for my father, the second for my mother, the third for my hometown ...."
Taro was regretting that he did not make much of his life.
He was sorry for being there just because he was careless.
The sight hurt me a lot.
I was hoping truly that he could make the tower of stones. But!
17.
This was hell. When the tower was almost completed, oni showed up.
"I am not going to forgive even a child. I am going to destroy this!"
Onis glared at the child and brandished his iron bar. He broke the tower of stones. Ah, poor kids! The tower of stones will never be completed. They cannot go back to their parents.
Children, do not waste your lives!
When I came to myself, I was in this life. I thanked Buddha. I do not want to go to hell. I want to go to heaven. That is why I have decided that I'll never make others sad.
You should be carefull, too!

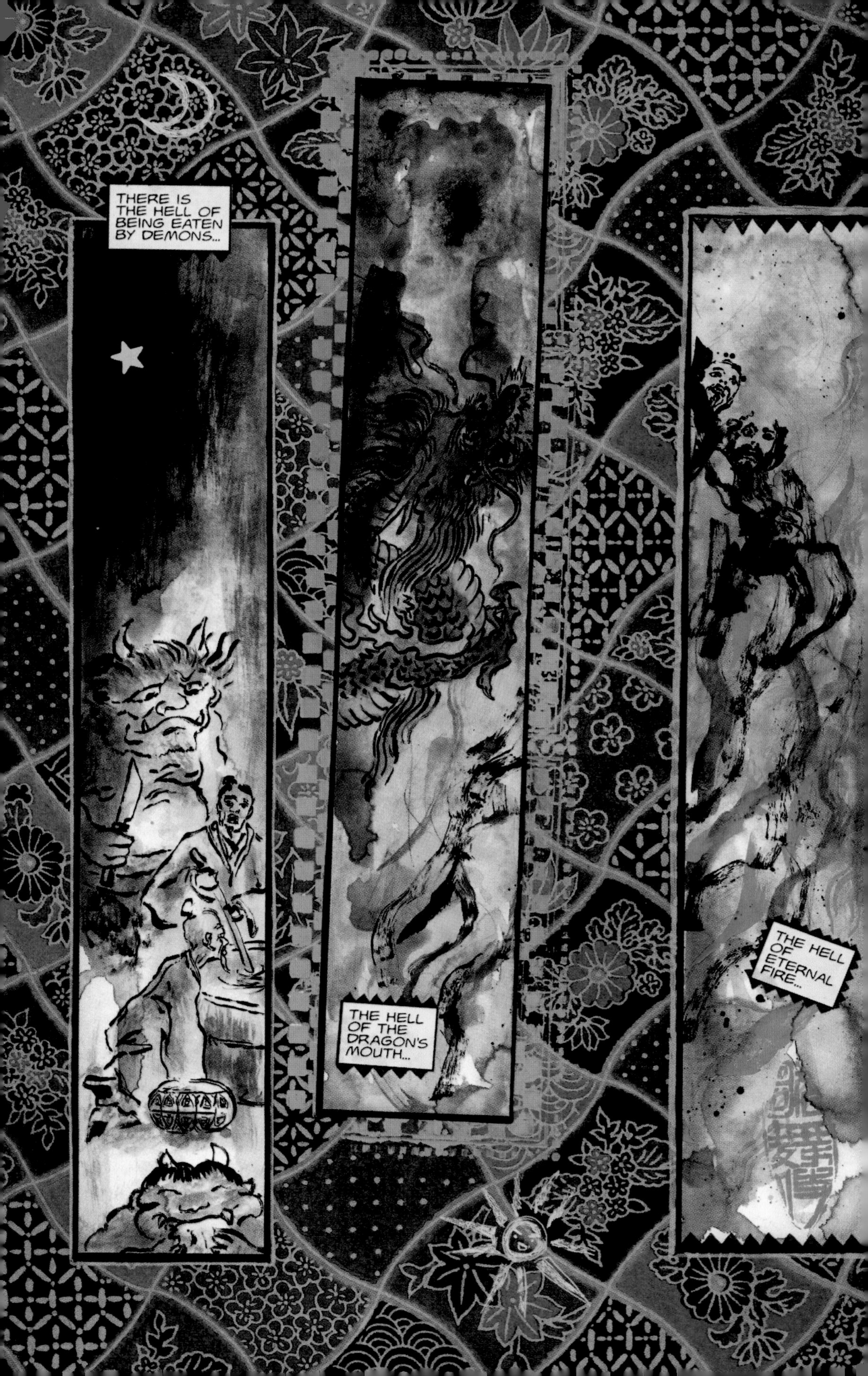
THERE IS THE HELL OF BEING EATEN BY DEMONS...
THE HELL OF THE DRAGON'S MOUTH...
THE HELL OF ETERNAL FIRE...

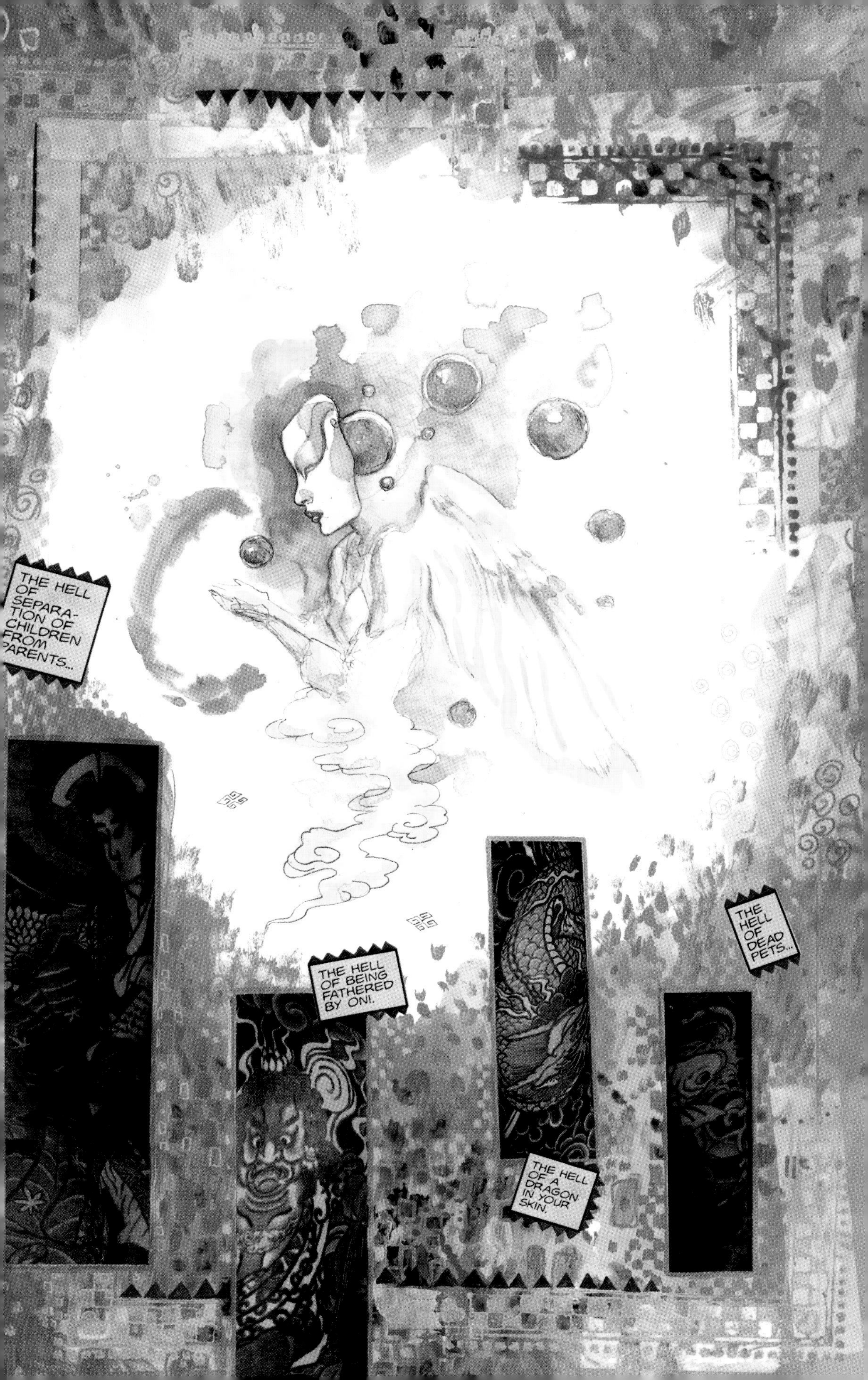
THE HELL OF SEPARATION OF CHILDREN FROM PARENTS...
THE HELL OF BEING FATHERED BY ONI.
THE HELL OF A DRAGON IN YOUR SKIN.
THE HELL OF DEAD PETS...

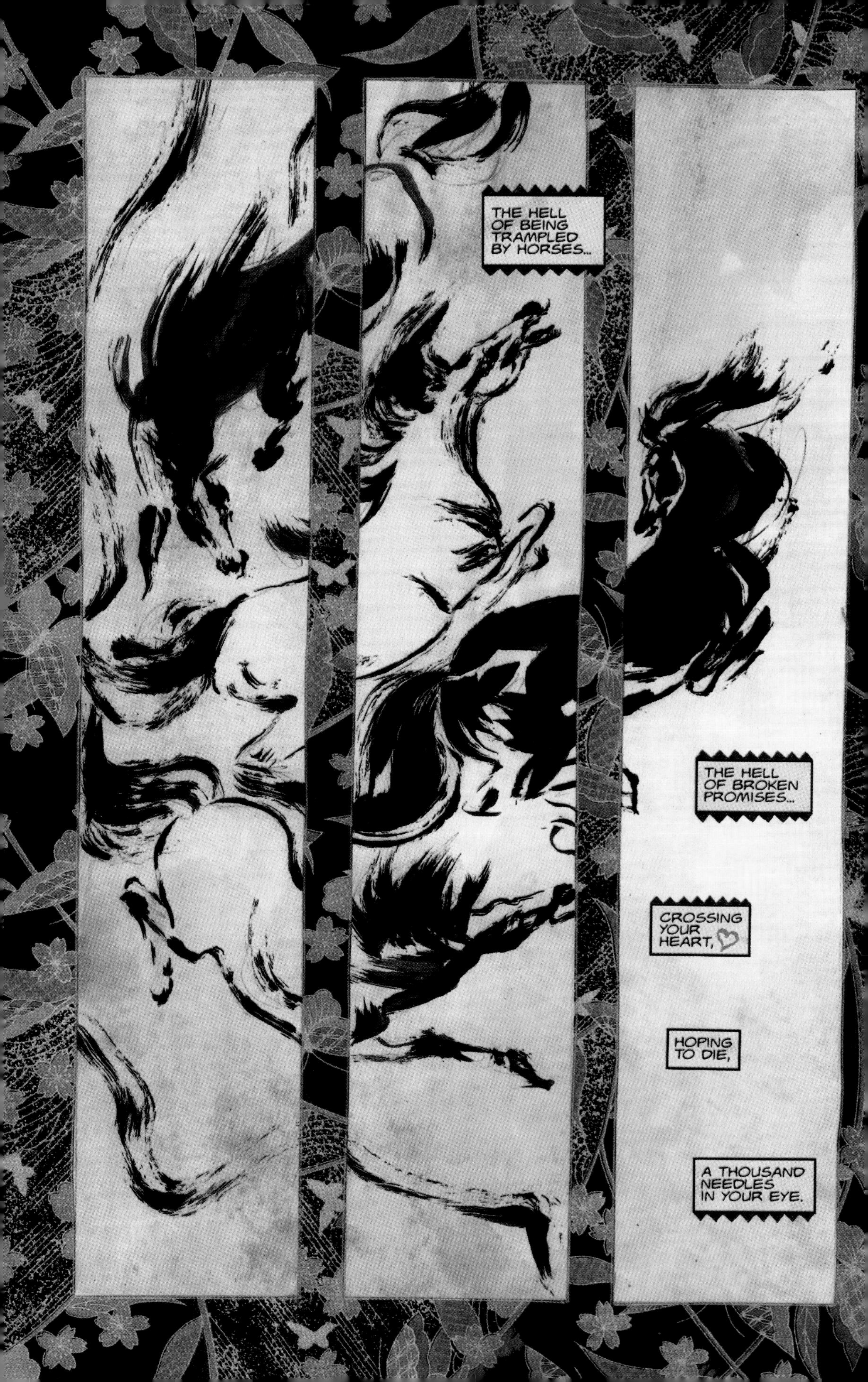
THE HELL OF BEING TRAMPLED BY HORSES...
THE HELL OF BROKEN PROMISES...
CROSSING YOUR HEART, ♡
HOPING TO DIE,
A THOUSAND NEEDLES IN YOUR EYE.

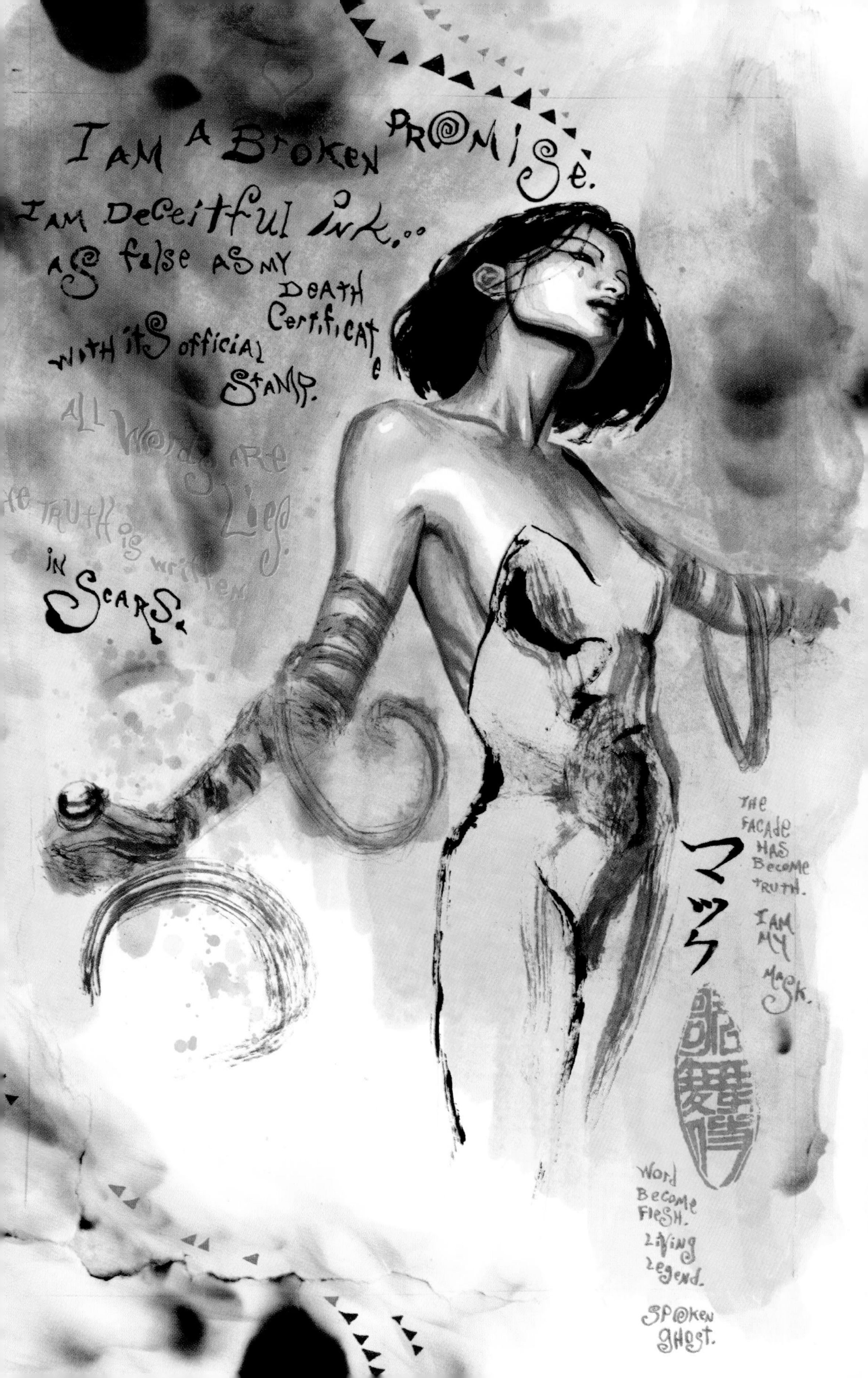
I AM A BROKEN PROMISE.
I AM DECEITFUL INK...
AS FALSE AS MY DEATH CERTIFICATE
WITH ITS OFFICIAL STAMP.
ALL WORDS ARE LIES
THE TRUTH IS WRITTEN IN SCARS.
THE FACADE HAS BECOME TRUTH.
I AM MY MASK.
WORD BECOME FLESH.
LIVING LEGEND.
SPOKEN GHOST.

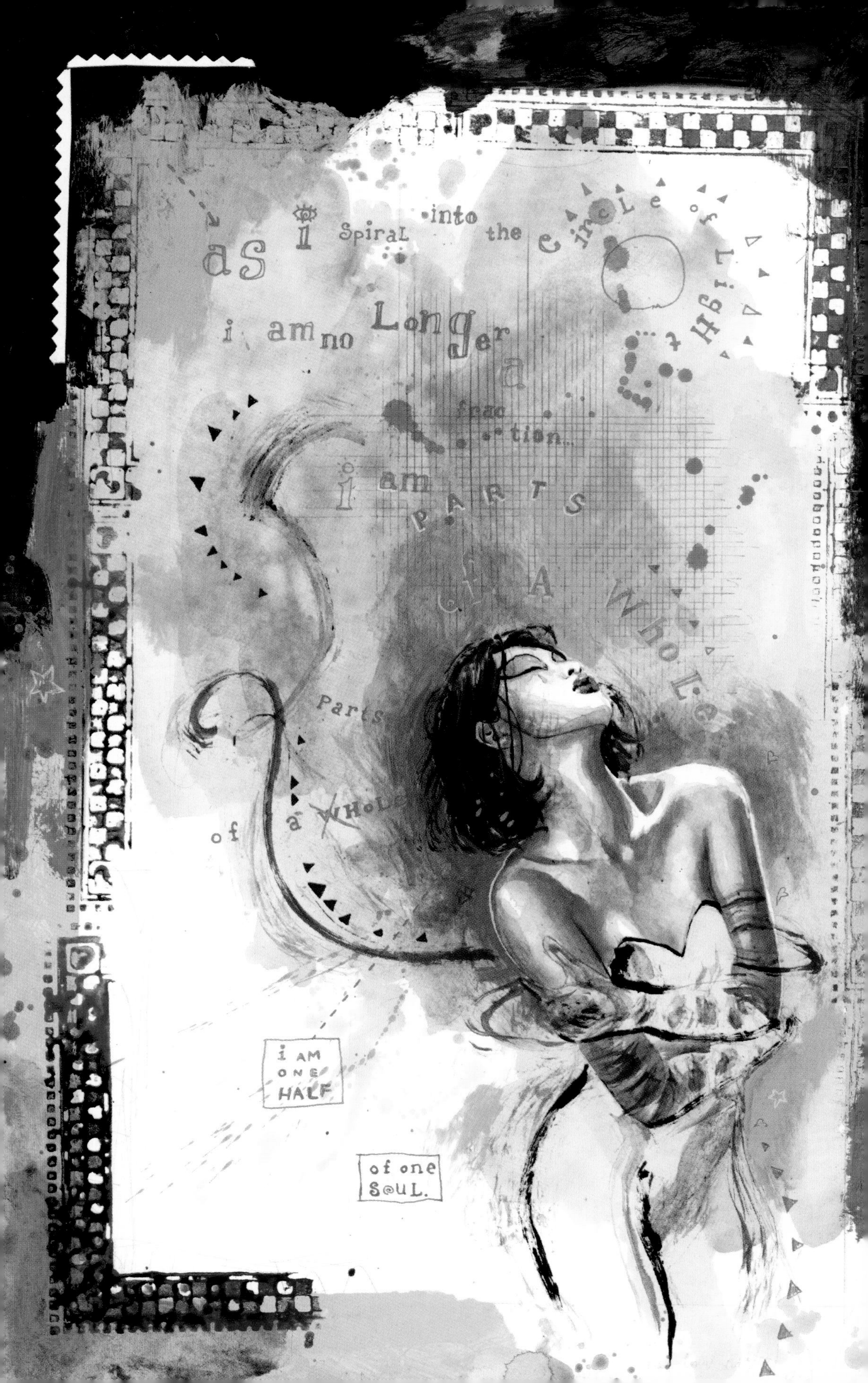
as i Spiral into the circLe of Light
i am no Longer a
frac tion...
i am PARTS of A WhoLe
Parts of a WHoLe
i AM ONE HALF
of one SoUL.

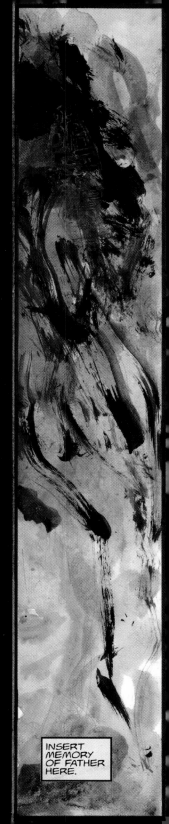

INSERT
MEMORY
OF FATHER
HERE.

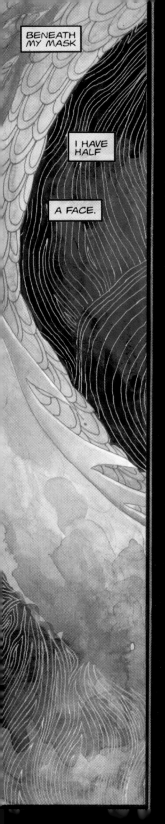
BENEATH
MY MASK

I HAVE
HALF

A FACE.

I BELONG
TO
ONE HALF

OF ONE
RACE.

MY
NAME

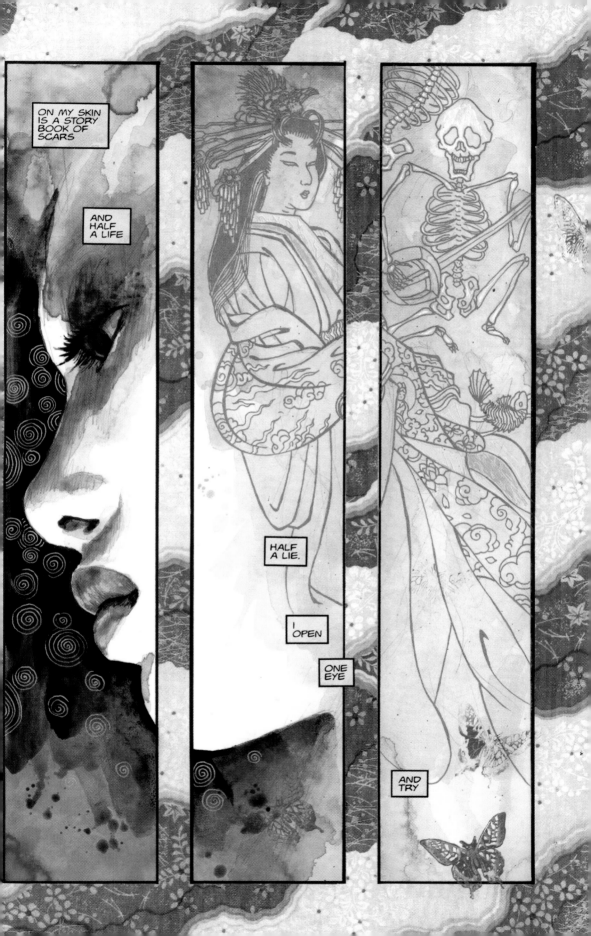

ON MY SKIN
IS A STORY
BOOK OF
SCARS

AND
HALF
A LIFE

HALF
A LIE.

I OPEN

ONE
EYE

AND
TRY

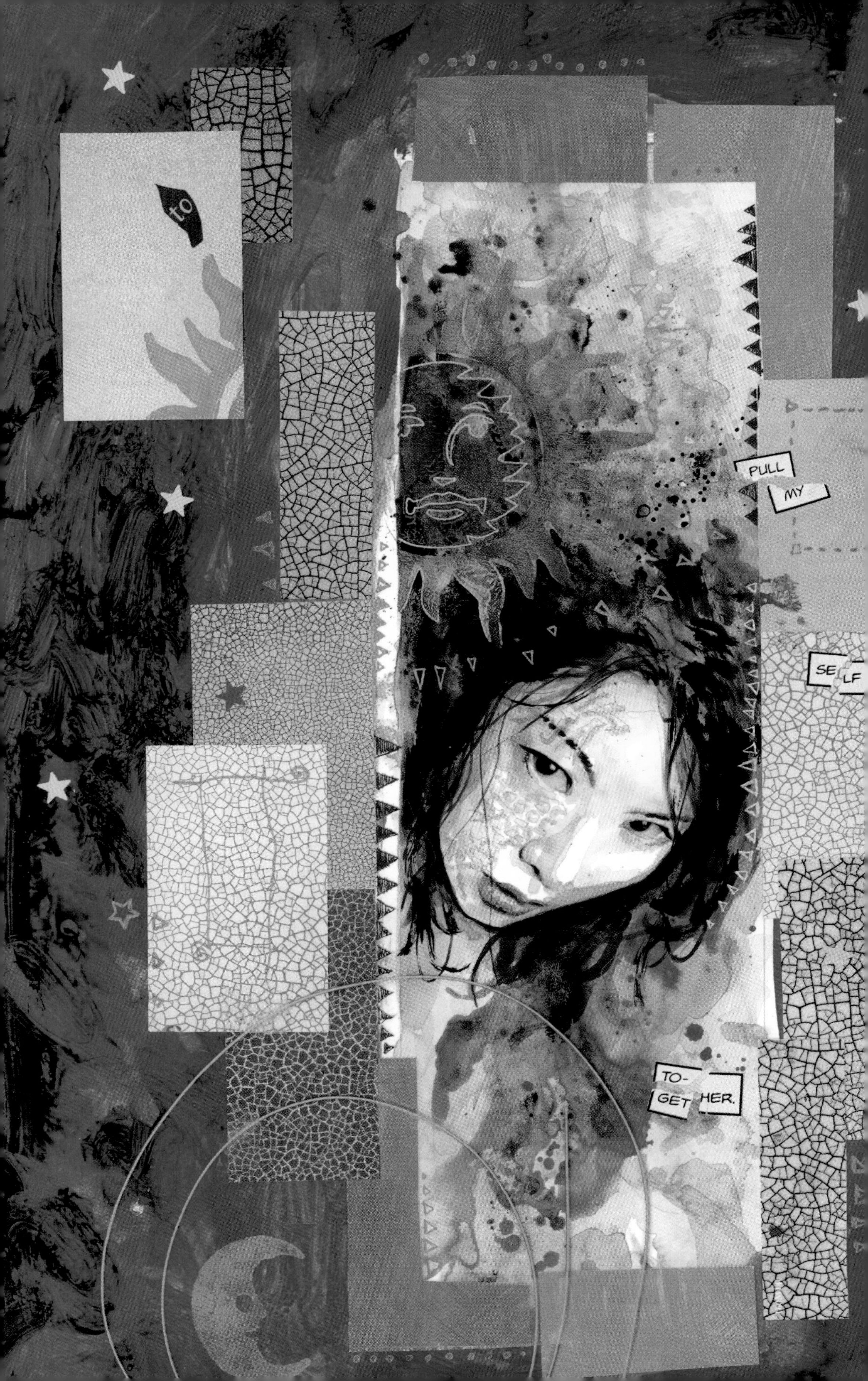
to
PULL
MY
SE LF
TO-
GET HER.

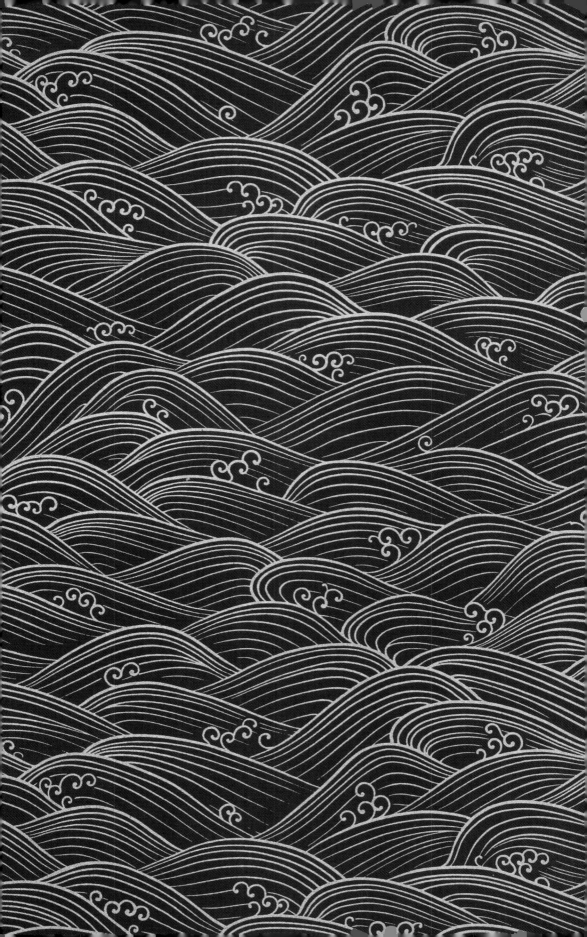

confront us in the Nō, and, as we look, they are the ghosts of our own hearts that meet us. -a faint dream gone with the dawn,—are to me the most real and terrible ghosts I know. For we have all felt them; we carry them, each of us, in our own bosom.

IV

Of course, by no means all the Nō plays are the habitations of ghosts; but many are the haunt of strange intuitions, of fallings from us, vanishings, worlds not realized; the moving within us of spirits who have moulded our being and whom we have never known. It is a twilight world, lit by waning moons. The ghosts who dwell there have been given over into the prison of their own Self-

hood; their passions and memories have made their cage; and they have no escape, in life or death, until they accept the law of self-annihilation.

Such a disease of the soul as hers could not escape the Nō, for it gives the woman chained to her misery, as Prometheus to his rock.

The special difficulties of translating Nō plays, with their mysticism, their allusions, their constant overtones and preciosity of language, have tended to make this peculiar and peculiarly Japanese form of religious drama little known to the occid... There is

These plays demand as much as they give; the audience must bring its gifts of imagination, intellect, knowledge, and poetic insight, and lay them before the stage, or the actors can do nothi... for them. It is not so in other parts of the world, so far as I k... I see a Western audience; the glaring obvious stage, tricke... with decoration that overpowers the story, the players, ... thought (if there should be such an irrelevance!); eve... feeling expressed in black and white before it can ... the heads that crowd the place. What does ... It has paid its money to be amused, ... done for.

But why dwell upon what all ... cial civilization throned in ... said that the Nō was an ... intellect. Poss... it...

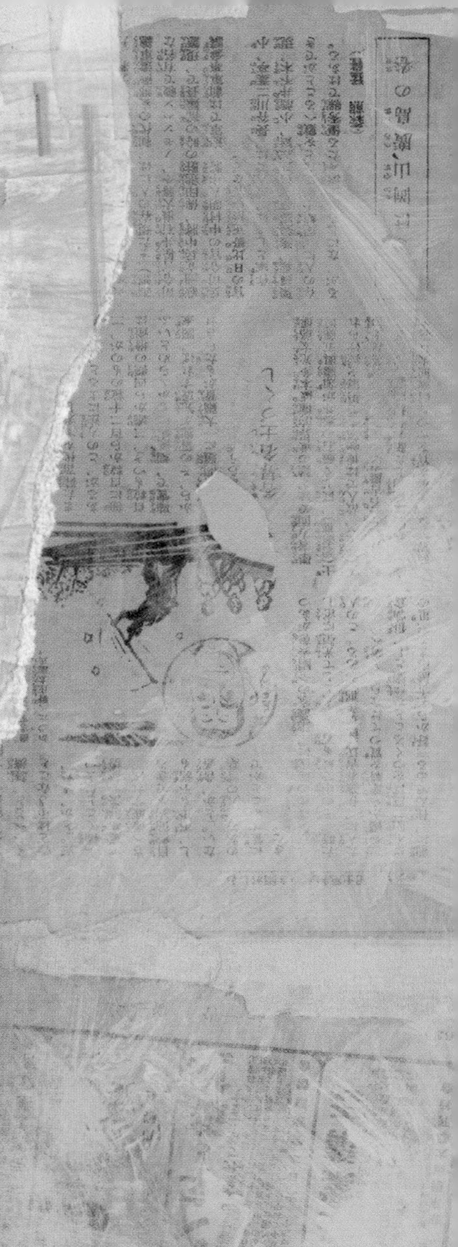

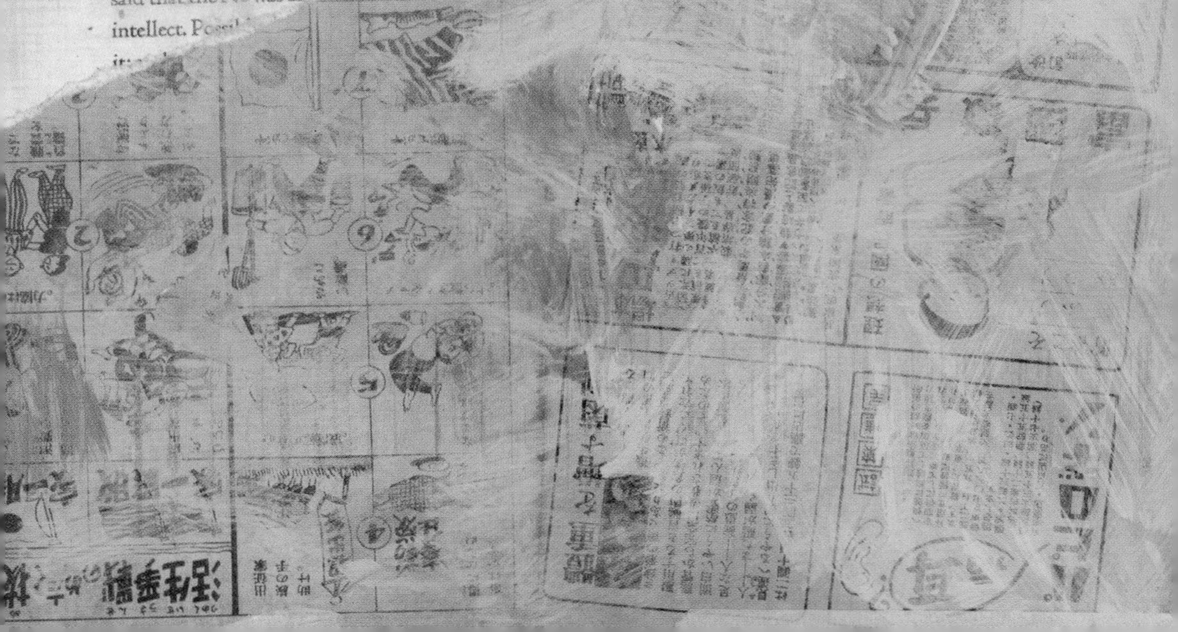

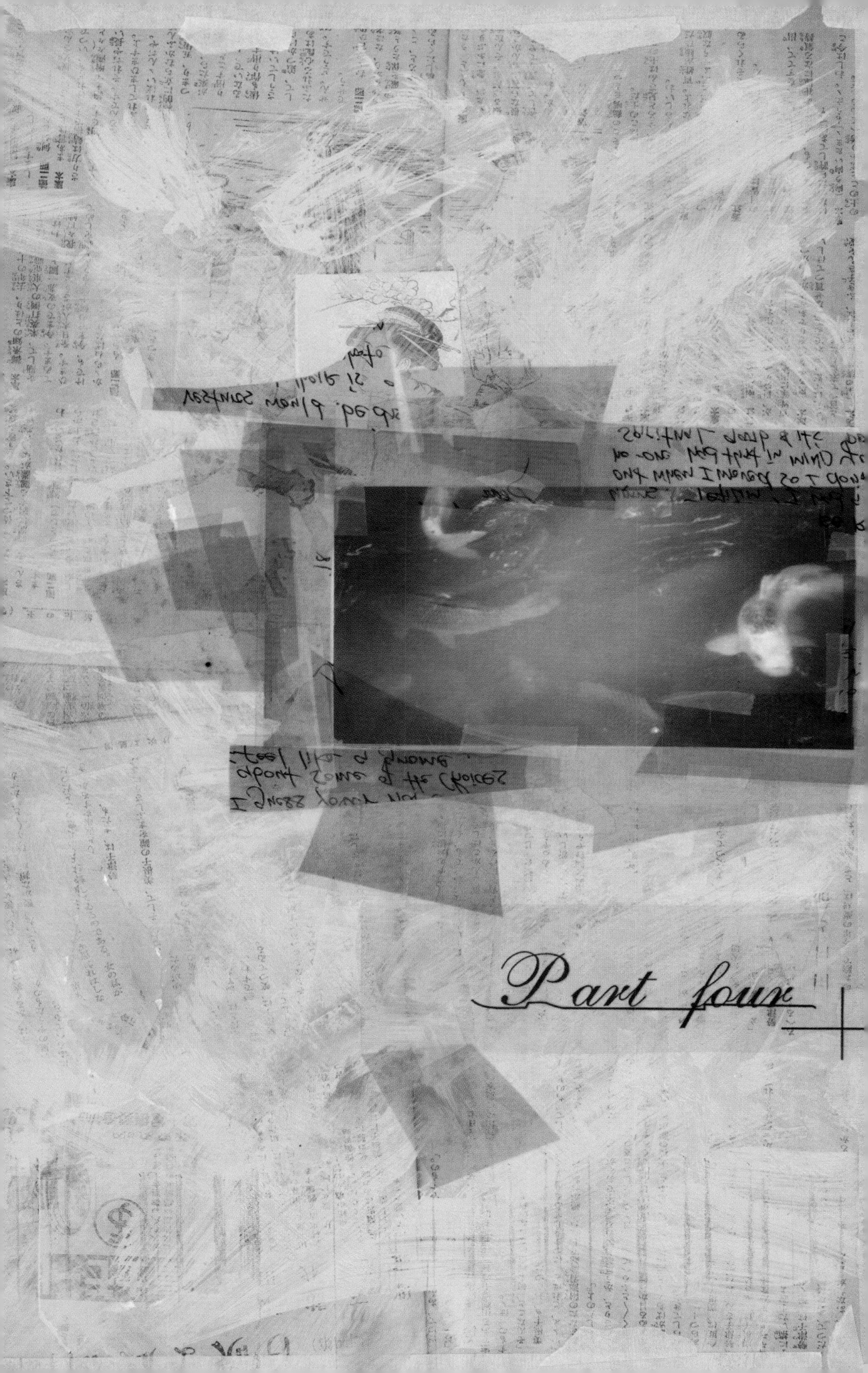

Part four

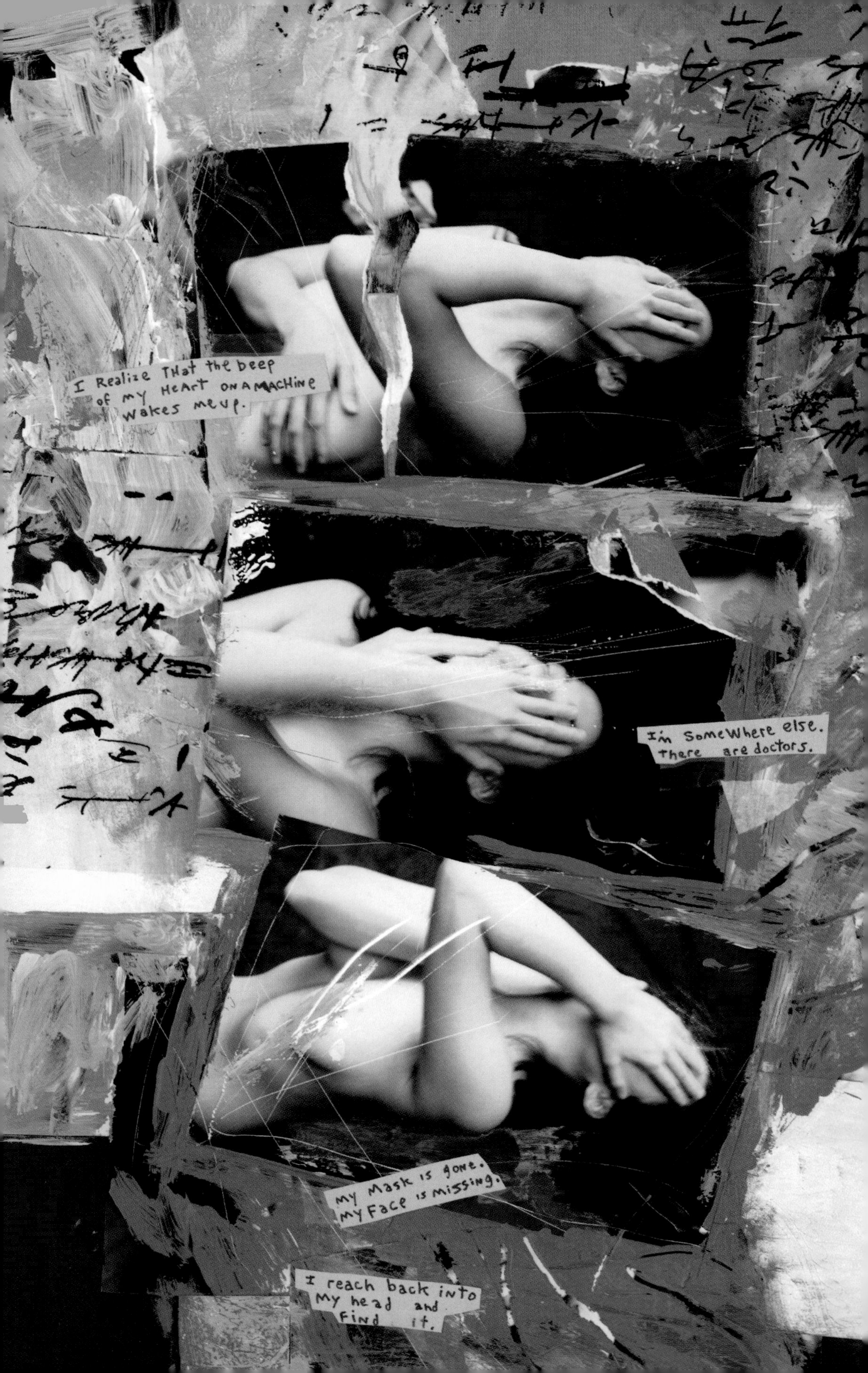
I Realize THAT the beep of my HEART ON A MACHINE wakes me up.
I'm SomeWhere else. There are doctors.
my Mask is gone. my Face is missing.
I reach back into my head and Find it.

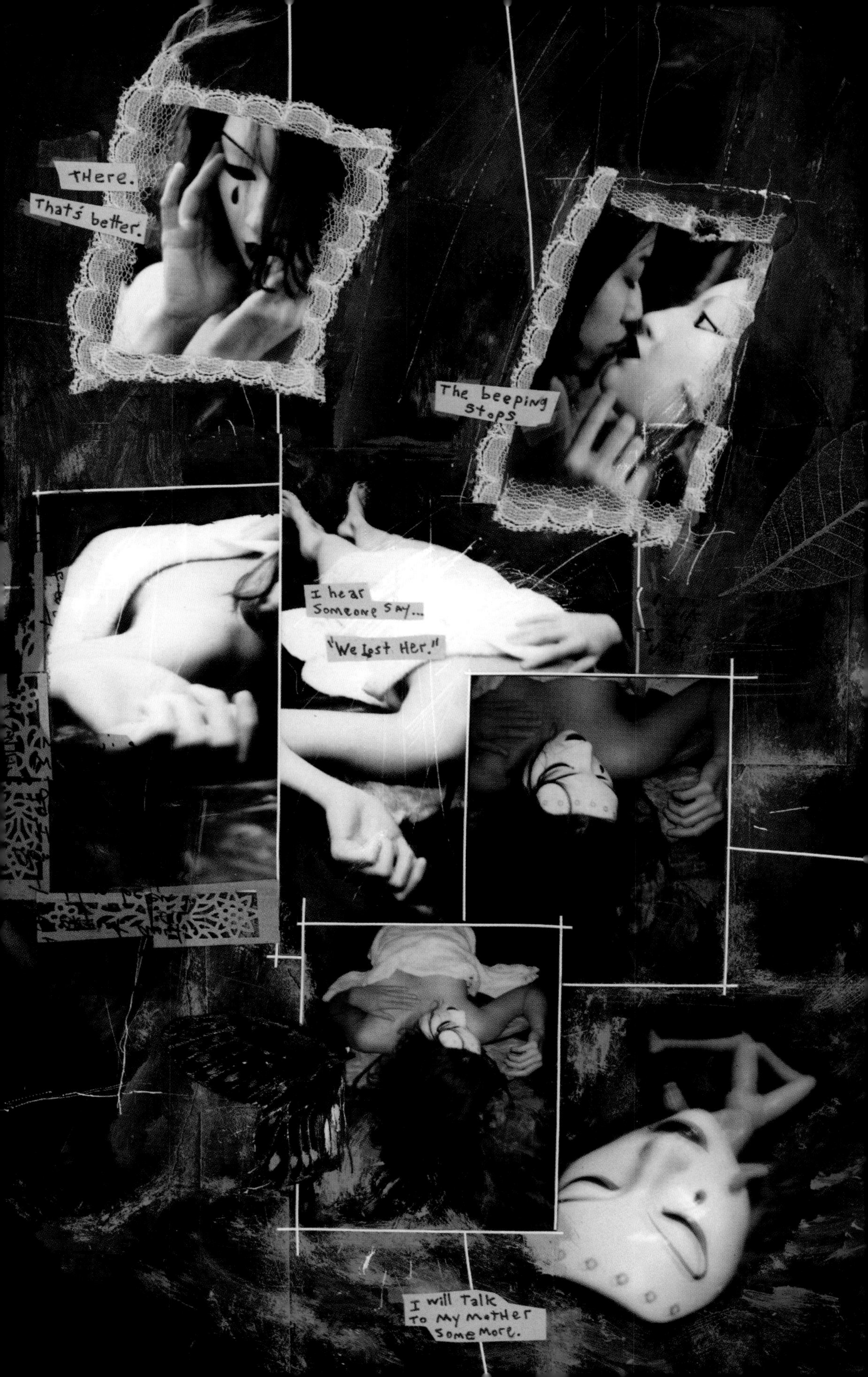
There.
That's better.
The beeping stops.
I hear someone say...
"We lost Her."
I will talk to my mother some more.

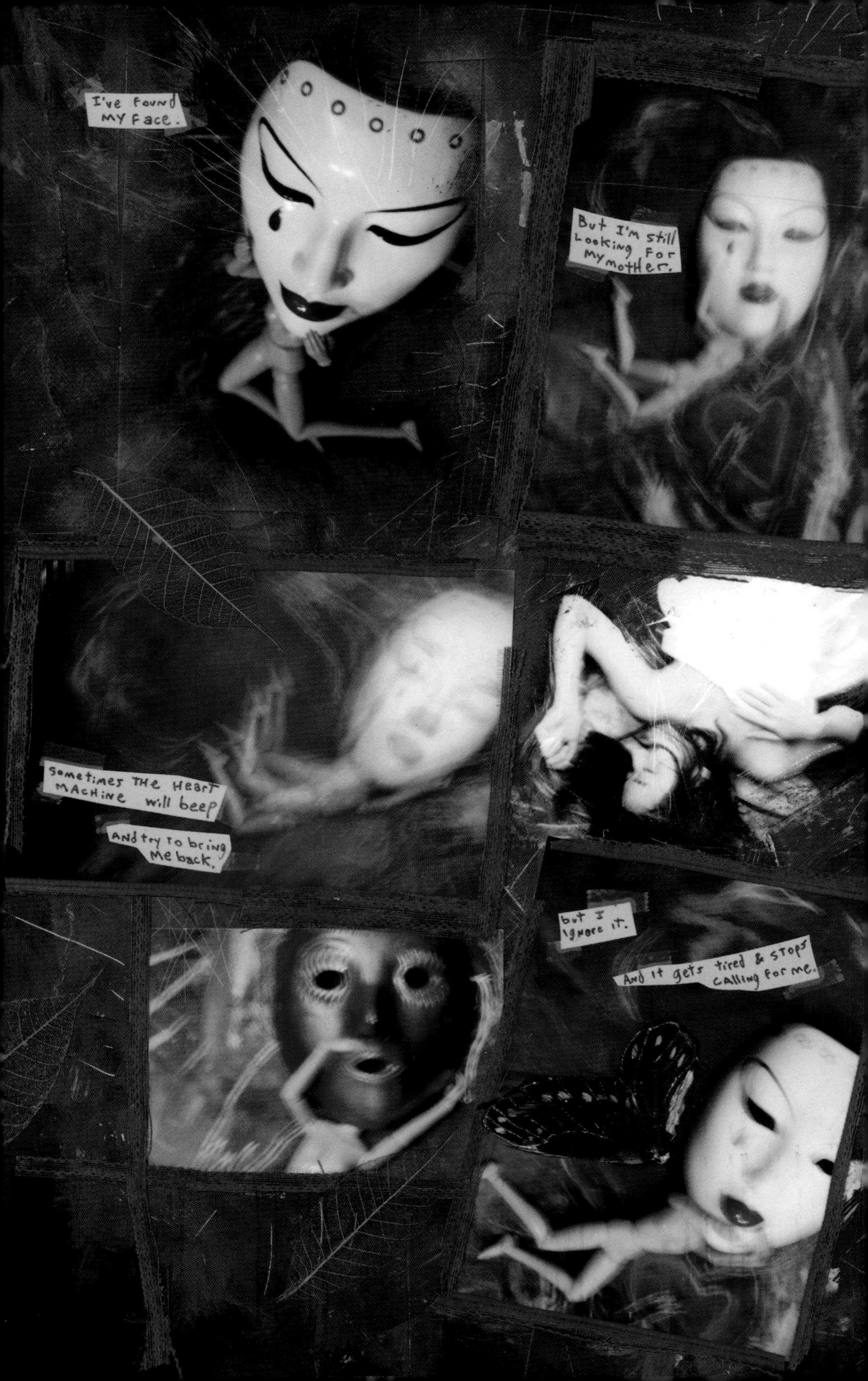
I've found my face.
But I'm still looking for my mother.
Sometimes the heart machine will beep
And try to bring me back.
but I ignore it.
And it gets tired & stops calling for me.

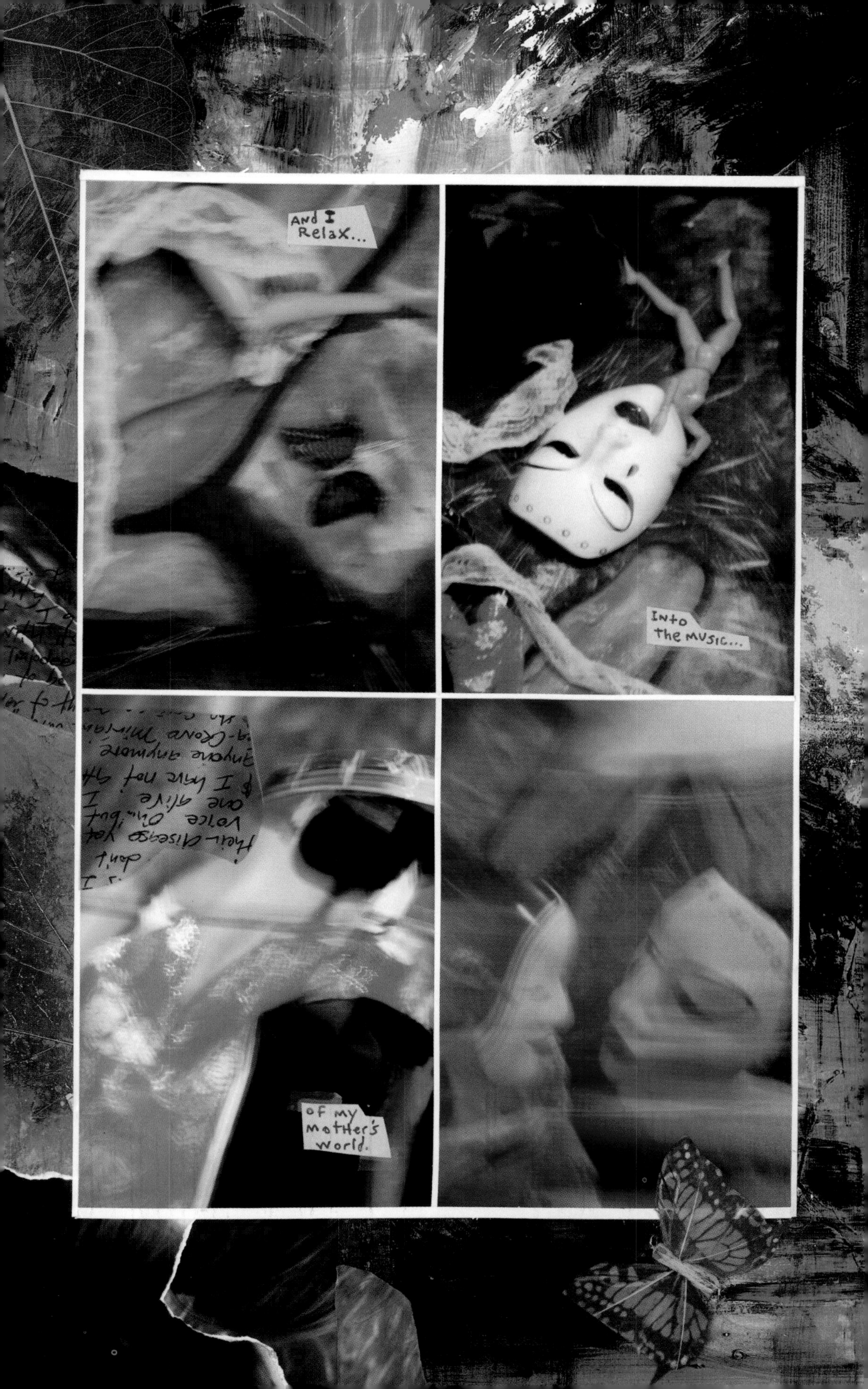
And I Relax...
Into the music...
of my mother's world.

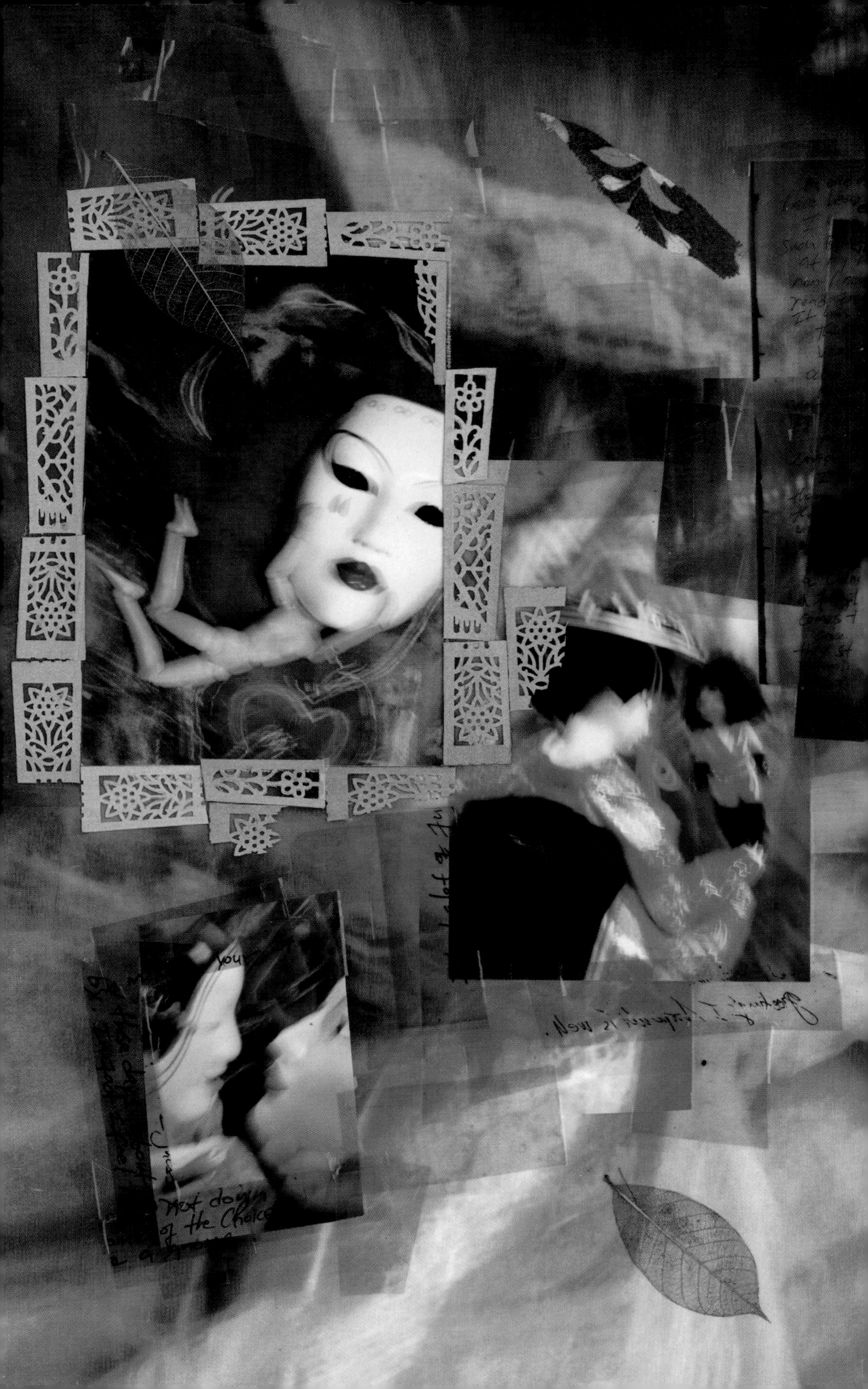

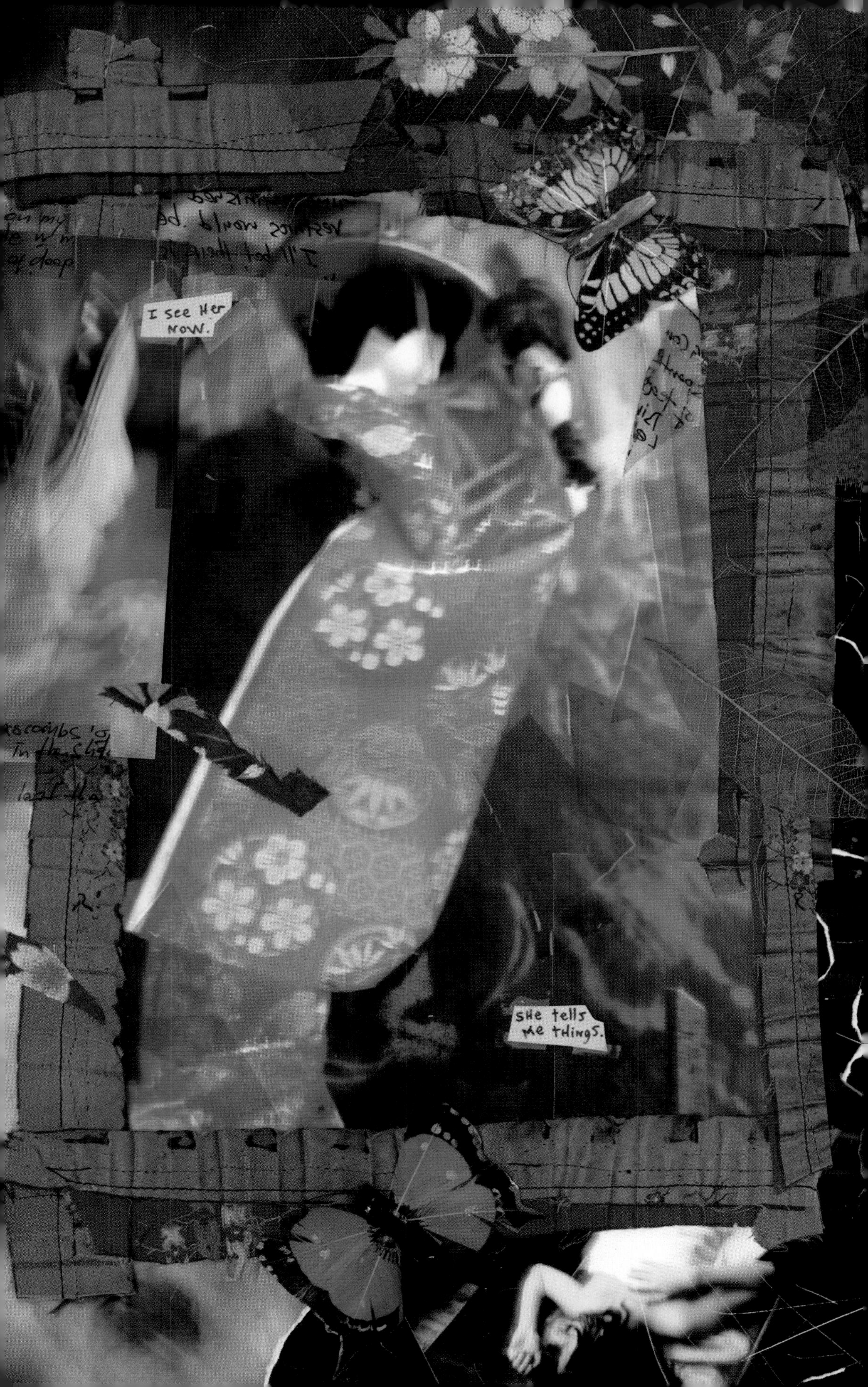
I see Her NOW.
SHe tells me tHingS.

As one of those Biblical rag wi[...] from that monastery as I
[...]e been living in the bottom of the babtiste's Well.
[...] have never felt more peculiar comming up for Gir from be[...]
[...] Black witors that toddy when I drank teh I did'nt dare [...]
[...]t my reflection in my tea-cup. Now for one of my Spectacular
[...]on-linner aside'shans. [...]
[...]end from that Zen Maste[...]
[...]t has become a memor[...]
[...] the ancient principals o[...]
[...]ry #8 & by the W[...]
[...] I have gotten some[...]
[...]horland fans[...]
[...] noble & sev[...]
[...]e Artwork[...]
[...]y goodness [...]
[...], lush & ext[...]

we Sort of Have
our OWN
LaNguage.

if you know

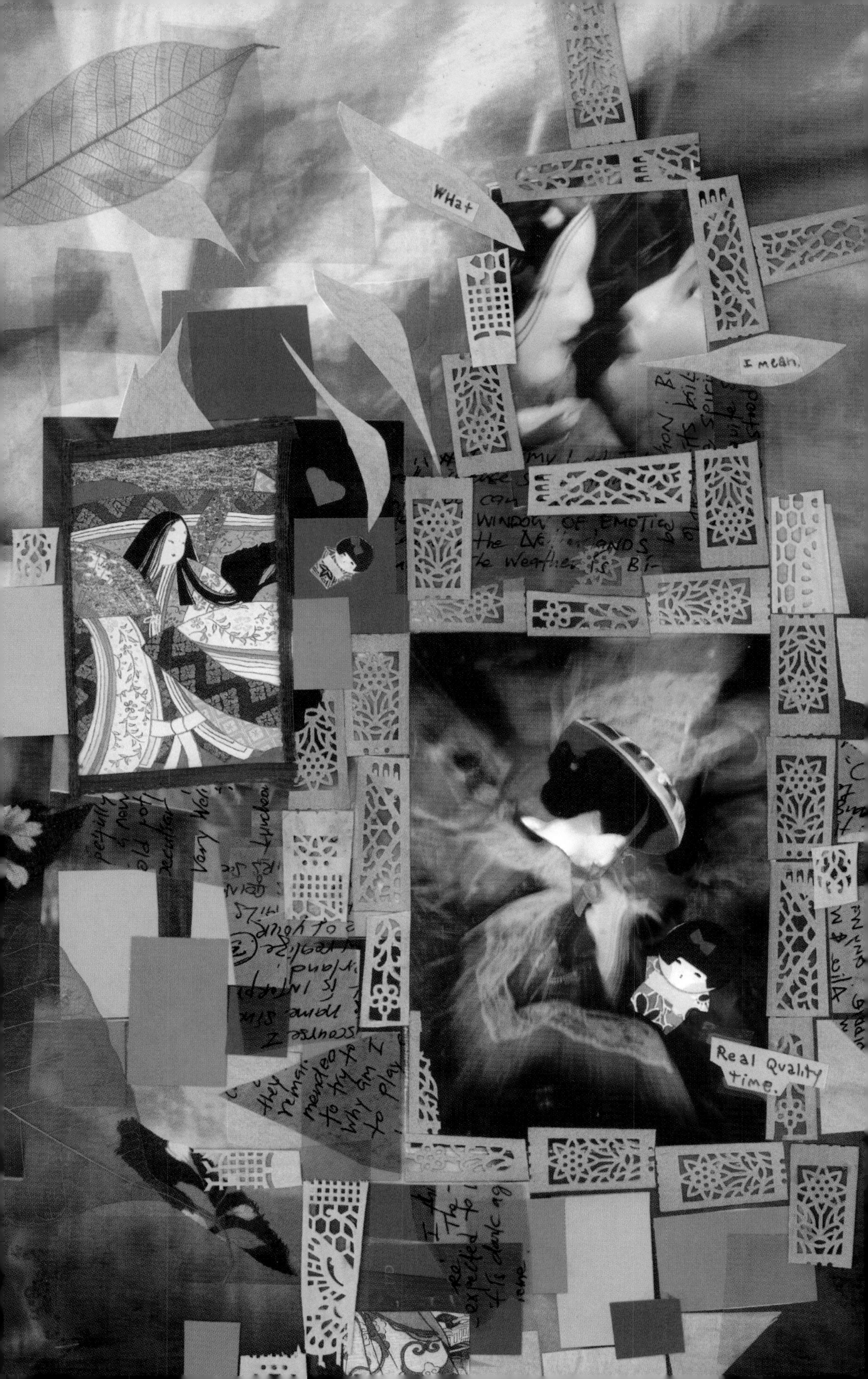
WHat
I mean.
Real Quality time.

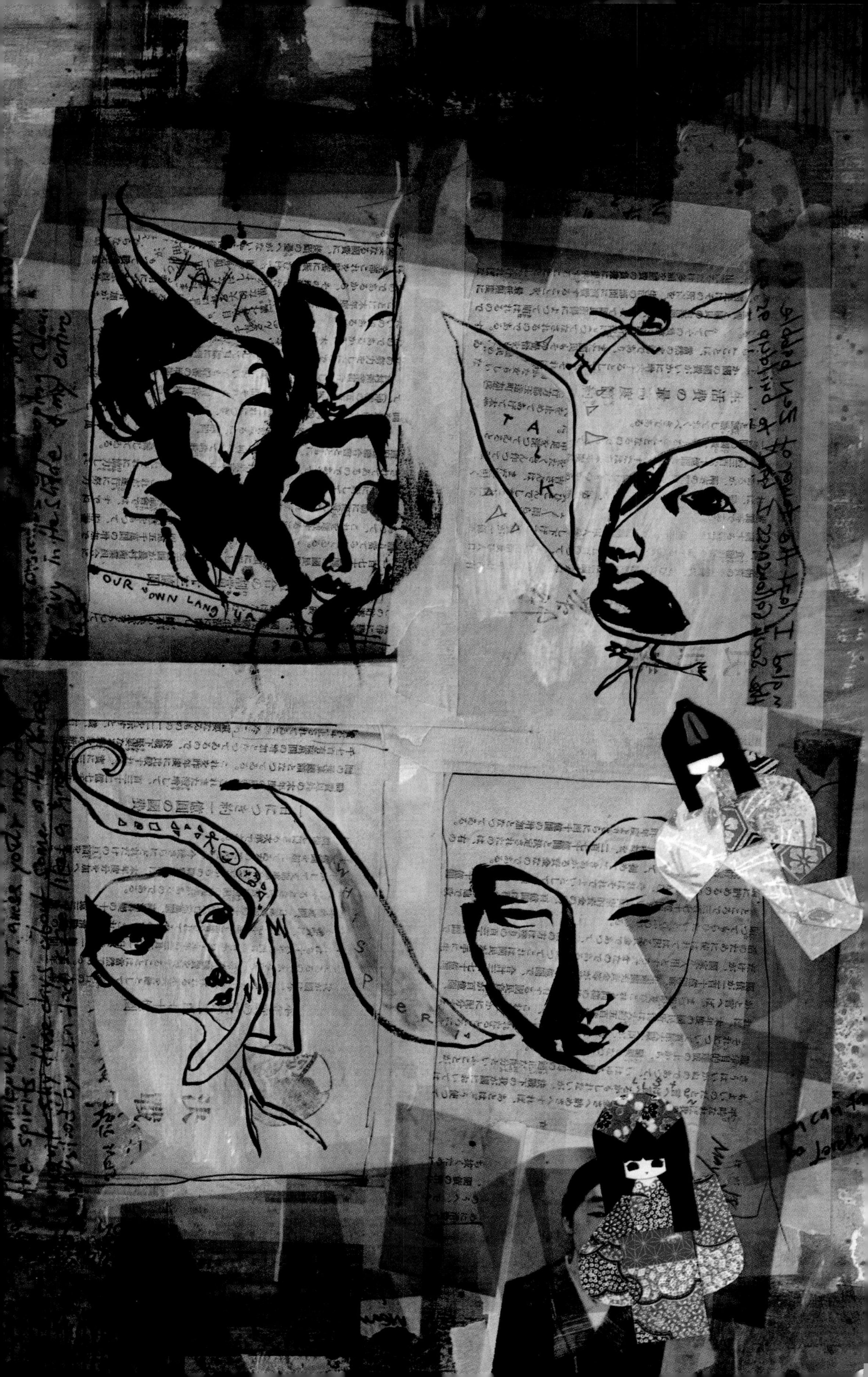
TALK
WHISPER

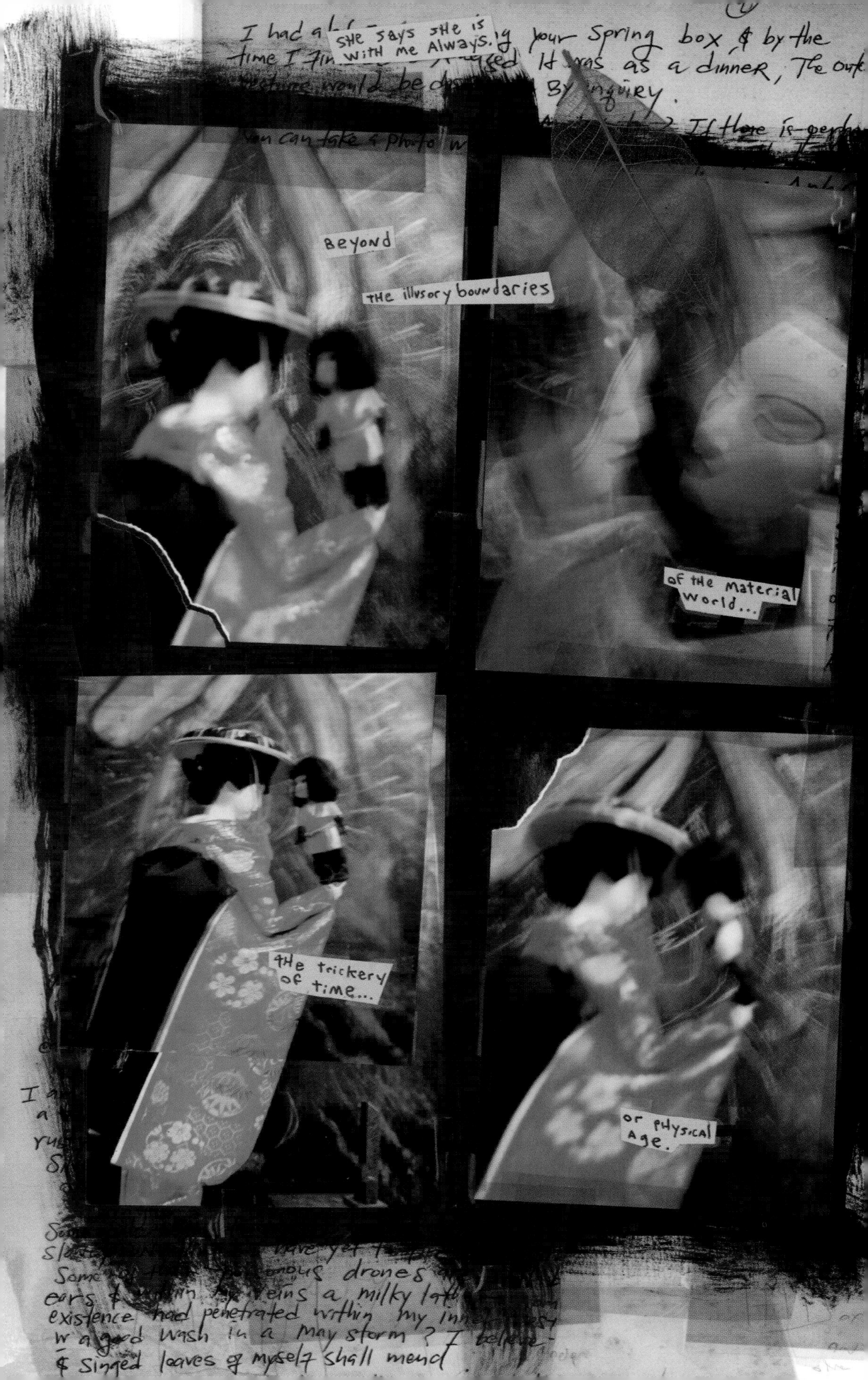

SHE SAYS SHE IS WITH ME ALWAYS.
BEYOND
THE illusory boundaries
of the material world...
the trickery of time...
or physical age.

be lovely to wear w an evening attire ok maye A
wear it but you will have to make a Cyber Toupee Fir
I wonder what will be next in kabuki > And I
don't expect anything for a while

She tells me
to grow up...

Become
MYSELF.

no avalanche

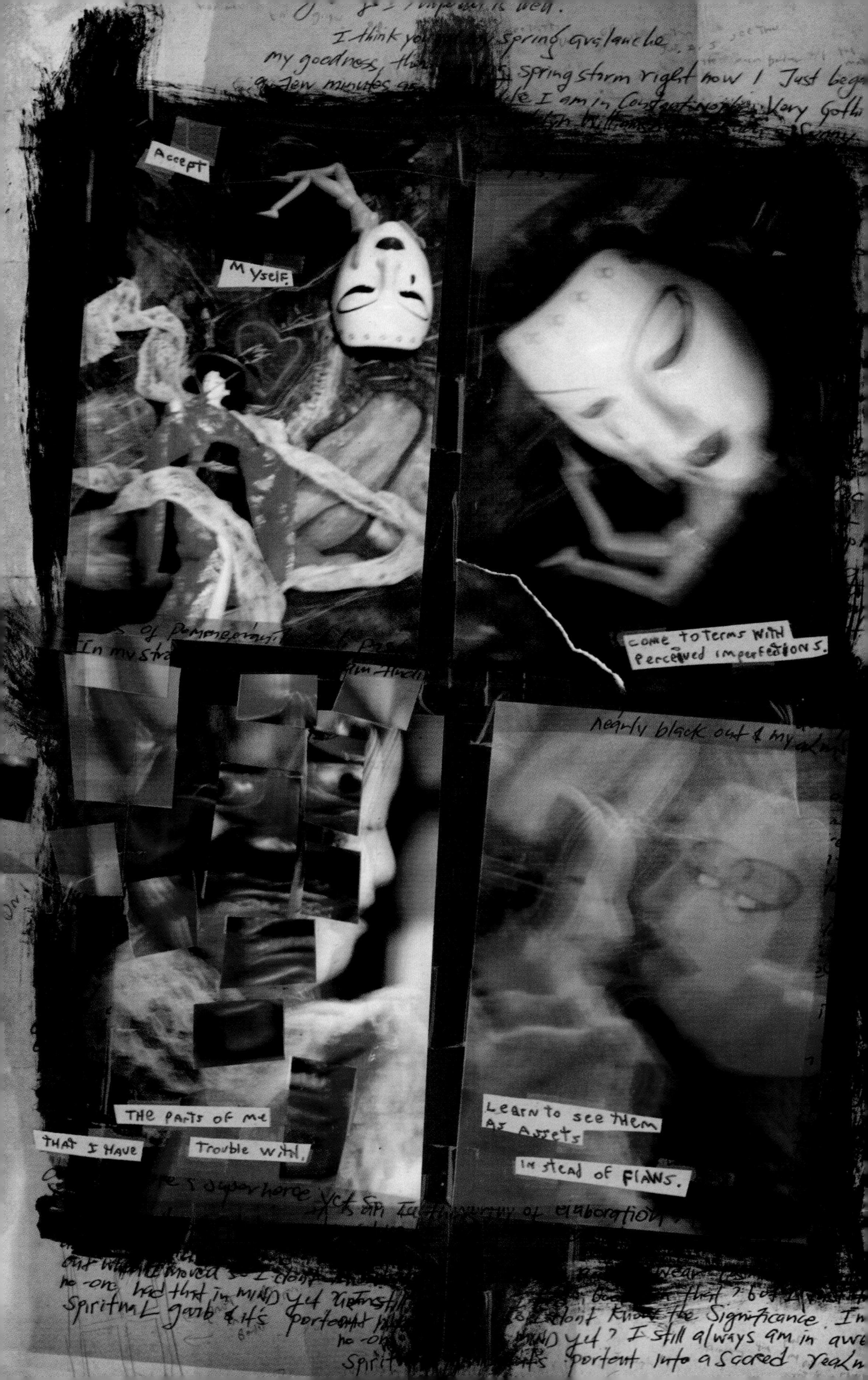

Accept

Myself.

come to terms with
perceived imperfections.

nearly black out & my ...

The parts of me

that I have   Trouble with,

Learn to see them
As Assets

in stead of FLAWS.

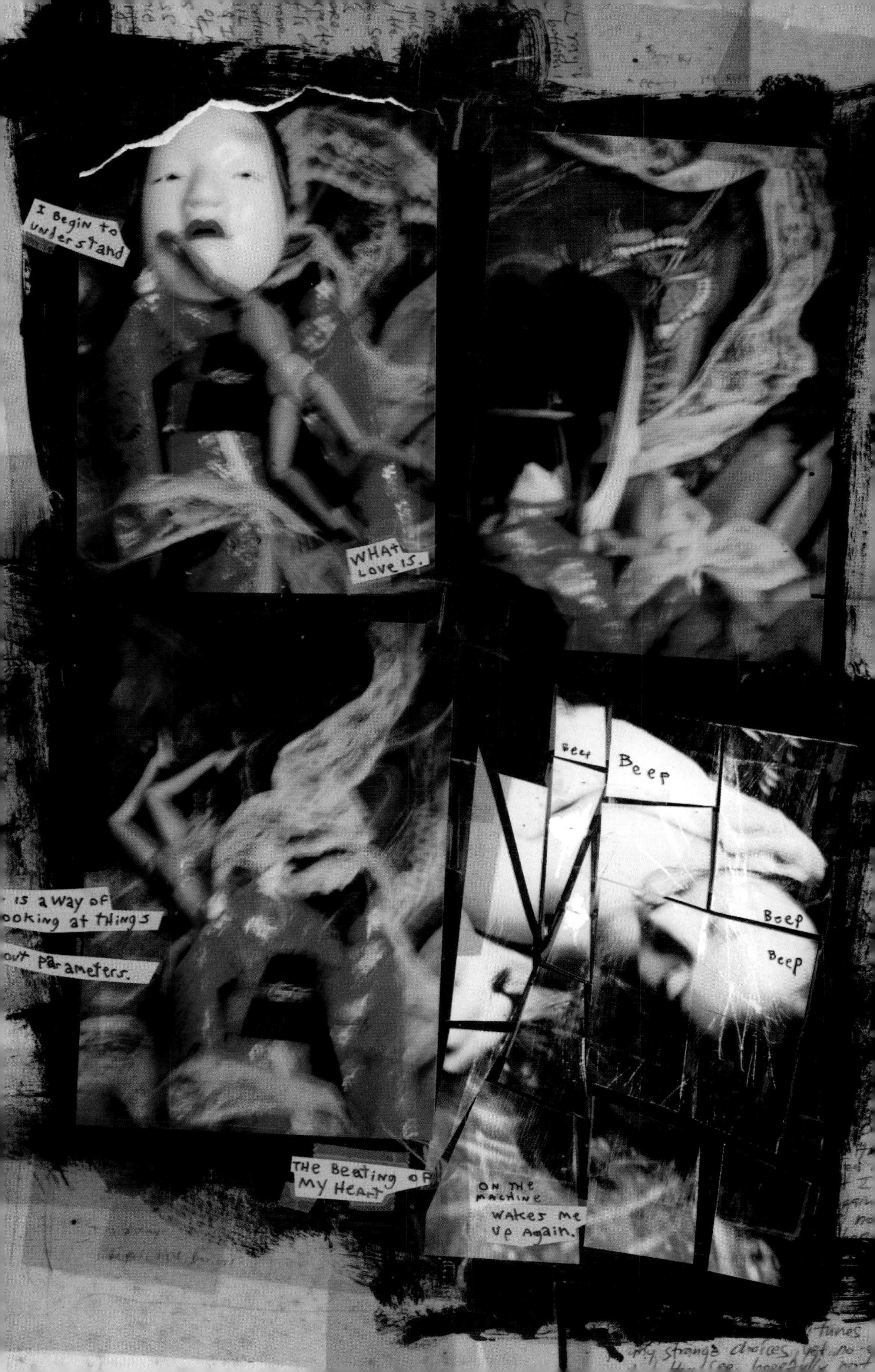
I Begin to understand
WHAT LOVE IS.
is a way of
ooking at things
out parameters.
Beep
Beep
Beep
Beep
THE Beating of My Heart
ON THE MACHINE
wakes me up again.

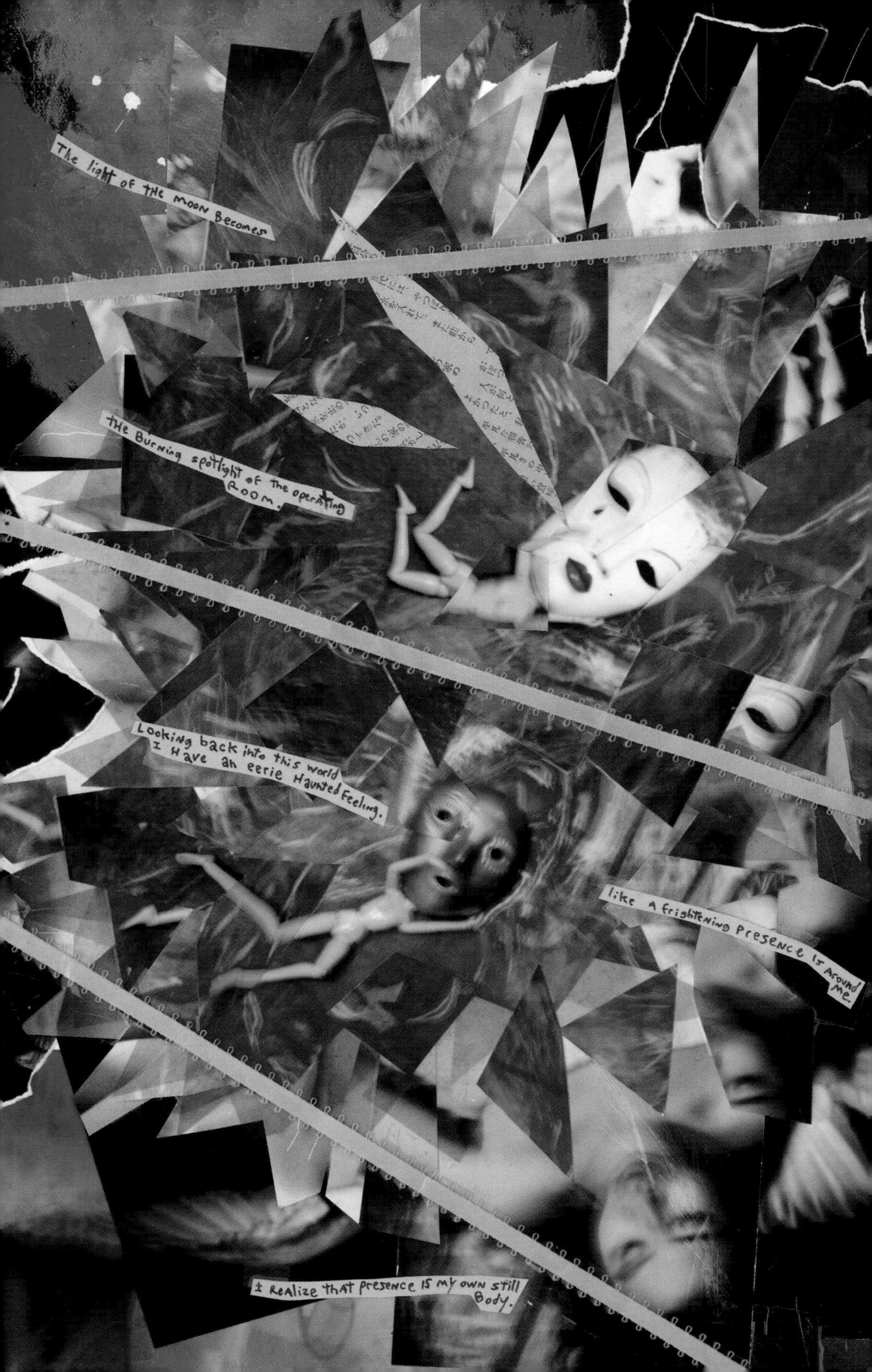
The light of the moon Becomes
The Burning spotlight of the operating Room.
Looking back into this world I Have an eerie Haunted Feeling.
like A frightening Presence is Around me.
I Realize that Presence is my own still Body.

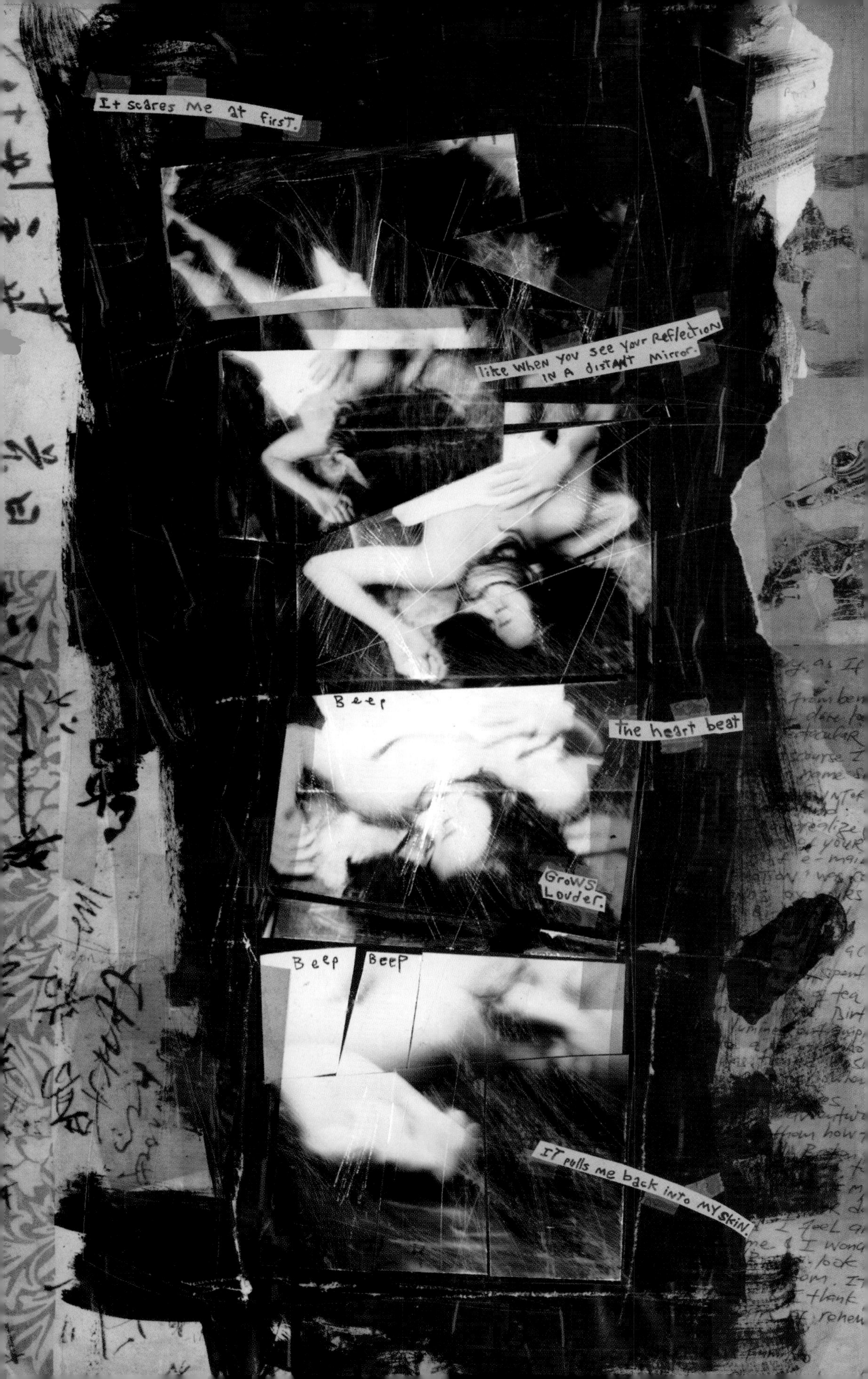
It scares me at first.
like when you see your reflection
in a distant mirror.
Beep
the heart beat
Grows
Louder.
Beep
Beep
IT pulls me back into my skin.

for my Mother

I d a   M a c k
1946-1995

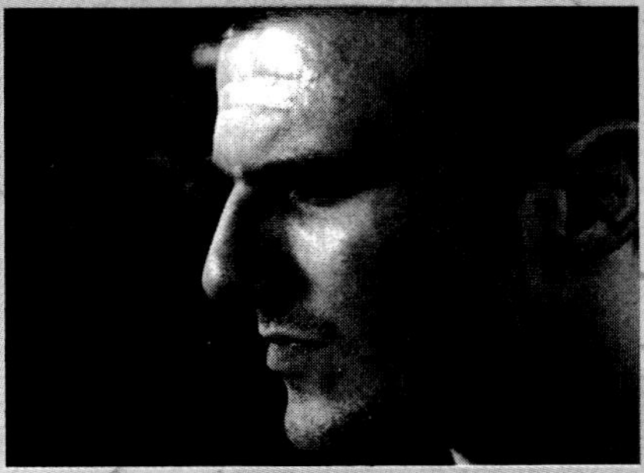

about the author

short Biography

school & carreer highlights

answers to frequently asked questions

David Mack is the creator, author and artist of *KABUKI* published by Image Comics and the writer and cover artist of *Daredevil (one of the top ten best selling comics in the United States) from Marvel Comics.*

Mack's work has garnered nominations for the 1999 **International Eagle Awards** in the categories of *Favorite Comic Artist* (Painted), and *Best Cover Art of the Year* (Painted), the **Eisner Award** (America's most prestigious comics award) in the category of *Best Painter*, and both the **Harvey** and **Kirby Awards** in the category of *Best New Talent*, as well as many other awards and nominations.

David Mack was born October 7, 1972 in Cincinnati, Ohio. By the time he graduated from high school, he had written and acted in several school theater productions, and won numerous medals and awards for the Science Fair, art shows, writing competitions, speeches, athletics, and foreign language.

Instead of a specialized art school, he attended a university for five years. He was awarded a four year scholarship based on his portfolio of art works and a fifth year Dean's Scholarship for academics. He began NKU in 1990 at seventeen years old. There, he studied multiple disciplines in art and academics, including: *Acting & Theater, Anatomy & Physiology, World Religions & Mythology, World History, Children's Literature,* and the *Japanese Language*.

He competed in the university's college-level *Karate* tournaments. As a freshman competing against upperclassmen, Mack won the gold medal for first place. He graduated with a BFA in *Graphic Design* (which included studies in *Sculpture, Painting, Drawing, Art History, Photography, Typography, & Bookmaking*) with a Minor in *English*. The first published *KABUKI* collection: *KABUKI – Circle of Blood*, was completed while in college and turned in for his senior writing thesis.

KABUKI has earned David international acclaim for its innovative storytelling, painting techniques, and page design. It is available in seven different languages. There are well over a million copies of *KABUKI* Comics, Paperbacks, and Hardcovers in print in the U.S. alone. Mack has toured and exhibited throughout Europe, Asia, and America. He was the first American to be nominated for Germany's most prestigious Max-und-Moritz Award in the category of *Best Imported Comic*.

David Mack is listed in *Wizard* Magazine's *Top Ten Writers* List. Articles about his work have appeared in *The Washington Times, SPIN, Carpe Noctem, Sketch Magazine, Hobby Japan, Tokyo Pop, Cincinnati Magazine, Giant Robot, Urb, Soma, CMJ New Music Monthly,* and others around the world. His books have been the subject of under-graduate and graduate university courses in Art and Literature, and listed as required reading. His work has been studied in graduate seminars at USC and hung in the Los Angeles Museum of Art.

Mack has illustrated and designed Jazz and Rock albums for both American and Japanese Labels (including work for Paul McCartney), designed toys and packaging for companies in Hong Kong, and ad campaigns for SAKURA art materials.

Currently, David is working on the *KABUKI* feature film for Twentieth Century Fox. Besides writing the treatment, his credits include, *Visual Designer, Creative Consultant,* and *Co- Producer.*

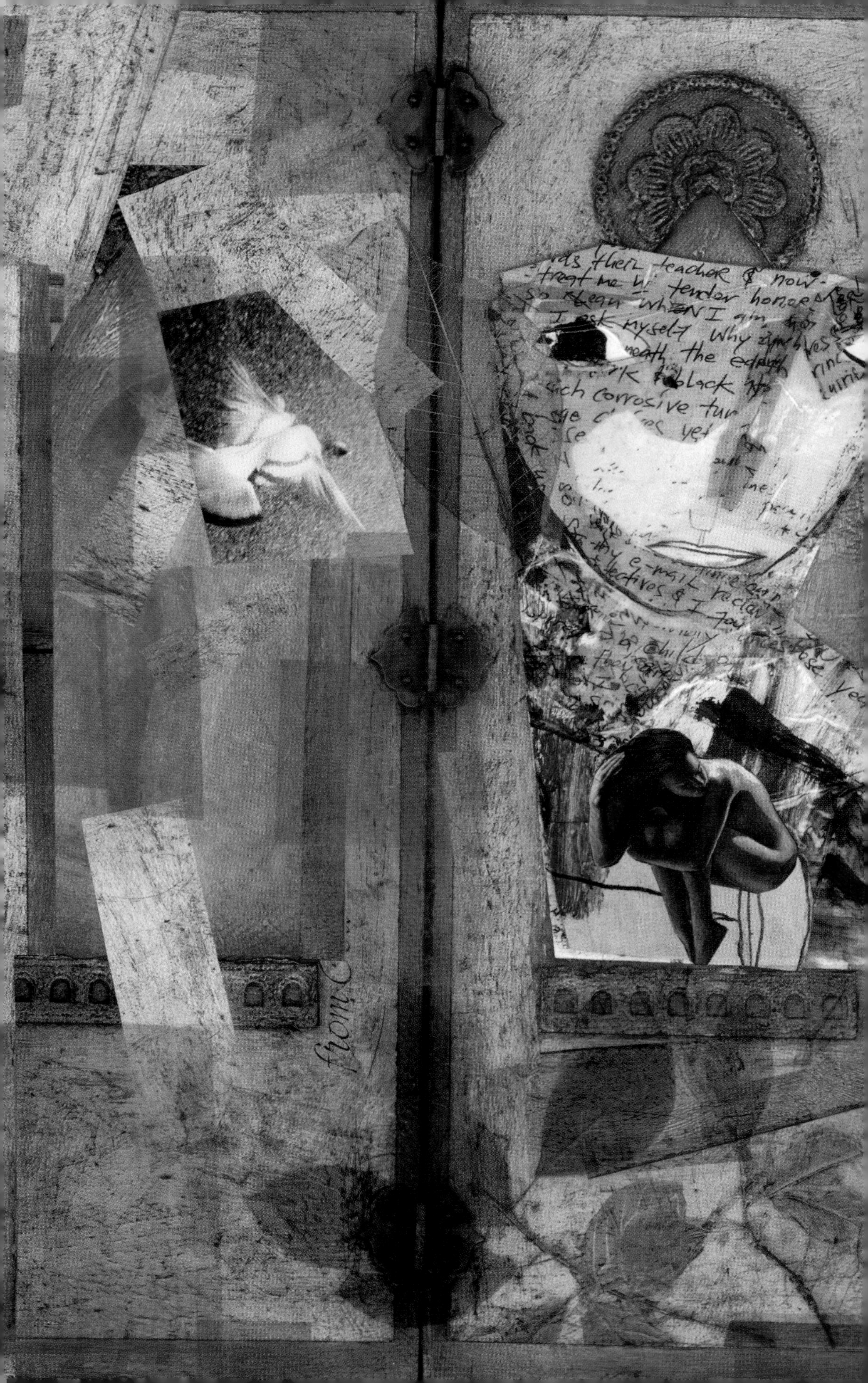
from

AfterWORD

By David Mack

This story began as an epilogue to my first Kabuki
story (Circle of Blood). Some of the pages in Dreams
weave in and out of the pages in the conclusion to
Circle of Blood and throughout parts of Masks of the
Noh. Sort of a glimpse between dimensions and
perspectives. Both of those stories are in black and
white. So I wanted the goings on of the conscious and
material world that bookends the stories in Dreams
to take place in black and white also. These moments
begin the book, end it, and are peppered throughout it
(whether in black ink, black and white photos, or
shades of gray). When the character drifts out of the
material story and crosses into the unconscious or
spiritual realm, the use of colored media signifies
the transition and provides the atmosphere for this
new theater of experience. I wanted the art and
narrative to change form and rhythm to fit the shape of
the new laws of physics that apply to the character's
perceptions as she journeys back and forth between
both of these realities.

As the first two stories in this book were the very
first painted books that I ever did, I began to
realize that working in color and texture added
entirely new dimensions in storytelling. Sometimes
it was necessary for me to scrap my plans, plots, and
preconceived notions of the story, and let the color
tell things that could not be told by other means. I
realized that the words and pages did not work in the
order that I had designed them when they were pencil
sketches and text scribbles. Some of the pages looked
better next to other ones simply based on their color
and compositional contrasts. I realized that I had to
re-order the pages based on the system of
relationships between each of the pages rather than
the pre-ordered analytical sequence that I began with.
Stripping away these conventional rules of order and
sequence allowed me to work much more intuitively on
these stories. This seemed very appropriate for a book
titled Dreams. This is not to say that there is anything
random in the organization of the work, but rather that
the pages reveal their own natural, organic, inherent
order of sequence.

It is interesting to note, that every single painted
book that I have done since this first story in here
has worked in this fashion. I start by arranging the
pages based on my story. Then I realize that the
pages work much better in an entirely different order,
and I re-configure the sequence. The story reveals
itself this way.

The text followed a similar path. I usually have to rewrite each paragraph sentence by sentence in the exact opposite order that I originally jotted it. I don't know why, but it always sounds better this way. And more importantly, after I finish the art, I realize that I have to eliminate more than half of the words. In the case of this book, I realized that things did not happen in words. So I needed to cut out ninety percent of the text and fit the remnants together into something that more closely resembled a poem.

I used similar cut-up techniques for the words in between each chapter. Those lines are taken from a book documenting various Noh plays that deal with visiting figures in the afterlife (a favorite topic of both Kabuki Theater and Noh Theater). I cut out lines or words from different plays and mixed them together to make little poems that I felt related to this story as it's own Ghost Play of Japan.

Though both Dreams and Circle of Blood are constructed in a framework that correlates to the structures and themes of the Ghost dramas of Japan, they are also very personal stories for me. These stories focus on Kabuki coming to terms with the death of her mother, and her communication with her mother, just as they do the same for me with the death of my own mother, my relationship with her, and my own brushes with life after death. If I was to analyze it, I might consider that much of these stories are, in effect, my own way of dealing with the death of my mother, a document of my own after death experiences, and communication with my mother in my own dreams. Perhaps it is also about my relationship with her when I was a child. The stories that she read to me. The way that she shaped me. The way she taught me how to look at things. The lessons that I did not fully understand until much later.

The walls and doors between imagination and reality, past, present and future, or between the material and the less physical worlds seem to be just a matter of perception and acknowledgement. I believe that the veil between these worlds is thin. My work on these books is, for me, a bridge that integrates all of these realities into the present moment. This is where I deal with the conscious and the unconscious alike. I'm speaking in both of these languages simultaneously.

NOTE: When I was in college, I had a teacher named Howard Storm. He was the chairman of the art department. His office had a rich thick smell from the pipe he smoked and the room displayed a very large painting of a circular composition. I remember looking closely at the texture and composition of it and the other paintings that I would later see at one of his gallery shows. I remember that he had died in France and that the paintings reflected his experiences before he came back into the land of the living. I've listened to his story of the afterlife on several TV and radio shows (most recently: Oprah, Unsolved Mysteries, and Art Bell). He was one of the teachers whose art, lectures, and demeanor fascinated me in class, and I think some of those paintings inspired a page or two in this book.

The following pages are a peek into some of my sketchbooks and journals that have not been reprinted anywhere before. It is a sort of short story from one of my sketch journals called "Rapid Eye Movements". Following that is a gallery of original covers from the stories in this book and the Kabuki spotlight from Ekllipse Magazine.

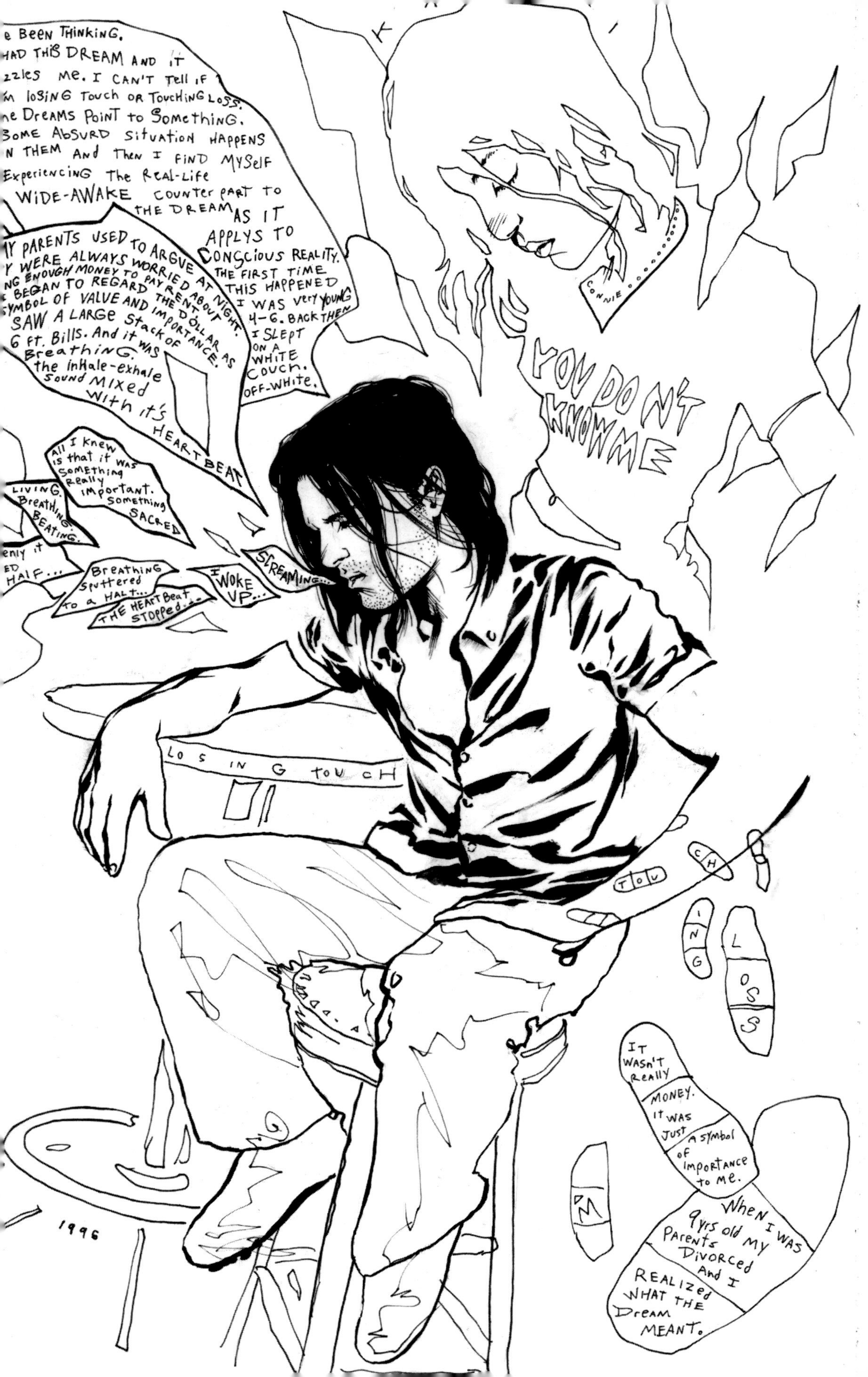

e BEEN THINKING.
HAD THIS DREAM AND IT
zzles ME. I CAN'T TELL IF
'M LOSING TOUCH OR TOUCHING LOSS.
ne DREAMS POINT to SOMETHING.
SOME ABSURD SITUATION HAPPENS
N THEM AND THEN I FIND MYSELF
EXPERIENCING THE REAL-LIFE
WIDE-AWAKE COUNTERPART TO
THE DREAM AS IT
APPLYS TO
CONSCIOUS REALITY.
THE FIRST TIME
THIS HAPPENED
I WAS VERY YOUNG
4-6. BACK THEN
I SLEPT
ON A
WHITE
COUCH.
OFF-WHITE.
Y PARENTS USED TO ARGUE AT NIGHT.
Y WERE ALWAYS WORRIED ABOUT
NG ENOUGH MONEY TO PAY RENT.
BEGAN TO REGARD THE DOLLAR AS
SYMBOL OF VALUE AND IMPORTANCE.
SAW A LARGE STACK OF
6 FT. BILLS. AND IT WAS
BREATHING.
THE INHALE-EXHALE
SOUND MIXED
WITH IT'S
HEARTBEAT
LIVING. BREATHING. BEATING.
ALL I KNEW IS THAT IT WAS SOMETHING REALLY IMPORTANT. SOMETHING SACRED
enly it
ED HALF...
BREATHING SPUTTERED TO A HALT...
THE HEARTBEAT STOPPED...
I WOKE UP...
SCREAMING...
CONNIE
YOU DON'T KNOW ME
LOSING TOUCH
TOUCH
INGLOSS
IT WASN'T REALLY MONEY. IT WAS JUST A SYMBOL OF IMPORTANCE TO ME.
WHEN I WAS 9YRS OLD MY PARENTS DIVORCED AND I REALIZED WHAT THE DREAM MEANT.
1996

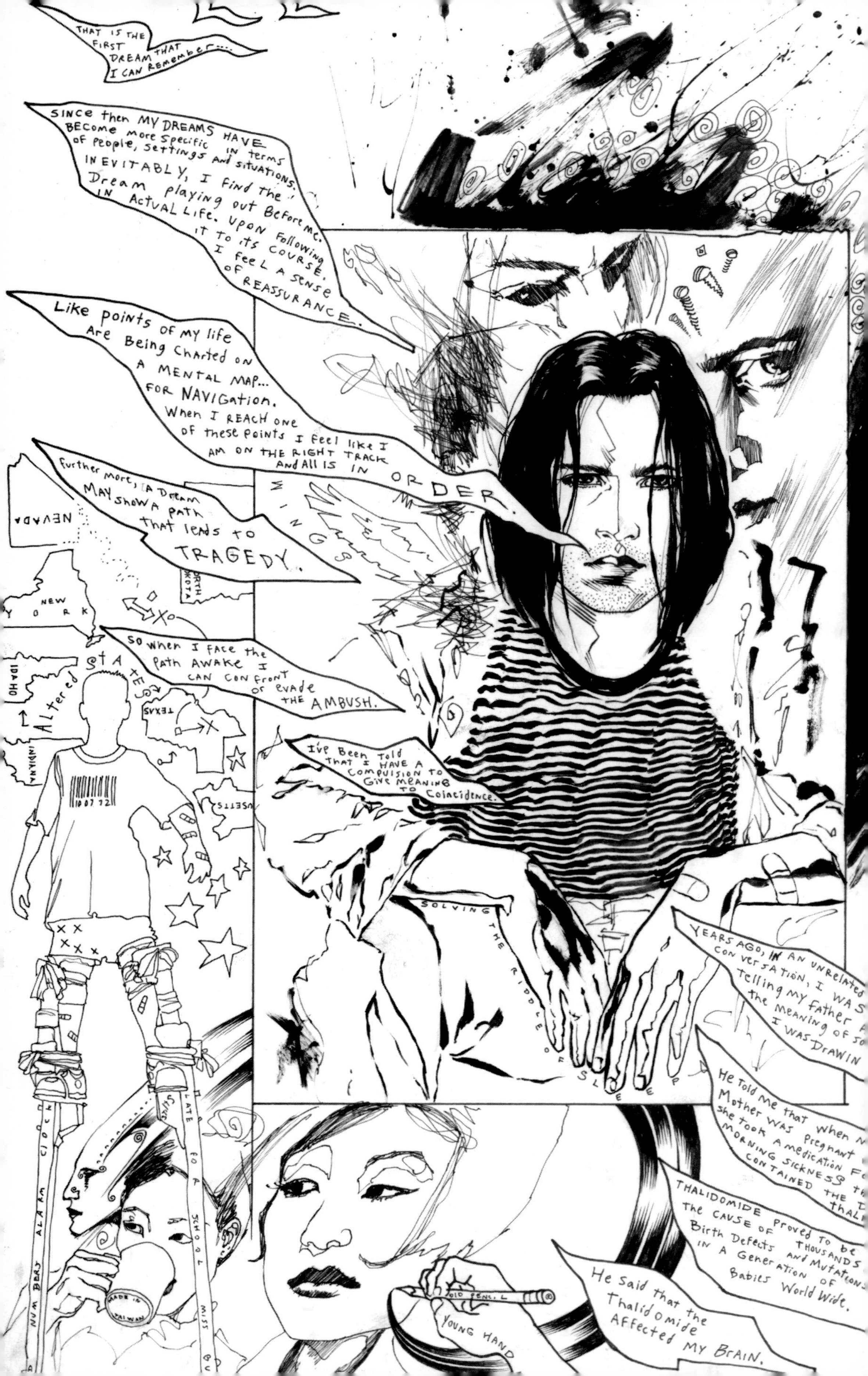

THAT IS THE FIRST DREAM THAT I CAN REMEMBER....
SINCE then MY DREAMS HAVE BECOME more Specific in terms of People, settings and situations. INEVITABLY, I find the Dream playing out Before me IN ACTUAL LIFE. UPON Following it to its COURSE, I FEEL A SENSE OF REASSURANCE.
Like points of my life Are Being Charted on A MENTAL MAP... FOR NAVIGATION. When I REACH one of these points I feel like I AM ON THE RIGHT TRACK And All is IN ORDER
WINGS
Further more, A Dream MAY show A path that leads to TRAGEDY.
NEVADA
NORTH DAKOTA
NEW YORK
So when I face the path AWAKE I CAN CONFRONT or evade THE AMBUSH.
IDAHO
Altered STATES
TEXAS
INDIANA
SETTS
1007 72
I've Been Told that I HAVE A COMPULSION to Give meaning to Coincidence.
SOLVING THE RIDDLE OF SLEEP
YEARS AGO, IN AN UNRELATED CONVERSATION, I WAS telling my father the meaning of I WAS DRAWIN
He Told me that when Mother WAS Pregnant she took A medication MORNING SICKNESS CONTAINED THE
THALIDOMIDE Proved to be The CAUSE OF THOUSANDS Birth Defects And Mutations IN A Generation of Babies World Wide.
He Said that the Thalidomide Affected MY BRAIN.
STILTS
LATE FOR SCHOOL
NUMBERS ALARM CLOCK
MADE IN TAIWAN
YOUNG HAND

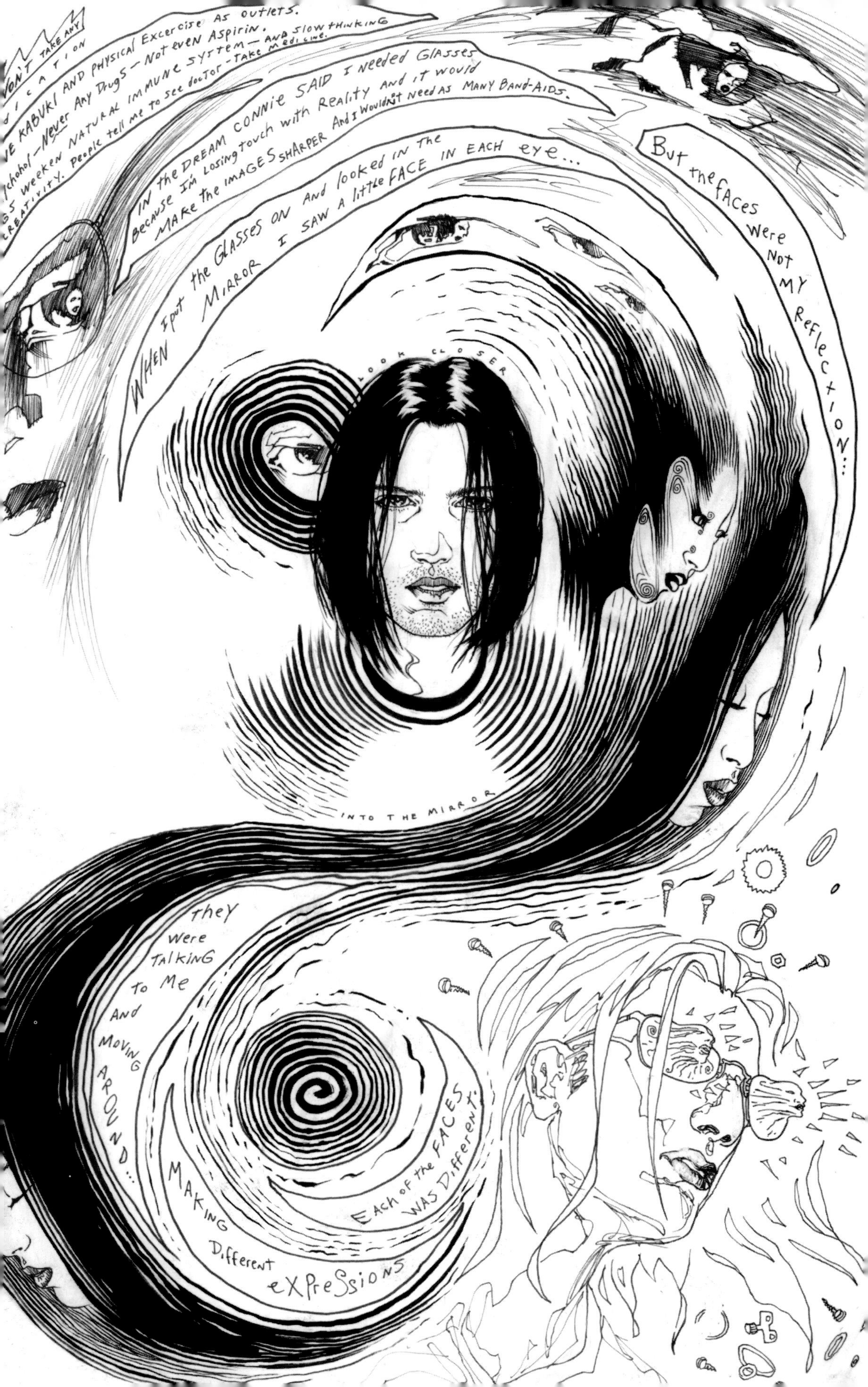

WON'T TAKE ANY
D I C A T I O N
VE KABUKI AND PHYSICAL EXCERCISE AS OUTLETS.
LCHOHOL—NEVER ANY DRUGS—NOT EVEN ASPIRIN.
GS WEEKEN NATURAL IMMUNE SYSTEM—AND SLOW THINKING
CREATIVITY. PEOPLE TELL ME TO SEE DOCTOR - TAKE MEDICINE.
IN THE DREAM CONNIE SAID I NEEDED GLASSES BECAUSE I'M LOSING TOUCH WITH REALITY AND IT WOULD MAKE THE IMAGES SHARPER AND I WOULDN'T NEED AS MANY BAND-AIDS.
WHEN I PUT THE GLASSES ON AND LOOKED IN THE MIRROR I SAW A LITTLE FACE IN EACH EYE...
BUT THE FACES WERE NOT MY REFLECTION...
LOOK CLOSER
INTO THE MIRROR
THEY WERE TALKING TO ME AND MOVING AROUND...
MAKING DIFFERENT EXPRESSIONS
EACH OF THE FACES WAS DIFFERENT.

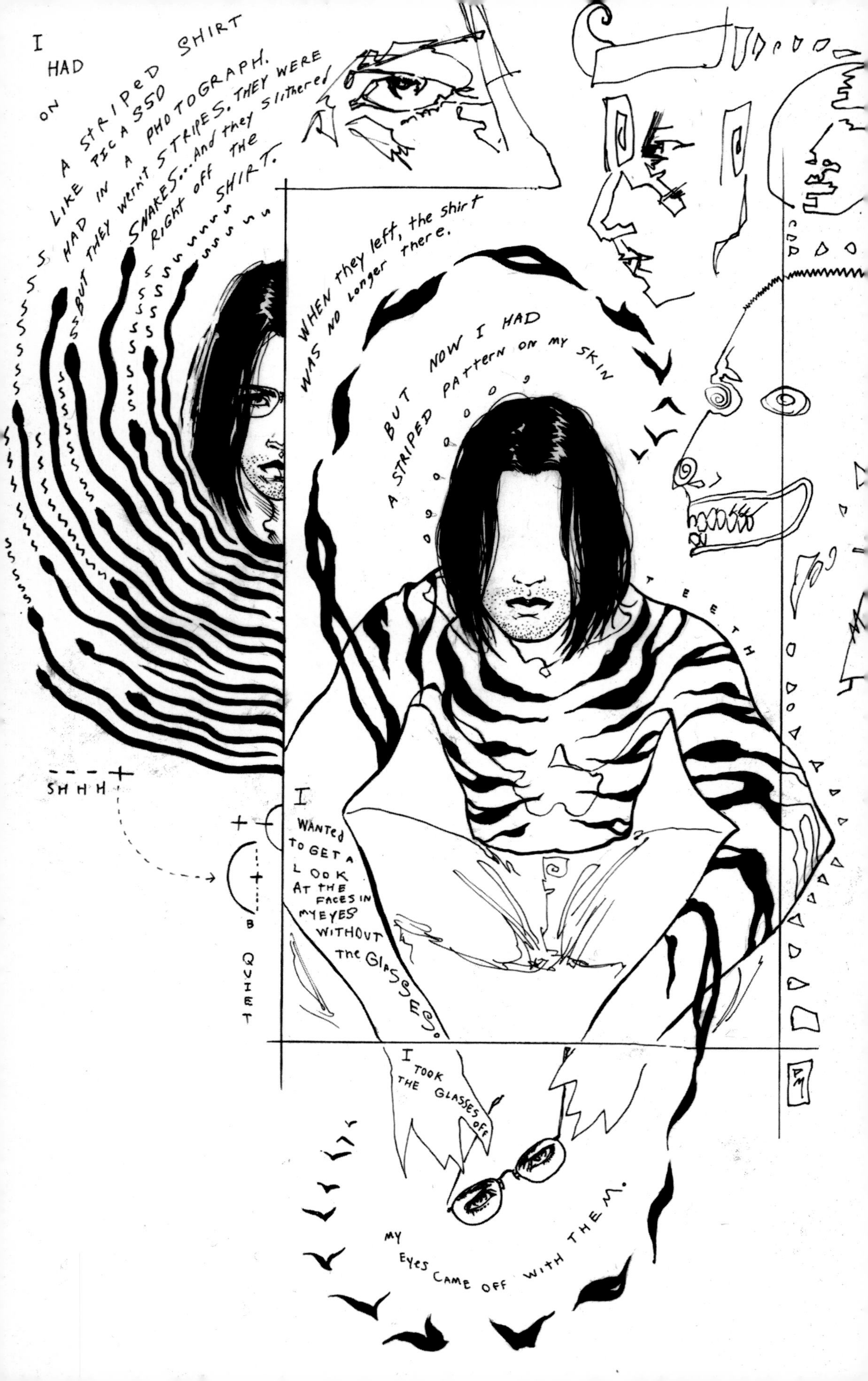
I HAD ON A STRIPED SHIRT LIKE PICASSO HAD IN A PHOTOGRAPH.
BUT THEY WEREN'T STRIPES. THEY WERE SNAKES... And they slithered RIGHT off THE SHIRT.
WHEN they left, the shirt WAS no longer there.
BUT NOW I HAD A STRIPED PATTERN ON MY SKIN
TEETH
SHHH
B QUIET
I WANTED TO GET A LOOK AT THE FACES IN MY EYES WITHOUT THE GLASSES.
I TOOK THE GLASSES OFF
MY EYES CAME OFF WITH THEM.

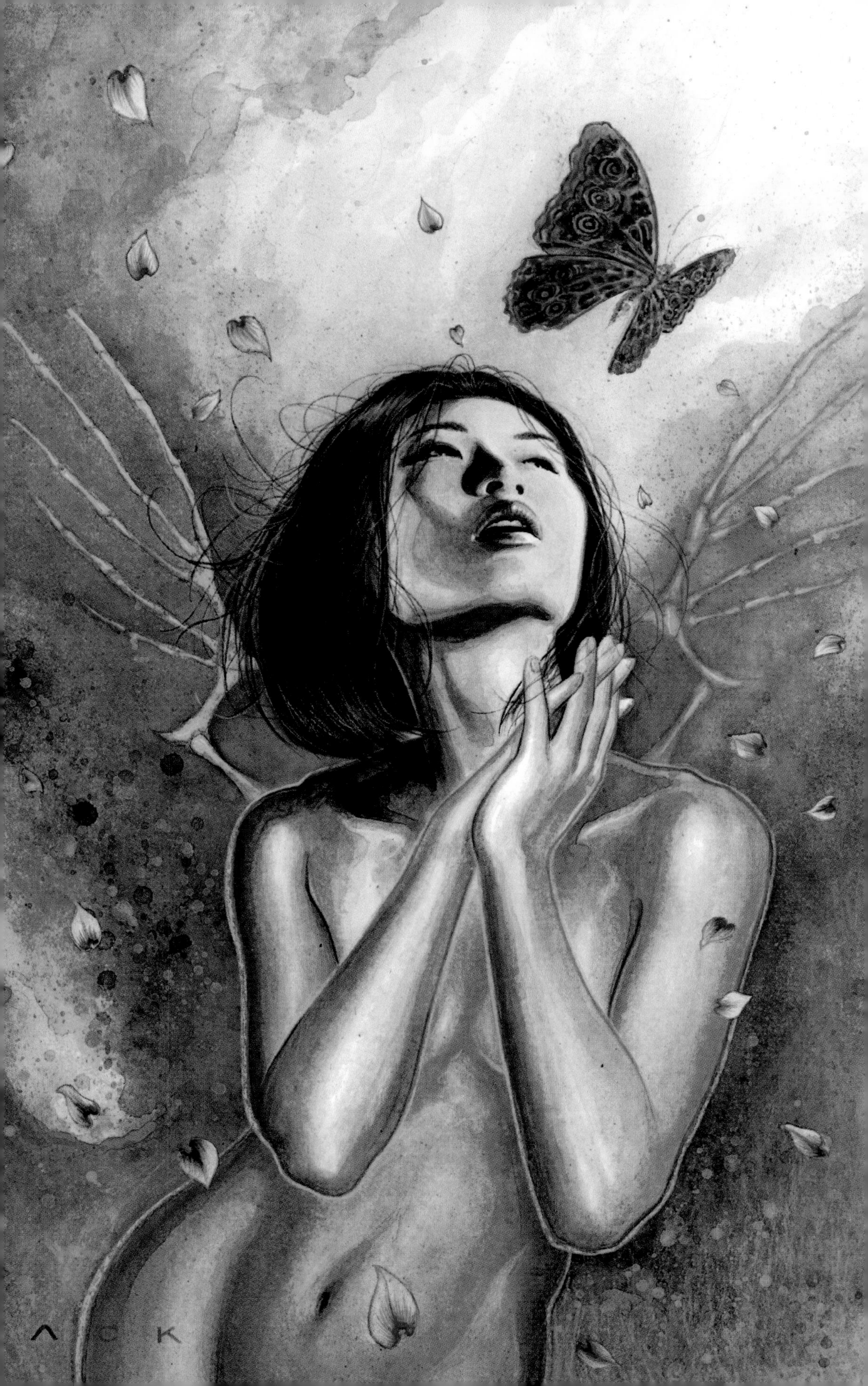

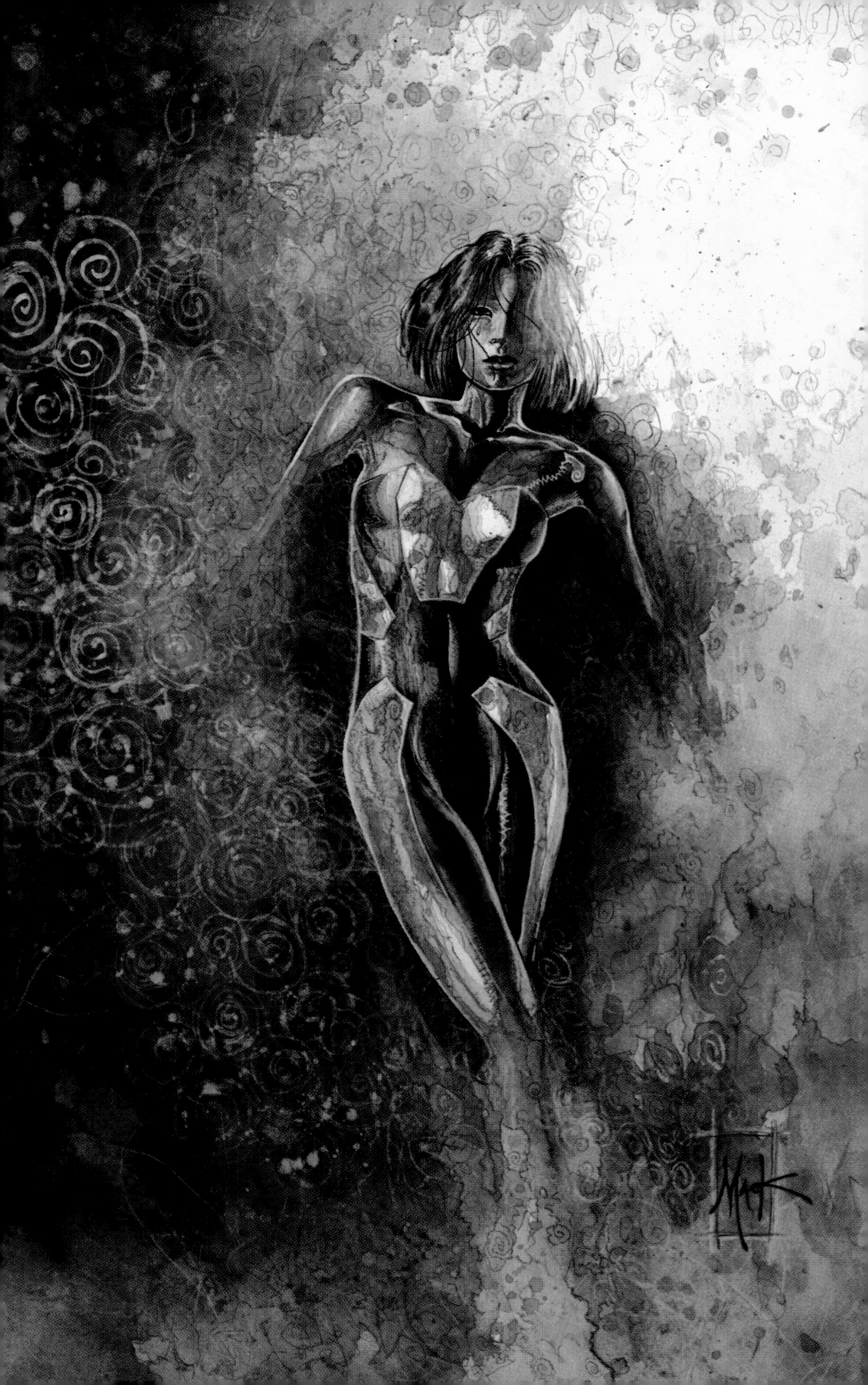
Mack

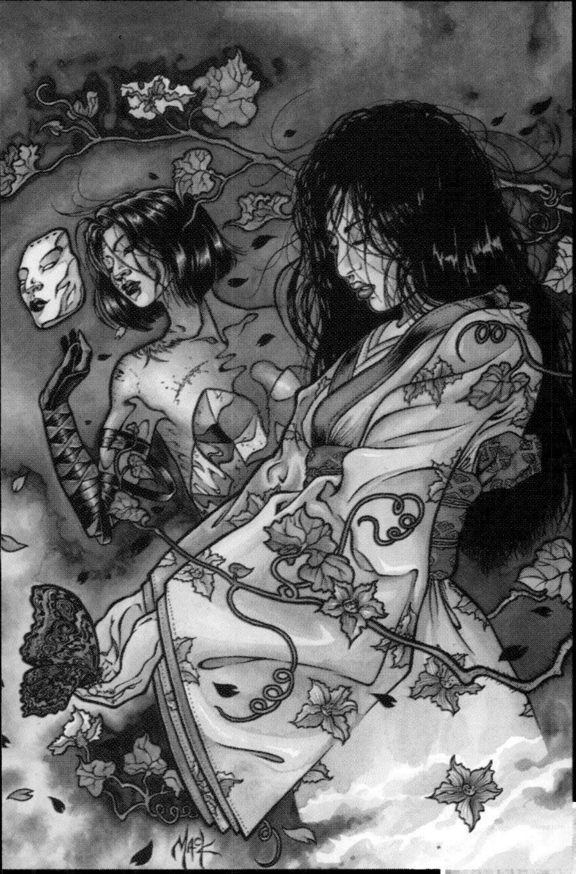

ORIGINAL COVER ART FOR Dreams of the Dead

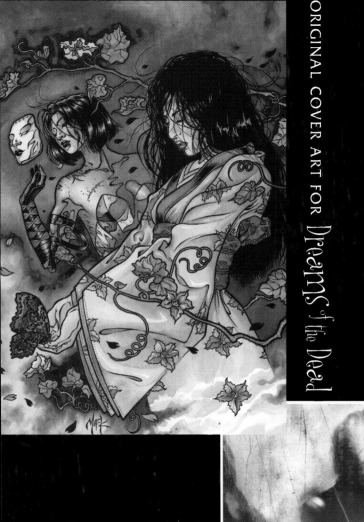

COVER TO

Kabuki Color Special

COVER TO

Kabuki 1/2

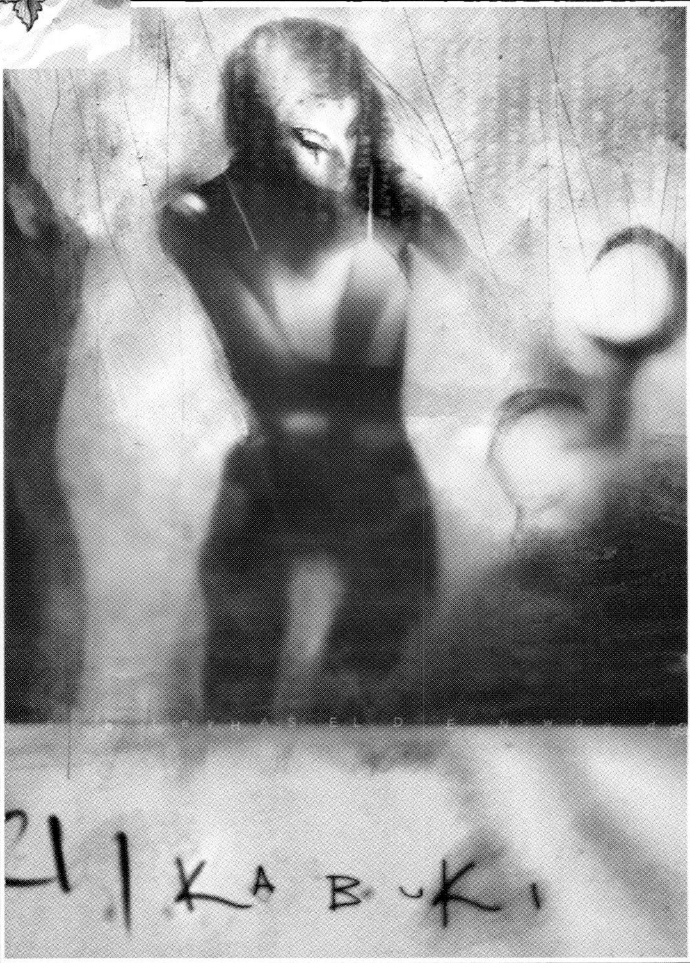
KABUKI

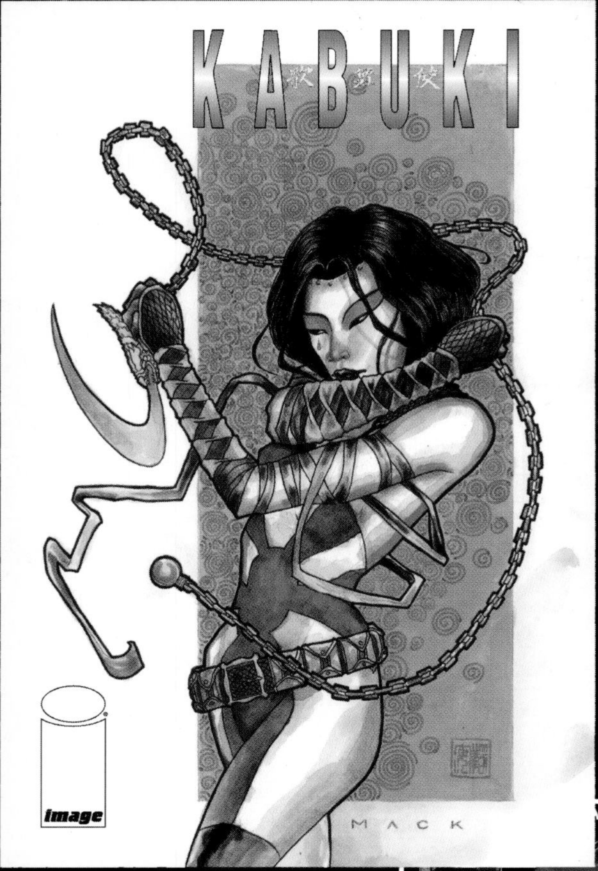
KABUKI
image
MACK

ORIGINAL COVER ART FOR Kabuki 1/2

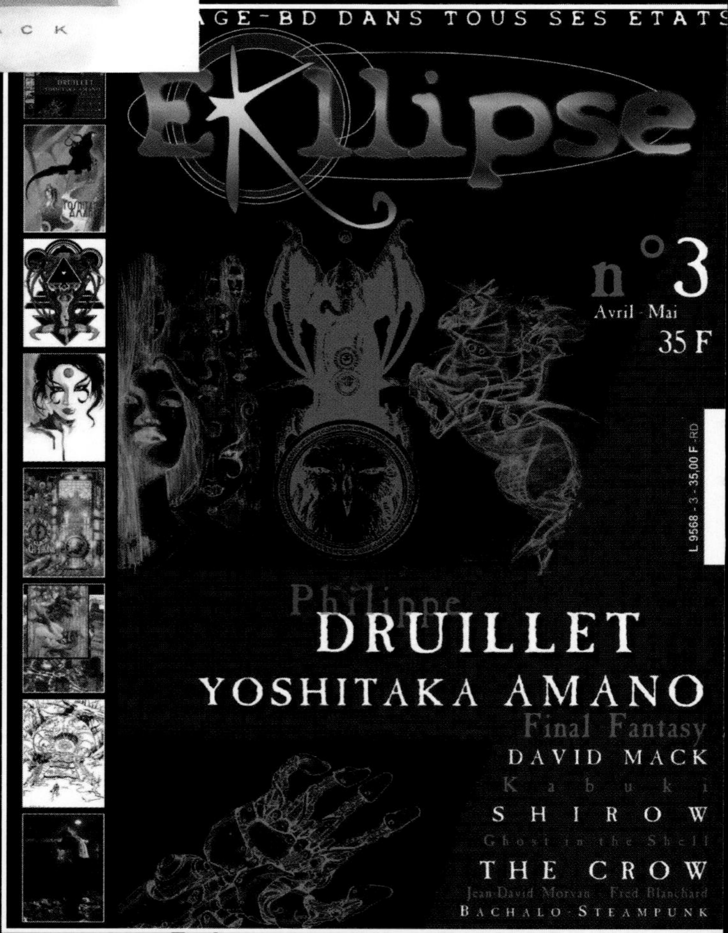
AGE-BD DANS TOUS SES ETATS
Ekllipse
n°3
Avril - Mai
35 F
L 9568 - 3 - 35,00 F - RD
Philippe
DRUILLET
YOSHITAKA AMANO
Final Fantasy
DAVID MACK
Kabuki
SHIROW
Ghost in the Shell
THE CROW
Jean-David Morvan - Fred Blanchard
BACHALO STEAMPUNK

COVER TO
France's
Ekllipse no. 3

SOLEIL COUCHANT

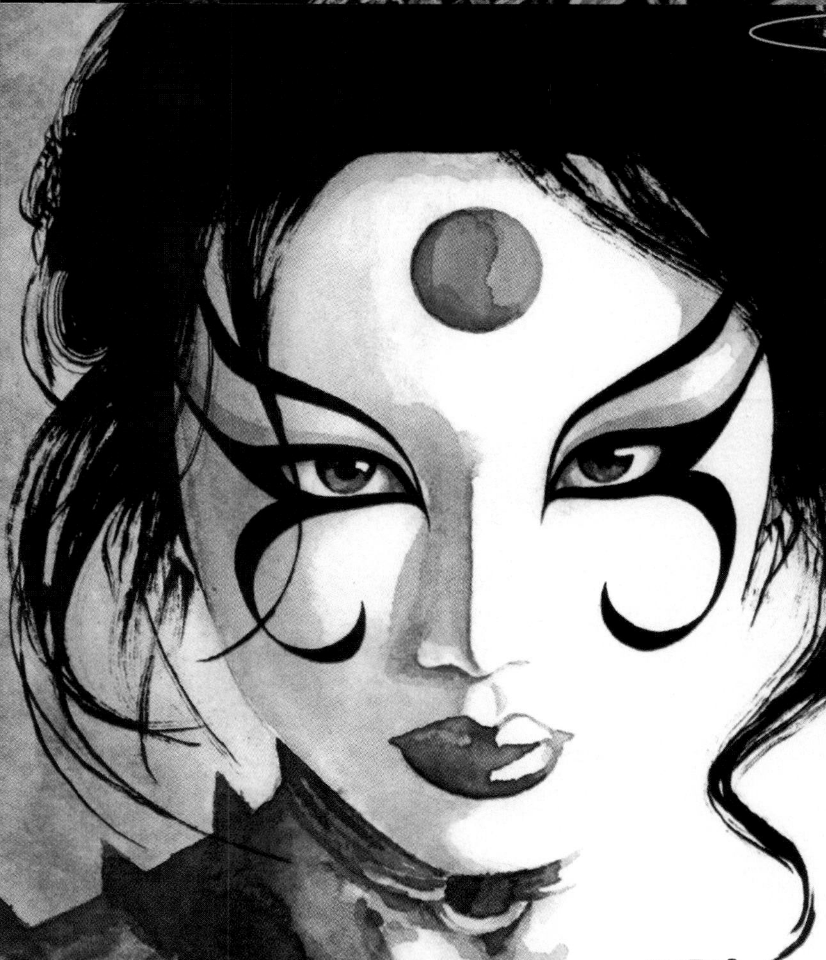

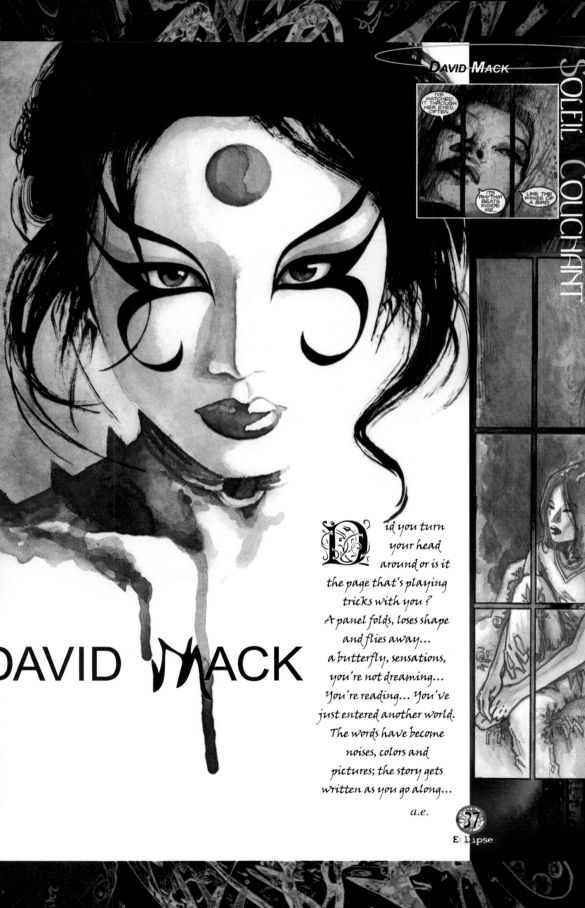

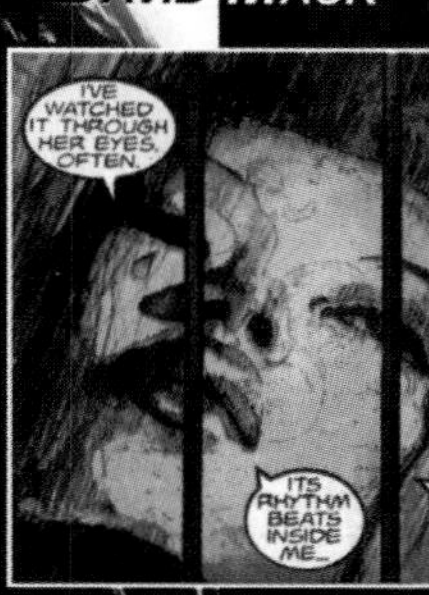
I'VE WATCHED IT THROUGH HER EYES, OFTEN.
ITS RHYTHM BEATS INSIDE ME...
LIKE THE WINGS OF A BIRD.

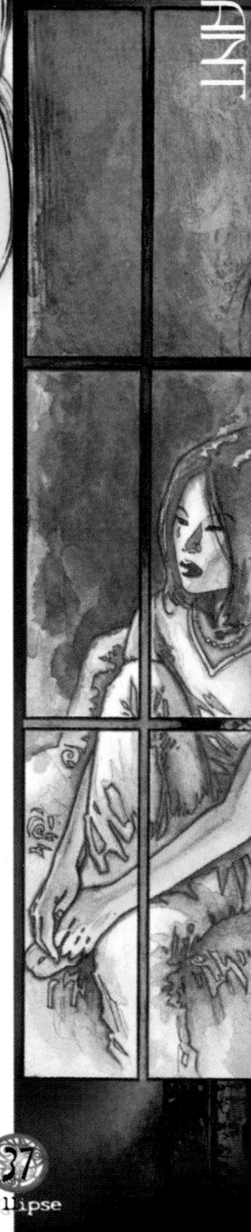

DAVID MACK

Did you turn your head around or is it the page that's playing tricks with you? A panel folds, loses shape and flies away... a butterfly, sensations, you're not dreaming... You're reading... You've just entered another world. The words have become noises, colors and pictures; the story gets written as you go along...

a.e.

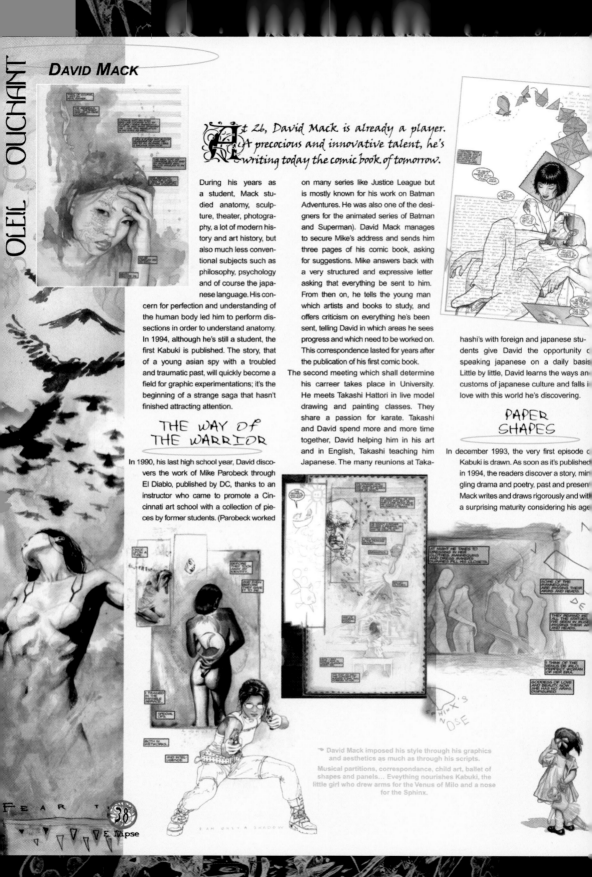

DAVID MACK

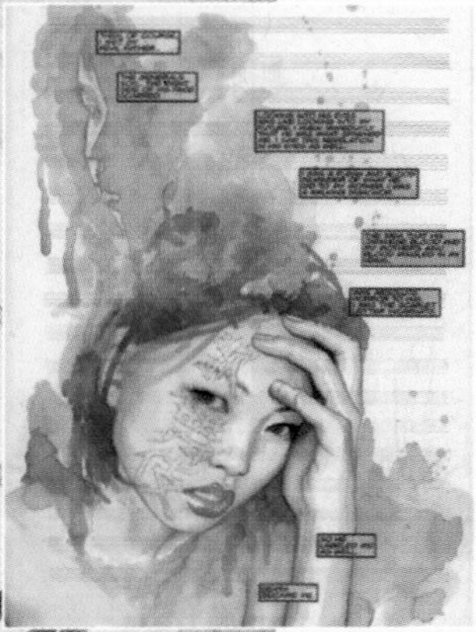

At 26, David Mack is already a player. A precocious and innovative talent, he's writing today the comic book of tomorrow.

During his years as a student, Mack studied anatomy, sculpture, theater, photography, a lot of modern history and art history, but also much less conventional subjects such as philosophy, psychology and of course the japanese language. His concern for perfection and understanding of the human body led him to perform dissections in order to understand anatomy. In 1994, although he's still a student, the first Kabuki is published. The story, that of a young asian spy with a troubled and traumatic past, will quickly become a field for graphic experimentations; it's the beginning of a strange saga that hasn't finished attracting attention.

THE WAY OF THE WARRIOR

In 1990, his last high school year, David discovers the work of Mike Parobeck through El Diablo, published by DC, thanks to an instructor who came to promote a Cincinnati art school with a collection of pieces by former students. (Parobeck worked on many series like Justice League but is mostly known for his work on Batman Adventures. He was also one of the designers for the animated series of Batman and Superman). David Mack manages to secure Mike's address and sends him three pages of his comic book, asking for suggestions. Mike answers back with a very structured and expressive letter asking that everything be sent to him. From then on, he tells the young man which artists and books to study, and offers criticism on everything he's been sent, telling David in which areas he sees progress and which need to be worked on. This correspondence lasted for years after the publication of his first comic book.

The second meeting which shall determine his carreer takes place in University. He meets Takashi Hattori in live model drawing and painting classes. They share a passion for karate. Takashi and David spend more and more time together, David helping him in his art and in English, Takashi teaching him Japanese. The many reunions at Takashi's with foreign and japanese students give David the opportunity of speaking japanese on a daily basis. Little by little, David learns the ways and customs of japanese culture and falls in love with this world he's discovering.

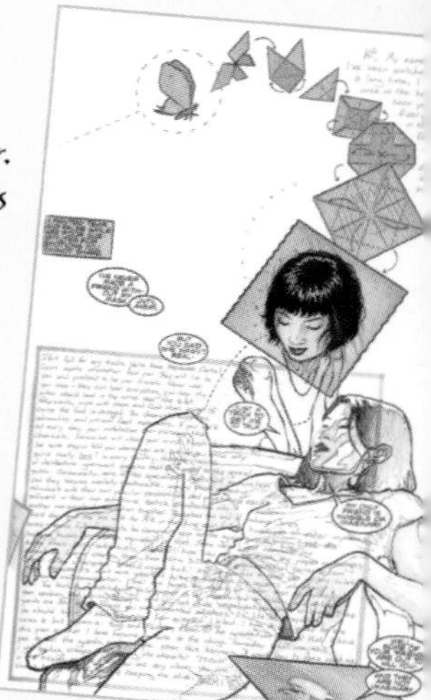

PAPER SHAPES

In december 1993, the very first episode of Kabuki is drawn. As soon as it's published in 1994, the readers discover a story, mingling drama and poetry, past and present. Mack writes and draws rigorously and with a surprising maturity considering his age.

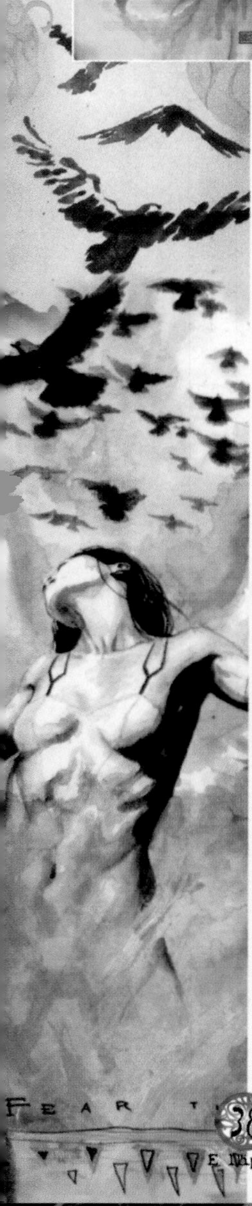

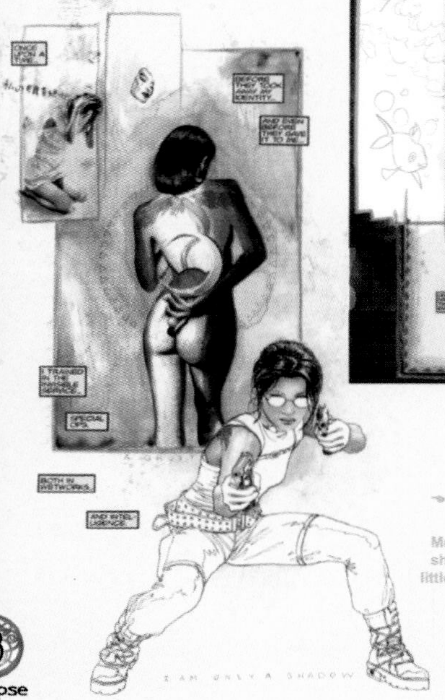
ONCE UPON A TIME...
BEFORE THEY TOOK AWAY MY IDENTITY.
AND EVEN BEFORE THEY GAVE IT TO ME.
I TRAINED IN THE INVISIBLE SERVICE.
SPECIAL OPS.
BOTH IN WETWORKS.
AND INTELLIGENCE.
I AM ONLY A SHADOW

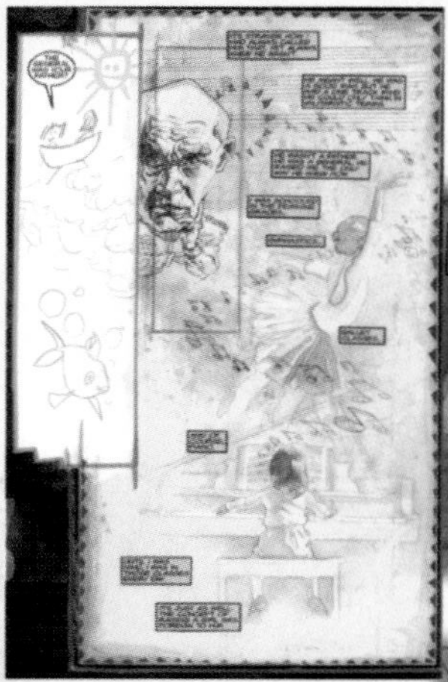

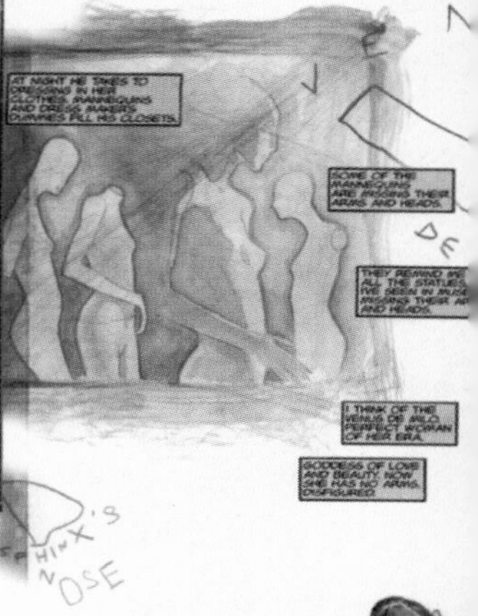
AT NIGHT HE TAKES TO DRESSING IN HER CLOTHES. MANNEQUINS AND DRESS MAKERS DUMMIES FILL HIS CLOSETS.
SOME OF THE MANNEQUINS ARE MISSING THEIR ARMS AND HEADS.
I THINK OF THE VENUS DE MILO. PERFECT WOMAN OF HER ERA.
GODDESS OF LOVE AND BEAUTY. NOW SHE HAS NO ARMS. DISFIGURED.
SPHINX'S NOSE

David Mack imposed his style through his graphics and aesthetics as much as through his scripts.

Musical partitions, correspondance, child art, ballet of shapes and panels… Eveything nourishes Kabuki, the little girl who drew arms for the Venus of Milo and a nose for the Sphinx.

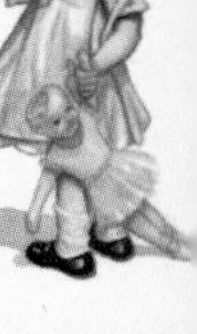

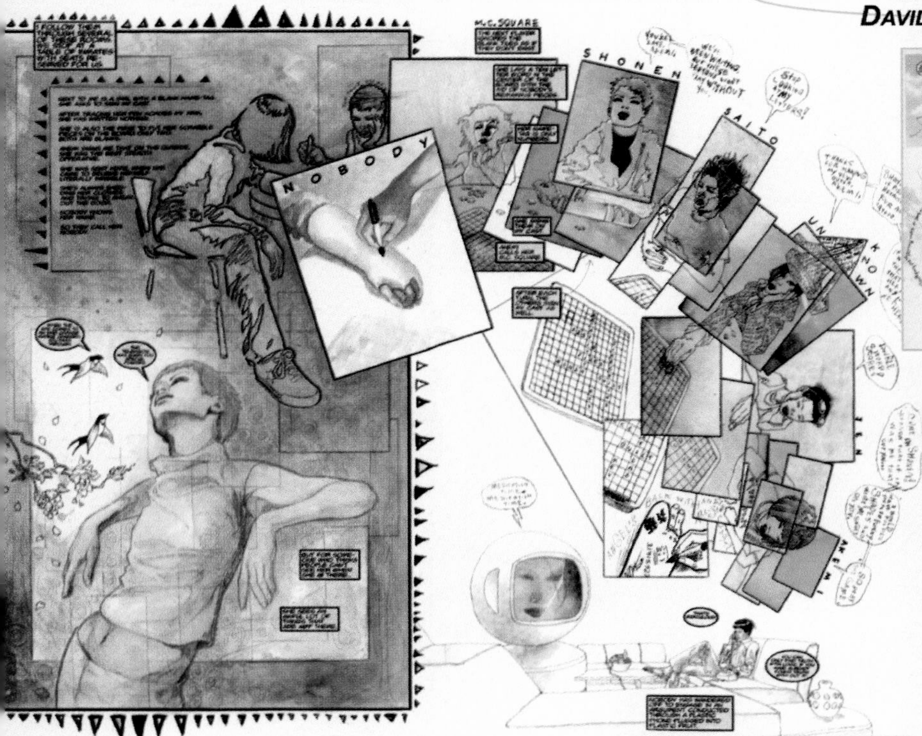
M.C. SQUARE
NOBODY
SHONEN
SAITO
UNKNOWN

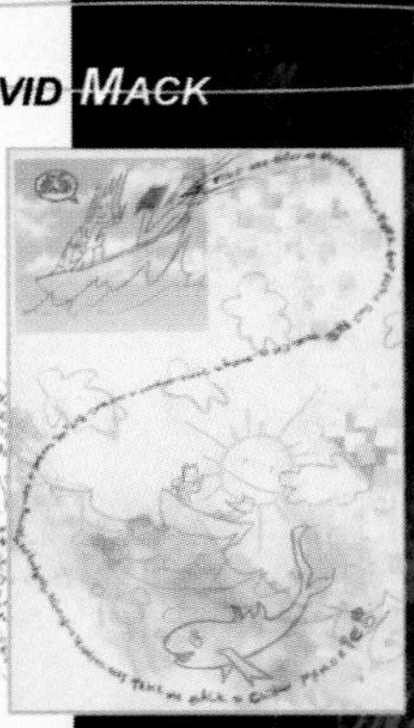

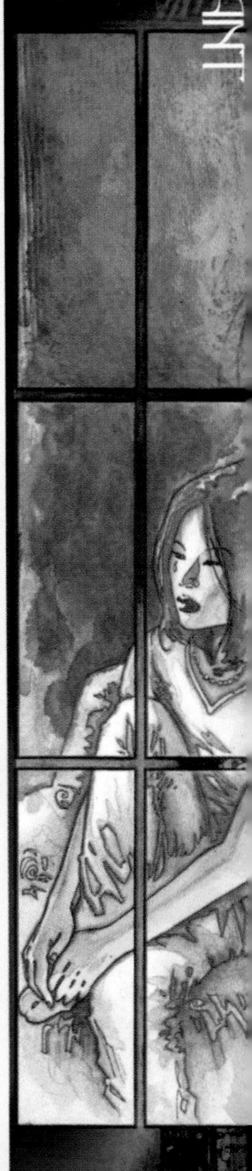

lack writes and draws rigorously and with urprising maturity, plus an unending and most obessionnal concern for perfection, ich compels him to keep on studying..."

plus an unending and almost obsessionnal concern for perfection, which compels him to keep on studying. He endows his work with a life and soul. The characters have depth, resolutely human feelings. Kabuki is no exception, it's even the main vector for it. As the story unfolds, the reader becomes closer to Ukiko and delves with her into her dreams, her thoughts and her life. The feelings, the impressions are communicated to us in a strong and poetic manner. The past collides with the present in order to move us, in a Japan branded with high tech, almost cold and free of emotion. If the atmosphere is chilly, the characters come out even better, in contrast to the setting. The separation between the private life and the professionnal activities of the nô members sets them clearly apart, to the point that the members only know each other under the guise of their masks, their identities being State secrets. But the personnalities seep through the masks, and in spite of the frozen features of those faces, friendships spark up and die out in an eclipse.

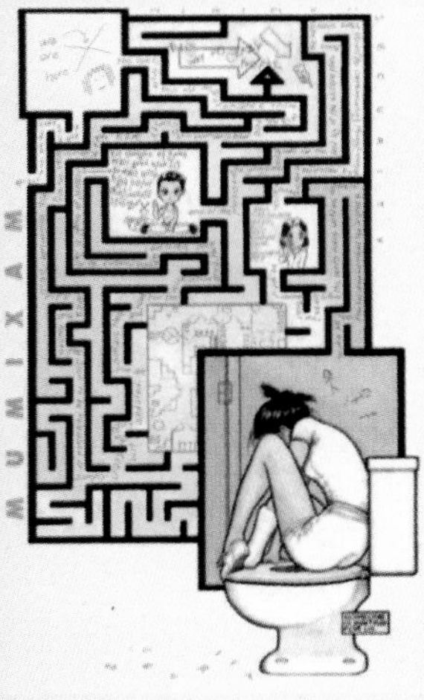
MUMIXAM

▲ Above, impossible to present the characters in a more dynamic manner, vertigo of an uncertain meeting around a game of Scrabble... Words always.

◄ Left : «If my characters are attempting to get out of an inextricable situation, I organize my page as a labyrinth». And the reader simply has to follow the thread of the storyline.

Right : from the little girl to the Noh agent : education ►

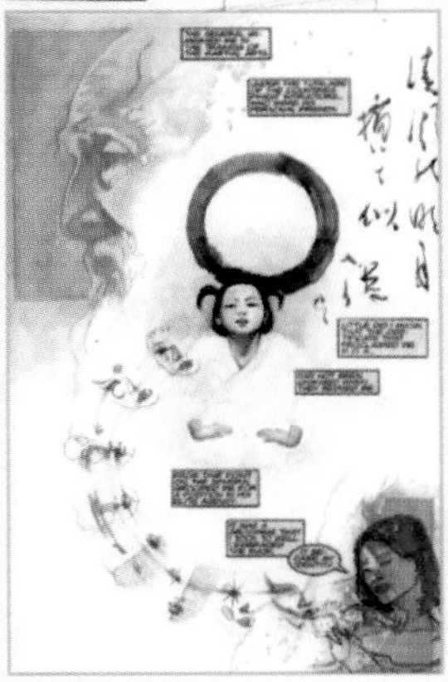

MEMORIES AND DREAMS

Memories are also a source of emotion; sometimes close, sometimes remote, they're a source of pleasure or pain. Kabuki remembers her father with horror, and creates an almost ideal picture of a mother that she has only known through the tales of her grandfather. The duality between her father and mother, immediately evokes the dualities man and woman, sun and moon (Tsukiko), good and evil.

DAVID MACK

The quest for purity is also to be found in the origami that Akemi practices. As in the origami, Kabuki metamorphoses, so that, from her basic matter, a new and pure being may rise, but the transformation is never without pain : she loses a part of her self through it. Like the legendary cat, she dies to live again, but the new life doesn't live up to expectations. New trials await her, there and then, maybe paving the way to wisdom.

PUPPET THEATER

Mack also enjoys toying with contradictions. Both the japanese popular theater Kabuki and the nô, theater of the priviledged japanese classes, are part of the story; originally these dramas are to be exclusively performed by men, replaced here by women, whom under the appearance of geishas, play the double role of prevention and repression. Just like Kabuki and nô both are divided in a precise number of scenes, the action domain of the nô is perfectly defined : the roles and missions are dictated by the leader of the nô, and just as in the plays, it seems impossible

to deviate from there. Kabuki, Scarab and the other executants have a preventive role, thanks to the mythical character of the roles they play, with frequent features on japanese television. They also play a regulatory role in maintaining the fragile balance of the statu quo between the government and organized crime.

lism. He has proven he has perfectly unde[r]tood the laws of realistic illustration, onl[y] bend them, when he adds them to the stor[y]

▸ Above : Unknown who dresses in folded [...] papers. Perfection of detail: see how her clo[...] are made of real man[...]

➤ "Akemi is the first person to accept Ka[...] without the ma[...]

CALLI-GRAPHY LOGY

Besides the nô, Kabuki and origami, arti[...] representations flourish under multi[...] forms. If references to Degas or Leona[...] da Vinci are numerous, Mack also adm[...] as major influences: Piet Mondrian, Gus[...] Klimt and Vincent Van Gogh for painti[...]

Origami, directions for use or shadow show...

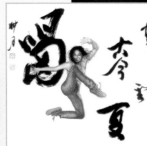

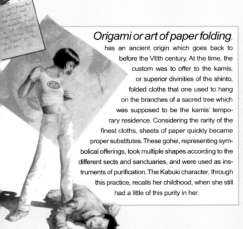

Origami or art of paper folding, has an ancient origin which goes back to before the VIIth century. At the time, the custom was to offer to the kamis, or superior divinities of the shinto, folded cloths that one used to hang on the branches of a sacred tree which was supposed to be the kamis' temporary residence. Considering the rarity of the finest cloths, sheets of paper quickly became proper substitutes. These gohei, representing symbolical offerings, took multiple shapes according to the different sects and sanctuaries, and were used as instruments of purification. The Kabuki character, through this practice, recalls her childhood, when she still had a little of this purity in her.

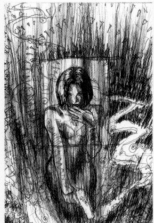

Pencil stroke or aerial calligraphy, Mack tames his material from the darkened page to the eloquent whiteness.

kira Kurosawa for cinema and William hakespeare in litterature. He's also insired by Frank Miller and Mike Mignola when he spawns "*Fear the Reaper*". With Mack, art also means dance. Waltzes whirl around, movements decompose themselves, and Ukiko appears as a Degas ballerina. Even the fights seems choregraphed like ballets, resulting in an ordered chaos. exploration of japanese tradition combines with a subtle mingling of imagination, violence and psychodrama. Spots or bloody strokes, frenetical hatching or child art, inevitably Kabuki finds a way to startle us, move us, especially if one is blasé by comics' predictability. Using an approach which mixes cinematics with surrealism, Mack has forged a new visual syntax in a form of art which hardly ever goes through change.

UNDER STATEMENTS

His philosophy, centered on the way of telling a story, isn't to tell the reader what is about to happen or even to show that, as many artists do, but to reveal the story to him. That revelation is provoked by a unique system of story telling which unifies the icons, the graphism and obsessive images in a sythesis of visual language. It's interesting to note that Mack doesn't feel bound to the laws of realism. He has proven he has perfectly understood the laws of realistic illustration, only to bend them, almost shatter them, when he adds them to the story.

David incorporates perfectly the japanese language into his story. Made up of different styles in relation to gender, age, professional and social status, Japanese has three alphabets : Hiragana, Katakana and Kanji. Kanji, based on chinese characters, is overly present in the comic book. The word Kabuki itself is made up of three characters : ka, bu and ki, which can be litteraly translated by song, dance and action. Mack takes the language concept up a notch. In Kabuki, each corporation and each social group has his own language, based on the lingo and slang of the organisation. That allows each of them its own family secrets. The agents of nô speak the language of nô, employees of Snow television speak in Snow language.

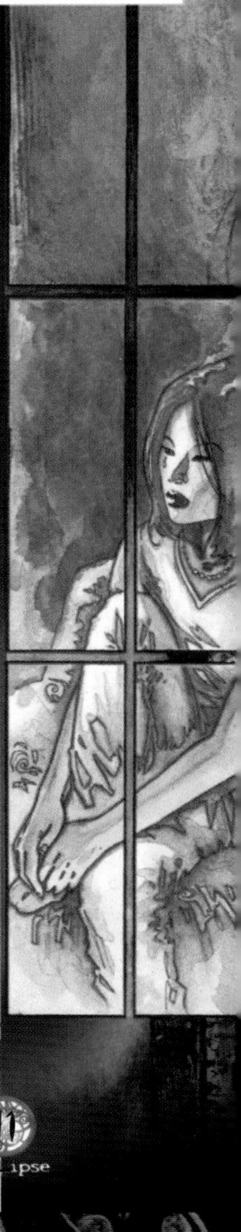

Theatre's Plays :

- KABUKI : (*Image Comics*)
Fear the reaper.
Dance of death.
Circle of blood, 6 issues.
Color special.
Dreams of the dead.
Masks of the Noh, 4 issues.
Skin deep 1.
Overstreet's Fan edition.
Skin deep 2 et 3.
Kabuki, Ongoing Serie, 9 issues as far.
Kabuki 1/2 (*Wizard Press*)
Kabuki agents : Scarab, 1 to 3 (written by D.Mack, illustrated by Rick Mays)

- Other contributions or projects :
Vision.
Frank Frazetta Magazine 1.
Devil's Requiem. Grendel : Black, White & Red 2, *Dark Horse*)
Daredevil 9 to 12, written by D.Mack, pencilled and inked by Joe Quesada and Jimmy Palmiotti. (*Marvel Knights*)
Sketchbook Magazine 1.

ONE THOUSAND NINE HUNDRED SIXTY NINE

the psy's notepad or Akemi's toilet paper haunt the pages.

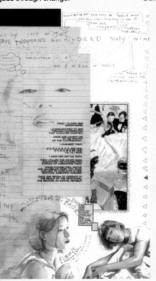

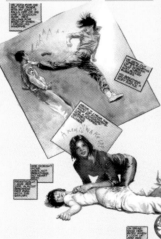

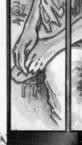

DAVID MACK

The Master of Masks :
Interview with David Mack

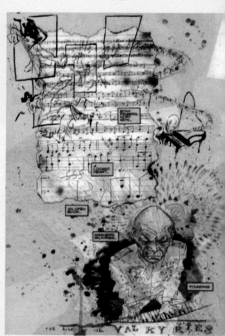

E : *We've noticed the cameo appearences in the pages of Kabuki of many painters and authors such as Degas, the monk Toba, Tezuka, and many more... You also seem to love music and piano. Are the partitions present in your pages related to actual existing pieces ?*

They certainly are ! I use specific pieces of music when it supports the atmosphere of a scene. When I do, I credit it either on the page or in the back of the book. The notes of music you are referring to are probably from the musical scenes in Kabuki #5. Most of that is Wagner's «Ride of the Valkyries» (which harkens back to the music that Kabuki could hear the General playing when her face was scarred). There is also a page in that issue in which two spirals of music come from a piano and intertwine in a double helix like DNA. These two different streams are Wagner's «Ride of the Valkyries» and the Japanese National Anthem. In light of the context of these pages, supported by the text, I think that you can see the deeper meaning that these musical pieces add to my message. The choice of the titles and tone of the music but also the visual presentation of the musical notes, call for differents degrees of interpretation. These can range from order to chaos, or spring up in a spiral geometry, through the recurring metaphor of the entanglement of two separate sides. They are synonymous of the essence of Kabuki, of her mixed blood, hence the DNA helix and the two different kinds of music. Wagner's Valkyries represent her journey from life to death and back again. It also represents the part of her that was scarred. The Anthem represents the façade side of the Mask, the constructs of her previous life in which she was groomed for patriotism and nationalistic duties in which she wore the flag.

E : *More generally, what are your influences ?*

I've tried to train myself to learn from everything I observe. I try to find something useful to apply to my art from every experience I have. I have been influenced by hundreds of writers, artists, musicians, scientists, architects, actors, etc.

E : *What are your intentions, your objectives when you start a story ?*

I should begin answering this question by stating why I've chosen to currently work in comics instead of telling the story in another medium. I have always enjoyed many different kinds of art. All my life I have always drawn, painted, wrote stories, sculpted, acted out stories, etc. As a child I always did this. As I got older (in high school) I continued to improve my craft at the things and I also developed additional interests. When submit a portfolio for a scholarship, I was able to include a diverse ran of disciplines. For the final piece I included a comic book th created. In the process of creating it I realized that comics w the medium in which I could integrate all other mediums. Com became my way to unite all my other interests into one artform In fact I got my first paying comic job my first semester in coll and I continued working in comics the entire time. I Created Kab as a book to not only incorporate the different mediums, also what I was learning in history, Japanese, philosophy, Kara Moreover I wanted, through my metaphors, to express my o experiences.

or my Senior Thesis in writi I was taught graphic design wa «synthesis of type and image». Thi the way that I approach comics

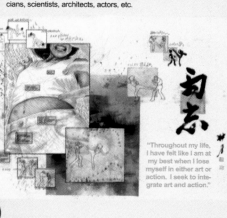

"Throughout my life, I have felt like I am at my best when I lose myself in either art or action. I seek to integrate art and action."

SOLEIL COUCHANT

▶ Left, the history of the mask, of Kabu-
&'s parents, 2 page drama
▶ Opposite, the shadow of Degas looms
ver the little girl. Below : it's Wagner's.

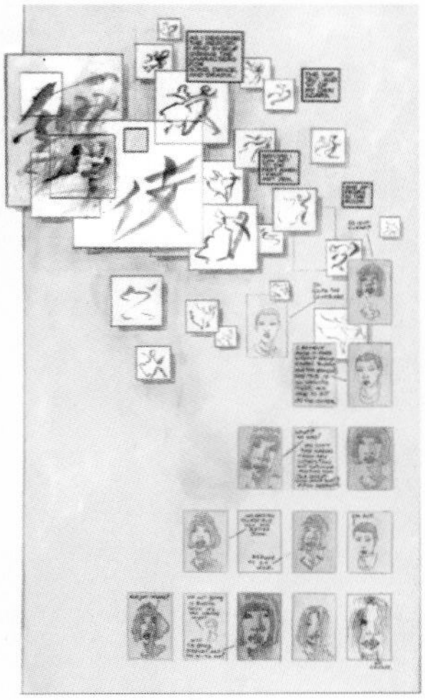

I turned in Kabuki Circle
of Blood for my Senior
Thesis in writing. I was
taught Graphic design
was a *"synthesis of type
and image"*. This is the
way that I approach comics.

Right. From
dance to words,
real play on the
Kanji and on
the layout of
the page ☞
Below : the
double helix of
musical DNA ¶

Often people like to put the emphasis either on story or on art. People often like to label creators into distinct and separate fish tanks.
My whole philosophy depends on integration not segregation. The
art and lettering and story are to be one. They should be indistinguishable from the other. The art is the story. The words are part
of the art. That is one of the reasons that I integrate Japanese
Kanji characters into my designs. The Japanese Kanji characters
are similar to words. They hold meaning. But they are also a visual
artform. They are a perfect integration of type and art. My words,
pictures, collages, designs, layouts, and pacing are meant to be
integrated to at point that they form a new kind of graphic language.

The point of my work in Kabuki is not only expression or integration, but more importantly, communication. The book is designed
to be a very interactive experience with the reader. In fact, the art
is not finished until th3tegrate the efforts of both the creator and
the reader. Hence: *communication.* And a new **language.**

E : *Your characters are closely linked to traditional art in Japan,
such as the Noh, the Kabuki, and the origami. What symbols
did you conceal in there ?*

First, Kabuki is part of the history of Kabuki's mother, of her
past in the camps. Second, Kabuki dramas are often about
ghost stories and the avenging of the wronged death (which is
one way to view **Circle of Blood**). Kabuki is an artistic drama
(literally meaning song, dance, drama) which is what that story
is meant to be.

The Noh is the style of theatre in which all of the actors wear
masks to delineate their roles. I thought this was a natural title
to give the agency whose operatives all wear masks. Of course
the mask is a central theme in the books.

As for origami, Akemi introduced it. Literally *"folded paper"*
it represents transformation and metamorphosis in the story.
It is folded from 2-D into 3-D. Kabuki must literally
create a new dimension to her identity. Akemi is
her guide, her catalyst needed to undergo her
own metamorphosis.

She escapes from what she was made into, and
becomes a self-aware individual. Besides
being an actual Japanese name, Akemi is
the phonetic pronunciation for **"Alchemy"**
the science/art of transformation. The first
Origami creature was a moth. A creature that represents re-birth and
metamorphosis.

E : *Kabuki is very different
from the other comic books,
where do you start off ?*

I wanted to write a very personal
and often autobiographical story. But

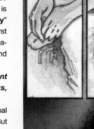

SOLEIL COUCHANT

DAVID MACK

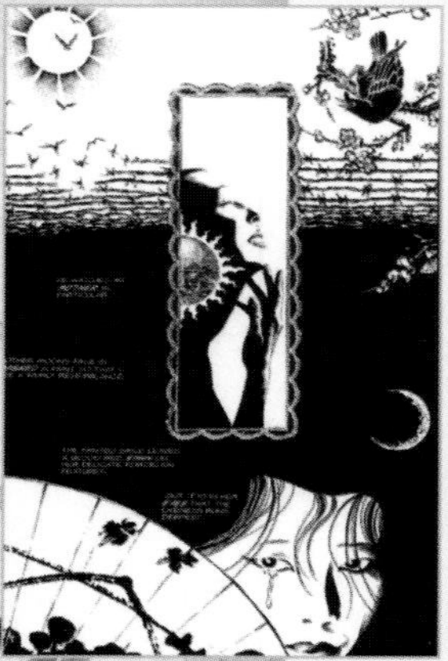

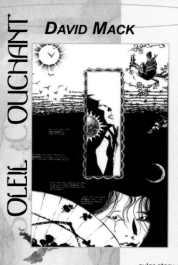

I wasn't ready to tell my story directly; I wanted to veil it through another character. Often when artists do this, they make the protagonists just an idealized version of themselves. So I decided to counteract on that and conceived every thing as opposite as possible. I would make the protagonist female. I would write through the lens of a different race, gender, culture and geography. I changed as many physical facts as possible. This way I kept the universal truths. Essence through metaphor.

E.: *Kabuki has evolved enormously, first in black and white, to become what we read today…*

I always start with the story. Then I design a different art style and choice of medium, depending on what I think best supports and sets the tone for that particular story. Circle of blood takes place in both the past and the future. I chose black and white because it had a sense of timelessness to it. It's like looking at black and white photographs, they are frozen in time and they instantly transport you to a different time. Movies use this method to great effect in Schindler's List, Seven Samurai, Raging Bull, or The Elephant Man. At the same time I wanted the beginning of the story to be accessible to new readers. I knew that I would be introducing a dramatic twist to the inherent language of comics but I needed to introduce it to readers gradually in order to have

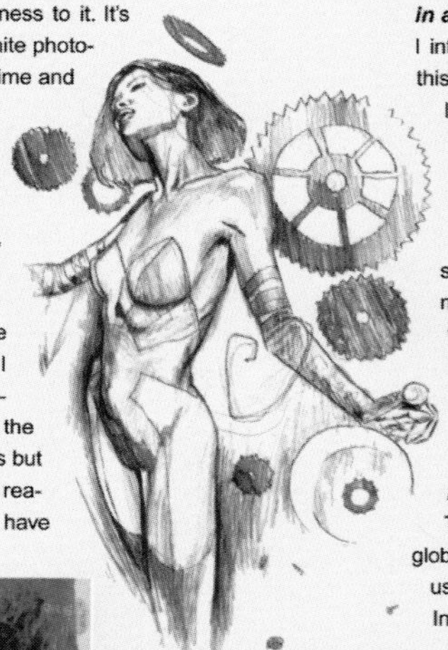

it support the story instead of distract from it. So in the f issue of Kabuki, I used my own style in a way that was s accessible to readers coming from experience with more mai tream books. Issue by issue the story telling twisted little by li and brought the readers step by step into my own world.

E.: *You bring forth a very original way of composing yc pages, the shape of your panels is really part of your s rytelling. How do you plan your layout ?*

I choose the layout, not only visually but for what is also a me phor of the story that is happening. For example, if the characte are piecing information together, I may design the page and pan like the pieces of a puzzle. If the characters are trying to find th way through a situation, I'll design the page as a Labyrinth. All t visual elements support and emphasize what is happening in t story. It is very important not to choose a motif that distracts fr the meaning of the story. The story comes first. Everything else into place in support of that central idea.

E.: *You use associations of ideas to a point seldom equall in a comic book !*

I integrate an object associated with a particular event. Oft this is an image associated with something in Kabuki's pa If you link the object correctly, it becomes an Icon. You m not realize the association at first. But when you show t icon again in a new context, its significance becomes cle and the object becomes more important than its intrin value. See, for example, the sickles, the halves of the Ja statue, Akemi's origami creatures, the design in the Jap nese flag, the crescent moon, the sun, the scar, the ma the tear, the missing finger…

E.: *Your characters wear a mask that has a proper ide tifiy. The bearer can be replaced, yet, there is alwa someone behind him. This duality, which can be fou in Superman who is not totally Clark Kent, is magnifi in your stories…*

The mask is a powerful metaphor. Every culture around t globe uses the mask in one form or another. Figuratively each us uses a mask of our own on a daily basis in social situatio In Kabuki's case, her true face is scarred. She feels ugly, dis

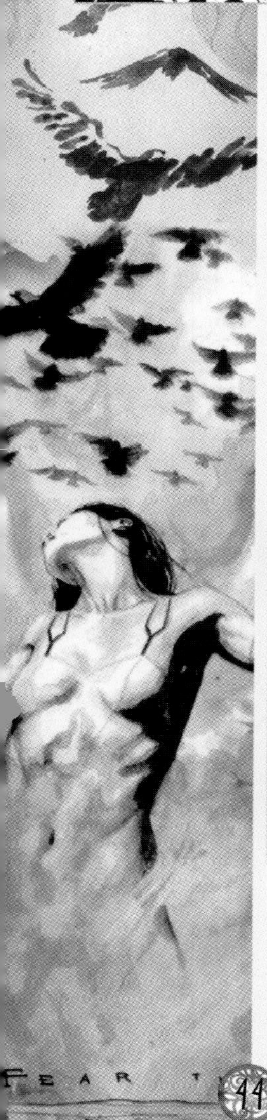

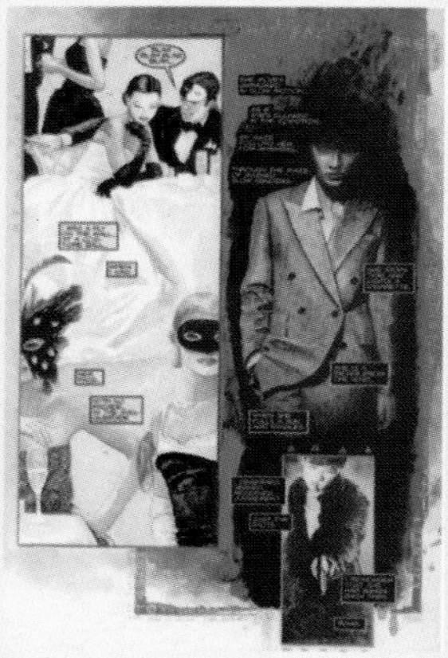

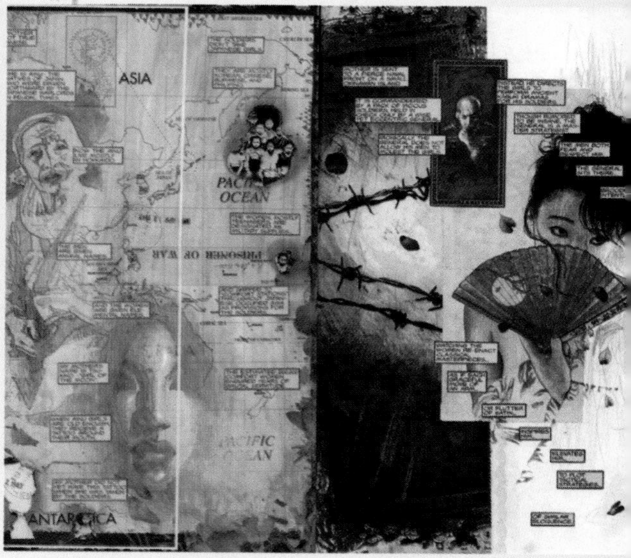

Framed, game of recurrent symbols, the sun, the moon or the barbed wire of Circle of Blood

Center, Design of the Kabuki cover, Classic 7.

Mask of social foreplay. Here the attention to detail make the character overlap his past. Journey in the Association of Ideas..

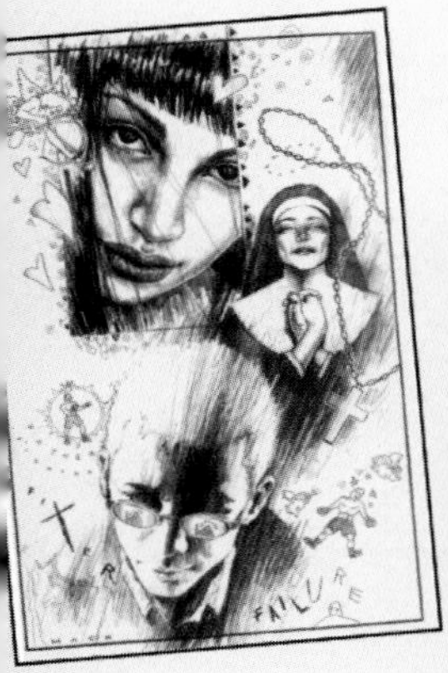
FAILURE

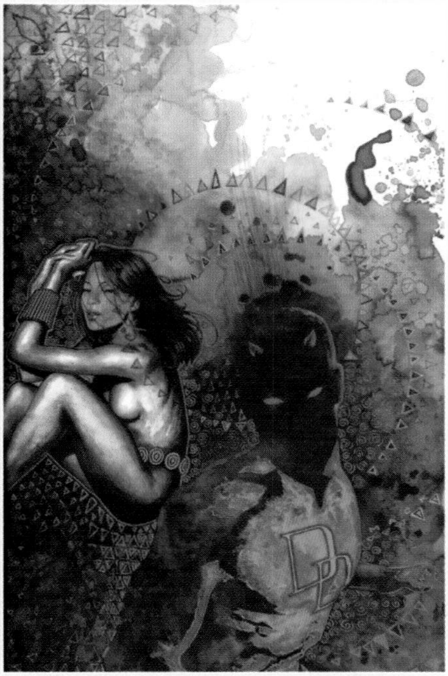

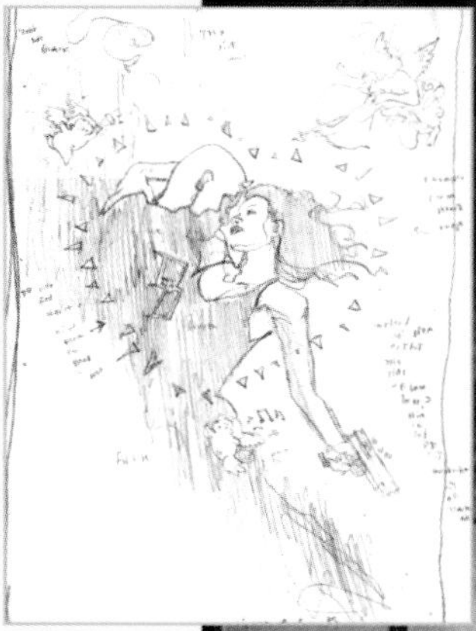

Opposite, Echo, Matt, Natasha and Daredevil. Or how to make a cover for Marvel Knights.

Below, a small drawing and David Mack himself who pictures himself in

even to have emotions. The mask has both a smile and a tear. The emotions that she does not have without it. Only through the mask is she comfortable to interact with others. Only in the mask does she feel in control of the situation. The identity that she has in the mask is either feared, or adored. Either way, she feels a sense of control from those responses that the masked identity gets.

Most of your characters are incomplete, they are missing something. It seems obvious with the members of the Noh, but, when you started writing Daredevil, who's blind, you had

wanted to write a very personal
ıd often autobiographical story.
ut I wasn't ready to tell my life
ory directly..."

him meet a deaf girl. Echo. Why ? Is it again a kind of metaphor, or is there a psychological explanation ?

Both, I think. In fact, Daredevil being blind and sensing the world in a way that others do not, is very detached from the rest of the people he interacts with. He can identify with someone else who must decipher the bigger picture from their own detached point of view. Also, I can not help but put my own point of view into my writing. In fact my writing is at it's best when It is based on my personal experience and view. That lesson for myself is to take what sets you apart, what makes you different, what others may consider your flaw, your imperfection, turn that weakness into your strength. Turn your handicap into your asset. This is part of my message.

: TYou're very "sensitive" in your way of telling a story. You use the perceptions or feelings of your characters as guides. Spaces and events are restricted by your characters perceptions. Do you create stories which shall be rather felt than read ?

This is true. But we all perceive reality not as it is in its entirety but from our own individual limited perceptions. In fact that is my handicap, my flaw. When I experience the same situation with others, I find that I saw something completely different than they did. Instead of letting that be my handicap, I turned that into my asset.

I try to make each of my characters a unique person. Each one interprets reality in a different way based on his own point of view which usually comes from his child hood. This is the case with the Kabuki characters, Daredevil, Echo and the Kingpin (whose childhood you will see more of in upcoming issues of DD). I try to restore the world as it's perceived by my characters, shaped by the experiences built in their childhood years. This is true of myself. I apply it to my characters.

E: *Do you have any other projects ?*

I do a lot of other work outside of comics. I am currently writing for the Kabuki film. I make CD's (for Geoff Keezer and Paul Mc Cartney recently). In the future I intend to work more in film and music, as well as poetry and painting. I'm interested by everything !

K.

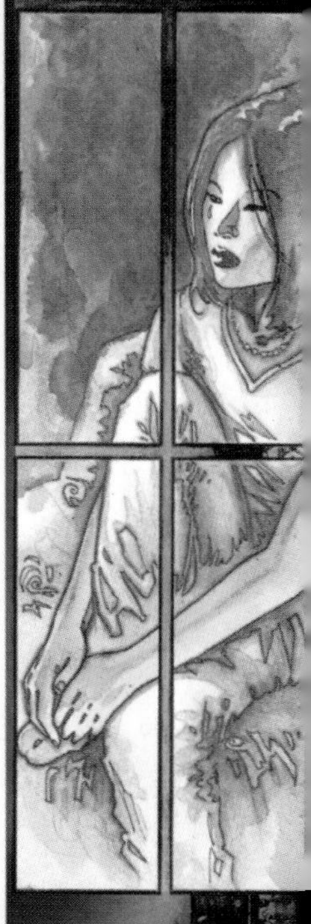

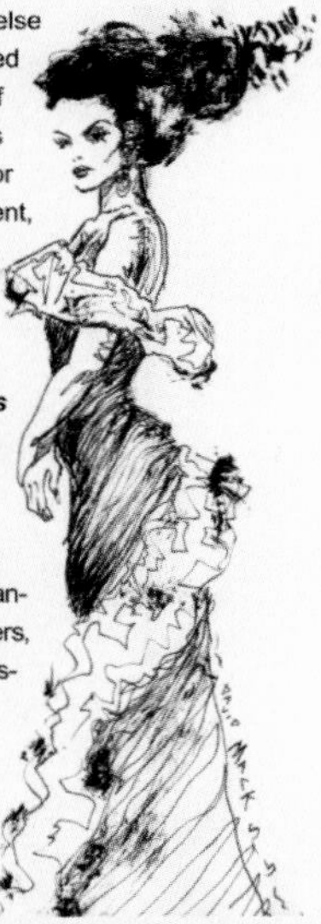

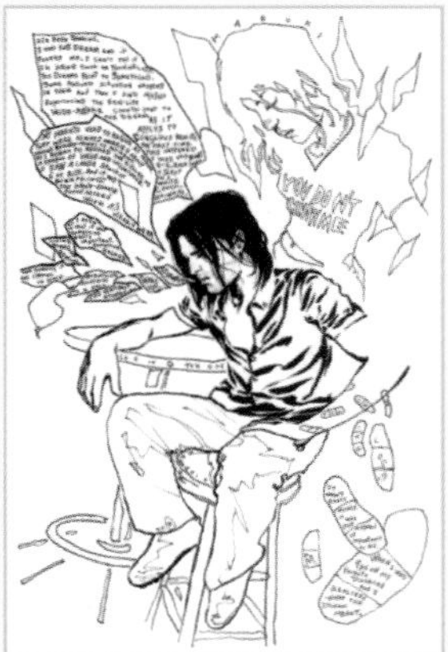

Interview: Aude Ettori.
Layout: Fabrice Deraedt.
Translation: Miceal Beausang.

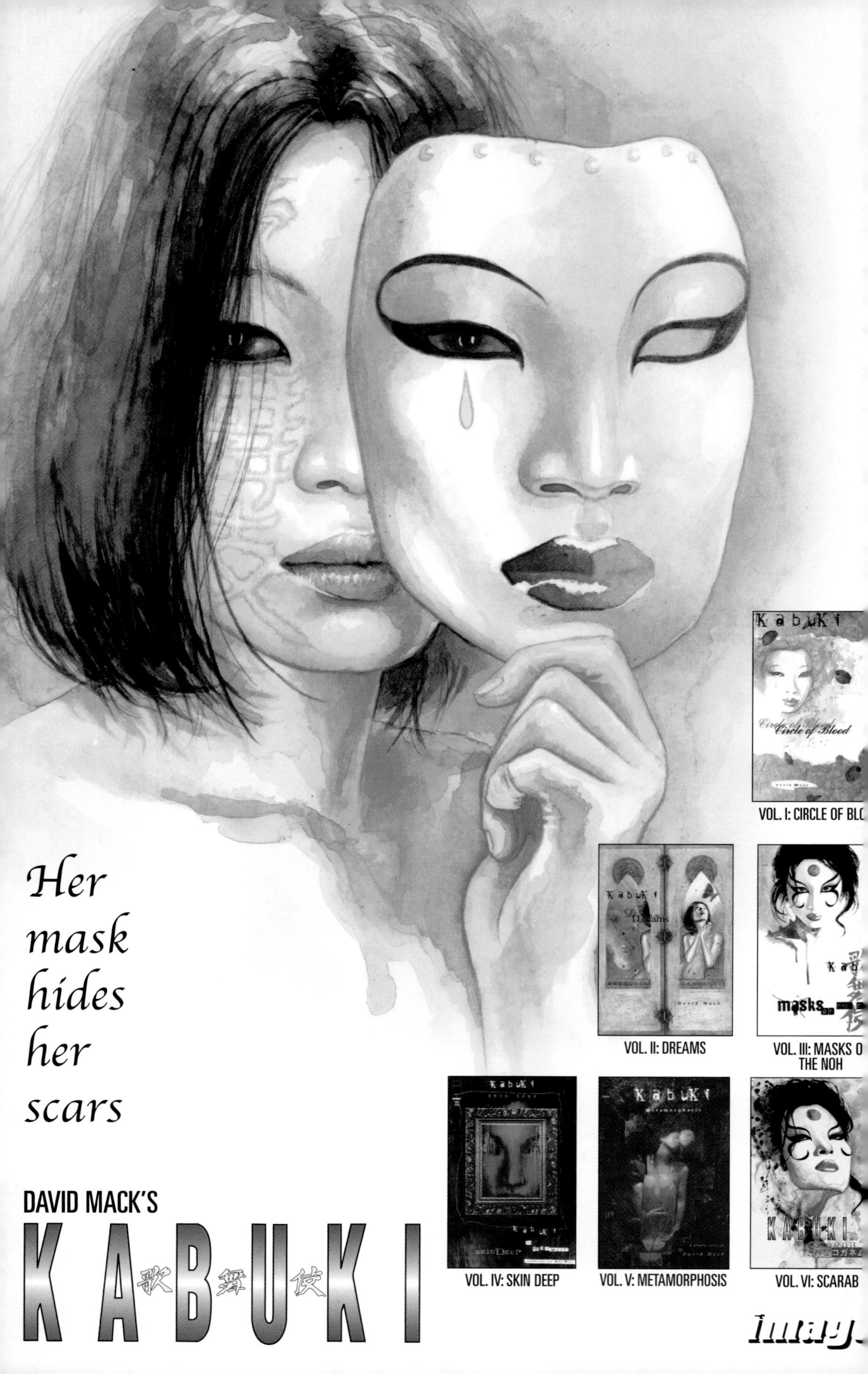
Her mask hides her scars
DAVID MACK'S
KABUKI
歌舞伎
VOL. I: CIRCLE OF BLO
VOL. II: DREAMS
VOL. III: MASKS O THE NOH
VOL. IV: SKIN DEEP
VOL. V: METAMORPHOSIS
VOL. VI: SCARAB
Image

Thank you to Anh Tran for her editing and design assistance,
and for modeling as Kabuki, Miss Fumiko of the First Zen Institute
of America for her inspiring mail and gifts (some of which I collaged
into the artwork of this book, including the antique Samurai helmet),
Brian Michael Bendis for his advice & friendship, and for making a
Kabuki mask that I used in the first part of this story, Ekllipse
Magazine for their help in including the Kabuki article and interview
in this volume, Steve Mack for helping me letter, my sister-in-law
Hiromi Oba for the handwritten Japanese translation of the book of
hells, Nancy Mao for modeling as Kabuki's mother, Connie Jiang for
advice & modeling, Rachel Steinberger for the gift of the handmade
"Baby Kabuki" doll that I collaged into the art, Andy Lee for his
artistic advice & for getting me into the university Science Lab so I
could use the bones of large animals to build the skeleton of a dragon,
Allen Spiegal, Rick Mays, Ryan Graff, Ashley Wood, Ean & Jan,
Larry Woolum, Jim Valentino, Anthony Bozzi, Brent Braun, & all
my friends at Image Comics, Bob Matson, Takashi Hattori, Clay
Moore, Ba & Ma Lee, Randy Quan, Bill Marlowe, Lee Hester, Paul
Mullins, Ron McElman, Justin Cheung, & Vince Locke for coloring
the three pages at the end of the second story.

Acknowledgements for inspiration from the works of Greg
Spalenka (thank you for the Kabuki art you sent me), R. Ward
Shipman, Andy Lee, Mah Win Shin, Gustav Klimt, Sandi Fellman,
Yoshi Toshi, Yoshitaka Amano, Bill Sienkiewicz, Anh Tran, Kent
Williams, Jon Muth, Dave McKean, Baron Storey, & Howard Storm.
The quote at the end of the second story is from the late Japanese
playwright, Yukio Mishima: "In this stillness was a beauty beyond
words. No more body or spirit, pen or sword, male or female. No
movement… no sound… no memories."
The quote at the beginning of the story is from Shakespeare's
Hamlet: "For in that sleep of death, what dreams may come?"